Mad Cow Disease in America

Something Special

and Other Plays

Other Theater Books by Lance Tait:

Edwin Booth: A Play in Two Acts

Miss Julie, David Mamet Fan Club, and Other Plays

2001 Dec.

Gordon,
    Not too long ago you mentioned to me that a number of playwrights my age were

MAD COW DISEASE IN AMERICA

SOMETHING SPECIAL

and Other Plays

writing plays that were looking back on life. I played with

by Lance Tait

this in The Swimming Pools of Paris (p. 87) — which I think you'll like. (The play also

with an introduction

by Michelle Powell

includes a mangled variation of Dumas' Camille).
    In part, hoping to counter

Enfield Publishing Company
Enfield, NH

the dumbing down all around. Theater audiences are ready for these plays — they are not the problem.
    Thanks for everything,
        Love, Lance

First Printing 2001

Publisher's Cataloging-in-Publication
(Provided by Quality Books, Inc.)

Tait, Lance.
   Mad cow disease in America, Something special, and
other plays / by Lance Tait ; with an introduction by
Michelle Powell. -- 1st ed.
   p. cm.
   CONTENTS: Dmitri -- The glass ceiling -- Mad cow
disease in America -- The swimming pools of Paris --
A family portrait -- Something special -- Read to me --
Betsy Philadelphia.
   ISBN: 1-893598-03-9

   1. Experimental drama, American.   I. Title.

PS3570.A326A6 2001   812´. 6
                 QBI01-701051

Printed in the U.S.A. by Morris Publishing, Kearney, NE

Published by Enfield Publishing,
P.O. Box 699, Enfield, New Hampshire 03748

Art Direction by Lise Geurkink
Book Design by Lise Geurkink

Cover Design by Jo Oskoui

Contents

Introduction

Only a few contemporary playwrights steer clear of the unwavering realism, the pathetic situations and voyeurism often found in American mainstream psychological theater. Lance Tait creates fresh and invigorating comedies of great depth and innovation that reach out to an audience who wants more than easy Naturalistic drama. Part of the power of the plays in this, Tait's second, anthology perhaps can be traced to what he has derived from his studies of Ionesco, Genet, Artaud, and others who come earlier: I am thinking particularly of Jarry, Pirandello, Witkiewicz, and, though he is not a playwright, Kafka. Without a doubt, the eight plays in this volume have a great deal in common with the works of these Continental writers and the influence of American playwrights such as Eugene O'Neill, Tennessee Williams, Arthur Miller, or even Sam Shepard, seems to be weak here. Tait's plays are not stage works that can be readily transposed to popular electronic media, made into "talking head" dramas. There is too much comic physicality in his work for that. Tait's dramas, some of which are classified "experimental" by American standards, are wedded to the live stage form; they resist adaptation to current film or television not only because of their physicality, but also because of their subject matter and their use of music and verse.

As the French and others before him, Tait is interested in an existential theater, one that examines the individual's place in the world, the possible purposes (or lack of purpose) of life, and the worth of the individual. But his characters are not as isolated or trapped as those that we see in Samuel Beckett's work, for example. (Could it be that characters are less trapped in Tait's work because they are in the United States, a large country with a range of opportunities not known previously in Europe?) Tait's characters usually find themselves in a less abstract and generalized (though still metaphoric) geography than we find in the plays written in Paris in the 1950s by the classic writers of that time. This is certainly another "American" characteristic of Tait. His characters are usually anchored in a particular city—such as New York, San Francisco, or Paris. This allows him to indulge in a kind of satire less common in the works of Ionesco and Beckett—to name but two earlier writers. Tait's satire is the satire of place and people from that specific place. There is no superior advantage to being able to engage in this kind of satire—it is simply something that sets Tait apart from his Continental predecessors.

Much has happened in the world since the 1950s, when the Theatre of the Absurd was in full flower. Now, the cold war is over. The iron curtain is gone. Fundamentalists have gained enormous power around the globe. Terrorism has increased. New Age religions and consciousness studies proliferate in the west. C.J. Jung, Antonin Artaud and countless other artists, scientists and thinkers have had significant impact upon our evolving cultures. Other important changes have happened over the last half century: television is ubiquitous; communications technology is highly advanced. With all this, the tragic-comedy of the 1950s is still relevant to today. However, every era has its art works that struggle to engage the public anew in dialogue. Lance Tait is part of a new generation of playwrights and theater practitioners from around the world—probably no one country or continent can claim to be the center of innovative theater today—that take considerable risks to create exciting, communicative, insightful and thought-provoking work for those people who still go to the theater in search of entertainment and enlightenment.

Like the plays in Tait's first book, *Miss Julie, David Mamet Fan Club, and Other Plays,* the plays here are challenging and full of wonderful rewards. They skillfully mix storytelling modes, such as monologue, comic dialogue, verse, **songs,** and movement, etc., making for an altogether thrilling kind of "total theater" that is a joy for actors to work in and a joy for spectators to be part of. Remarkable in Tait's work too is his interest in creating theater that leaves some space for the spectator to make up his or her own mind—this is in contrast to unambiguous reactions sought by Naturalistic theater. The spectator is not always given specific answers on how best to deal with the problems set before them. Not shy about expressing his opinions (often of political nature), the playwright nevertheless tries to bring charm into the drama when his editorializing is in effect. At times, he seeks to goad the spectator out of complacency; he wants us to disagree with him. Actually, Tait's politics are hardly objectionable: they are a mixture of common sense and a desire for a true egalitarian society.

In *Dmitri*, the first play of this anthology, we are given a setting that, despite its references to New York City, is more reminiscent of the generalized, almost allegorical locales of absurdist plays of the twentieth century. Dmitri is a waiter who has been thinking about committing suicide. The big city oppresses him but ironically Dmitri towers above the city—this is according to the set design. A hitman breaks into his apartment to put him out of his misery. Though Dmitri has been unable to make life "work", he is reluctant to let go of it—in fact, he stalls the hitman, by asking the hitman to sit down and act out what he says is the essence of his life. What follows is a skit within a play that uses a common waiter joke (that begins with "Waiter, what's this fly doing in my soup?) as a point of departure. What is fascinating about this play as a whole is the oblique way in which it informs us about Dmitri's character: we find out much about who he is and what is bothering him by the kinds of books he has in his apartment or by what he says to the customer in the restaurant (the customer is played by the hitman). Later we find out more about Dmitri in his face-to-face argument with the hitman but what seems to be underway for much of the play is the playwright's determination to dampen down many of the histrionic possibilities of the story. The design of this play is eclectic. I am struck by its viability despite the primacy of the waiter joke in the play—usually, in the theater, jokes can do more harm than good to a play's propulsion. One also sees in this play, in contrast to twentieth century European plays, what seems to me to be the very American kind of self-reliant spirit.

The Glass Ceiling is set with a vengeance (of the comic kind) in San Francisco. We all know the Bay Area is home to new ideas and experimentation. First addressed in this play for three women is a very real social problem: women's inequality in the workplace. Immediately though, this drama in a psychologist's office becomes a farce. And after we are acclimated to a satirical assault on New Age psychology, the play then swerves into a doctor/patient realm that has some unexpectedly profound possibilities for a patient's cure. This is all because of the machinations of Tamela, the doctor's bizarre assistant who has "gender-issues" concerning some of her role models (who are male). Tamela also happens to run a small museum that seems to be having trouble with limiting its mission to the world.

There are many excesses in this play but the play makes successes of these. We are treated to a comedy that has the kind of excitement we find in Ionesco's *Victims of Duty*—where there is also an unexpected, colorful "downward" mental journey. It should be noted that both *The Glass Ceiling* and *Dmitri* have their significant, snap impersonations which give new life to the concept of the "play-within-a-play". Much can be said concerning the shamanic, ritualistic elements of *The Glass Ceiling*; this work opposes Artaud only in so far as it refuses to take itself entirely seriously.

Mad Cow Disease in America is the first of Tait's "Paris Plays". (The four Paris Plays were either written about, or workshopped in, Paris.) In *Mad Cow Disease* we have one character, the Citizen. Partly through this character the playwright is sublimating his and others' anger and frustration over national policy, the American citizenry and entrenched, powerful special interests. Some recent events that are background to this play include the U.S. government's storming of the Christian fundamentalist cult compound in Waco, Texas and the election of George W. Bush to the presidency. The fact that the stories of the play are set in middle America emphasize that there is disfavor within the homeland itself about "how things are run." The play stays within the American borders; there is no need to criticize from a foreign vantage point, as we see in *The Swimming Pools of Paris*. This play, written before the attacks on New York and Washington in September 2001, is no less significant, despite these attacks.

Mad Cow Disease in America is participatory theater, with the Citizen front and center. The Citizen is an oracle. This oracle appears to be saying that when a democratic people does not think for themselves and seriously participate in the democratic process, then their democracy begins to rot. The fine juxtapositions between the natural, but simultaneously surreal, plains landscapes and the human events which are purported to take place in these landscapes are tension-producing, even shocking. The use of traditional songs is somewhere between the opaque and the sublime. The dark humor, as well as the political outrage, is reminiscent of European surrealism.

The Swimming Pools of Paris makes an entirely different set of demands upon the spectator, this time using melodrama and comedy of manners as bases from which to take off. Here we have the main character, Donald, a user, a manipulator, a rentboy (as the British say), a handsome man who looks back at his previous life in New York in the first half of the play and shows us in the second half what his new life in Paris is about now. The self-centered Donald gets us involved in different ways in each half of the play. In the first act he shamelessly elicits our pity and sympathy. We are looking through a kind of peephole into his New York life where events are in fast motion: there is scant time for most of the realistic details of what happened, only time for the moments that cause great emotional impact. Here places are fading with time and scene changes are unnecessary. The first act is a memory play in which Donald plays God. But God is in pain and eventually does something about it. He goes to France and there a few off-handed, complaining remarks about American culture take him a long, long, way.

The play's structure, even in the first half, peels some to reveal European influences—we are just over half-way through the first act when the actor who plays Tommy slips out of character and says, when cued by the word, "One": "There's one swimming pool in the fourth arrondissement of Paris." Tait explains that part of his intention here is that the spectator be separated from the unfolding emotional drama momentarily—in order that she or he may breathe, as is were, and think. It is my feeling that these interpolations owe something, in technique, to the dadaists. Tait's studies in physical theater and Etienne Decroux may have something to do with the ease in which he works against Naturalism here also.

In the second act of the play Donald has both feet firmly planted in Paris. It is now eighteen years since his New York experiences. Another country, another generation and there is a decidedly New Age—or is it Old Age—bent to the comedy. In this comedy of personal development where Donald says he has grown, has he really progressed that much? I wouldn't bet my life on it. We see in *Swimming Pools*, as well as many of the other plays, the particularly American notion of self-betterment and renewal that is absent from the Theatre of the Absurd. We remember that those writers were writing directly after World War II and Tait is writing after a number of years of relative peace and prosperity. Often, and it is the case here, Tait plays roughly with the notion of self-improvement. Two particular things that allow us to downplay our displeasure with Donald's antics are that he is surrounded by—there are no other words for it—the healing imagery of water, and that he can be awfully funny. The subtle criticism of sentimentality in this play mixes oddly, but well, with the poetry, comedy, and at times, swagger, of the rogue Donald. The originality of *The Swimming Pools of Paris* is not matched in any other recent theater work that I know of.

In *A Family Portrait* we have a family that is educated and eccentric, pro-active rather than re-active, and in fairly healthy shape except for their son, Brad. Brad, in contrast to the rest of the family is a bad seed, a cluster of evil genes, born to terrorize the world—despite the fact that he seems to know something about Systems Theory. What Tait is saying about the human race is not a pessimistic, I believe; it is an appraisal of the species and a warning that evil exists and that we should be ready for it. According to Tait and what is said in the play, *A Family Portrait* was ill received by some in its initial reading in Paris. Perhaps since the attack on New York and Washington in September, spectators will be more responsive to the portrait offered here by Tait. No solutions to the existence of evil are provided; this play is a comic *cri de coeur* where its characters are given music and dance at the end for some relief. The play's comedy of numbers, mysticism and symbolism, its satire on linking theory with practice, and its avoidance of religious dogma are very New Age—in all but their lack of self-certainty.

We have another family that is forced into existential questions and a dearth of answers in *Something Special*, a play with songs. In this comedy, the lawyer Tom Hazzitall has many things—a loving wife, a job that pays well and which he seems to like. However, he is not at peace; this is partly manifested physically in his eczema. There is no sign that he and his wife, Lisa, are going to have children, nor is there any mention of any sets of parents. Tom and Lisa are almost sealed in a cocoon of their own making. They live in material comfort in a new home, somewhere in a desert, in America. Tom first focuses his wayward fears upon his wife, whom he thinks is having an affair with her boss, Carl. This neurotic projection is disproved; the play gets complicated and the comedy of projections is replaced by a comedy of perceptions. Lisa is killed amidst the songs, the noise and the space aliens that are purported to have landed in the backyard. Another Lisa comes on the scene. Who is this Lisa? She is identical in appearance to the first Lisa. For what reason is she there? Who or what sent her?

The attack on materialism in this play is subtler than what one often sees in contemporary American novels. Tait has said that his plot is greatly influenced by Tirso de Molina's Spanish Golden Age play, *Damned for Despair* (1625), in which the protagonist of that play is condemned for having the unchristian quality of despair, instead of having hope. Other influences upon *Something Special* are Ionesco—not only his ideas, but his language in *The Killer* and *Exit the King.* Pirandello's *Right You Are* is another important play according to the playwright. (At the end of the Pirandello play the author lets stand the contradiction of who a mysterious woman might be.) Tait has also mentioned the influence of Mozart operas like *Don Giovanni* and *The Magic Flute.* In addition to these European plays and operas, the influence of the Negro Spiritual and the American pop song of the 1960s can be heard in the music of *Something Special*.

This play is terribly funny and has a surprising kind of charm to it— given its shocking deaths. Interestingly, after the first mention of a social problem, Lisa, the character who mentioned the problem, dies. This is as if to say that politics are not going to be part of the focus. There seems to be an operatic approach to the cosmos here. Pauline, the cleaning leading, appears to be generated from Italian *opera buffa* servant figures. However, her master is God. We never see any of the blood of those that die in *Something Special* and those who die don't really meet their end: Lisa comes back as another woman, Lisa Arny; we expect that the Christian believer, Pauline, is rewarded with eternal life, according to her faith. In form and structure this play is a long way away from most American comedies and the American musical. It is a spiritual comedy perhaps like that which T.S. Eliot attempted with his *The Cocktail Party.* It is a physical comedy the likes of which have not been seen since Preston Sturges made his comic film classics. Altogether, it is an extraordinary American hybrid, a Latin comedy cum Kafka that deals with human beings who find themselves in an incomprehensible universe.

In *Read to Me* we have a two people who are struggling to get by: one, John, is struggling, we suspect, for his sanity in the world; his material needs seem to have been met. For Barbara the struggle is both material and spiritual. John knows he can find peace and sanity in his appreciation of literature. The catch is that he cannot do it alone: he needs human interaction, he cannot be sane only among books, no matter how wonderful they are in and of themselves. Barbara has been forced into a life of prostitution in order to have enough money to bring up her child. She is hired by John to read him a story. In John's hotel room she is exposed to the powerful force of art and music and she breaks down momentarily.

This is a bittersweet play in which the playwright in part seems to be paying homage to the American short story writer, O. Henry. There is, however, no classic O. Henry twist to the end that ratchets up ironic prospects in the drama. This is a comedy of art and survival rather than a comedy of laughs and purgation. Of all the plays in this volume, this is most American in form. However the dramaturgy in the play is not totally realistic; what is exploited here is the aesthetic possibilities of memory play, minimalism and physical theater—something seen before in the first act of *The Swimming Pools of Paris*.

In the last play of this anthology, *Betsy Philadelphia*, we have what appears at first to be a fairly realistic political play. As in all of Tait's plays, the relation of story to location is tight. Here the setting is the "cradle of democracy," Philadelphia. Part of the intention of this play is to document, in a world of spin and instant revisionism, the feelings of some people during the 2000 American Presidential election. Interestingly, the play turns poetic in the third scene and in the fifth and final dramatic scene Betsy, a dominatrix, materializes. She commands Eddie and Lasko to worship the Hand, a symbol of strength, order, restriction and subservience. In the view of the playwright, the election of George W. Bush threatens democracy and liberty itself. The play is no ordinary social play; notable for its unpredictable structure, it departs from the social realm of the reactions to the presidential election and its aftermath and moves into a fantasy-dream realm full of symbols but still in possession of political values. Though some influence of Genet's dramaturgy is possibly here, an underlying sense of activism is one thing we do not see in Genet's plays nor in Ionesco. Tait shares with these two playwrights a great desire to communicate, but does not share their pessimism over the possibility of communicating.

Martin Esslin, when speaking of the Theatre of the Absurd, spoke about how the plays of that type attempt to make humankind face up to the human condition, and seek to help free the individual from illusions that are causing misery. In Lance Tait's comedies we see characters who have fallen after sustaining sundry blows, and who are given the option of picking themselves back up again—if they can pull themselves together. What these characters have to help them rise up is new information provided to them in each play. Lance Tait's plays, like many of the works in the Theatre of the Absurd, strive to free the individual. It is interesting that in a country that prides itself on freedom, more American writers have not taken up forms of existential drama. Arthur Miller has remarked that Americans are not interested in the drama of ideas. I would counter that they are; it is just that *Europeans* have in the past written the plays of this type.

Presently there are those in our society who are intensely interested in good health—and who embrace therapies of all kinds. "Inner work" is a phrase commonly heard among such people. Lance Tait has taken this last notion and brought it to the American stage with great comic assurance. His aim, like that of his Theatre of the Absurd predecessors, is, in the new jargon, "wellness." For Tait, wellness (a funny word, or not?) means good health for self, society and our planet.

Michelle Powell
Dramaturg
Los Angeles

Beginning Remarks

Each work here is a magic compass with which to explore our world. The direction the spectator heads toward is partially up to him- or herself and one hopes for learning and growth. Comedy does not provide trouble-free compass points. Comedy is a fabulous but natural response to the rigors of ideology, to orthodoxy, to fundamentalism.

It is not enough in art to just vent problems in a straightforward fashion. Style is integral to the process. Comedy is highly stylized. Style helps, as much as content, to make a work memorable so that the spectator might carry some of this work inside her- or himself possibly for a lifetime.

DMITRI

a one-act play

Characters

HITMAN   *Male. 30s-60s.*

DMITRI   *Male, 20s to 30s.*

Place: In a city, probably New York City.
Time: Present.

Notes

These send the message that reality is to be distorted: the small scale
of the buildings to the audience's left and the normal-sized restaurant
and apartment furniture to the right. A realistic acting approach to
most of the dialogue is best. The story of the play and the situations are
odd enough. How could the Hitman already know the lines he is supposed to be saying when he and Dmitri go to the restaurant table to
enact Dmitri's little play-within-a-play? Of course he wouldn't know
these lines. The Hitman is all in the mind of Dmitri.

The duration of the play depends in part on how long the Hitman
takes with his stage business while he waits in the apartment for Dmitri

to come home. It is no coincidence that the play refers to the "existential" writer Dostoevsky, and in addition, to books in general. There is tension between the older Hitman's life experience and advice, fictional experiences, Dmitri's life experience and need to survive, and the philosophy of Dostoevsky.

The first reading of Dmitri took place at Bretton Hall College of Leeds University, England on May 1, 2001. There some words of the play were anglicized ("skyscrapers" changed to "tower blocks", "apartment" to "flat", *The New York Times* to *The Independent*, the *Hackensack Weekly Register* to the *Romford Recorder*) and the actors, Dougie Hankin and Chris Yandell, used cockney dialect.

Dmitri

To the audience's left is the city: a small group of skyscrapers are there. These model skyscrapers are waist-high at their highest. There is enough space between some of the skyscrapers so as to be able to walk between them. Also a small restaurant table, with a checkered tablecloth is on the city-side of the stage. There is a chair for the restaurant table.

To the right of the audience is DMITRI'S *apartment. A rug is on the floor. There is a large chair—a recliner. Next to that, a bookcase. The bookcase is filled with books. On top of the bookcase there is a little lamp. There is the suggestion of a window at the back of the room.*

At the back of the stage there is a hint of a playground's jungle gym perhaps, and a strong wire fence—general cityscape stuff.

Lights up. The HITMAN *moves around the skyscrapers as if he were walking through a maze. Finally he winds up over by the window in* DMITRI'S *apartment.*

HITMAN: Up the fire escape goes the Hitman—that's me. Through the window and into Dmitri's apartment. You know, the window's supposed to have bars on it. Instead he's got some cheap flimsy gate. (*Pause.*) Why Dmitri? What's he done? Oh, he's done stuff. And it has something to do with what he is, who he is. I want him. He'll be back any minute.

The HITMAN *wanders around, restless.*

Not much here. No TV. What a weirdo.

Finally he goes over to the bookcase and takes a book from it. He turns the little lamp on. He starts reading a page from the book:

Hitman:

"This was a bitter disappointment. Roxy had for so many days nourished and fondled and petted her notion that Tom would be glad to see his old nurse, and would make her prod and happy to the marrow with a cordial word or two, that it took two rebuffs to convince her that he was not funning, and that her beautiful dream was a fond and foolish vanity. A shabby and pitiful mistake. She was hurt to the heart, and so ashamed that for a moment she didn't quite know what to do or how to act. Then her breast began to heave. The tears came. And in her forlornness she was moved to try that other dream of hers—an appeal to her boy's charity; and so, upon the impulse, and without reflection, she offered her supplication:

'Oh, Marse Tom, de po' ole mammy is in sich hard luck dese days; en she's kinder crippled in de arms en can't work, en if you could gimme a dollah—on'y jes one little dol—' "

Well, that's enough of that. *(He goes to the bookcase.)* It was right there I think.

He spots the place where the book was and puts it back on its proper place on the shelf. He walks around the room. Bored, he puts a toothpick in his mouth. He walks around some more, looks around. He sits down in the recliner chair. He reaches over and plays with the lamp on top of the bookcase, turning the lamp on and off again and again. He reclines in the chair. He reaches back over to the bookshelf and takes another book from it. He finds a place in the book and reads from it:

"The crowded courtroom was silent, and Bonanno listened impassively as Morgenthau went on to describe the extensive but futile efforts of the FBI and other law enforcement agencies to uncover him."

Real life. For some.

He stops reclining in the chair. He takes care to put the book back on the shelf where he found it. Pause. He reclines in the chair again.

Ah, this is the life.

He tries to relax. Long pause. He cannot relax. he decides to play a game with himself. He does not look at the bookcase. With his hand feeling around, he touches some books in the bookcase and selects one book at ran-dom. He looks at the book. He starts to read from a page:

"The gods assented, well pleased with the two. A long time they served in that grand building, and the story does not say whether they ever missed their little cozy room with its cheerful hearth. But one day standing before the marble and golden magnificence they fell to talking about the former life, which had been so hard and yet so happy. By now both were in extreme old age. Suddenly as they exchanged memories each saw the other putting forth leaves. Then bark was growing around them. They had time only to cry, "Farewell, dear companion.""

Yeah, goodbye, goodbye. Whatever this is all about.

(Continuing to read from the same book.) "As the words passed their lips they became trees, but still they were together. The linden and the oak grew from one trunk."

Oh, isn't that nice?

Footsteps are heard coming up the stairs. The Hitman *puts the book back in the bookcase quickly. He does not turn off the little lamp. He gets up out of the chair and listens. The footsteps pass by the apartment and continue, then fade out. The* Hitman *sits down again in the big chair. He tries to rest again. But he gets fidgety. He can't decide whether or not to keep the lamp on. He keeps it on. He plays his game again. Without looking at the shelf, he selects a book at random. He starts reading from the book:*

"This is no accident. The Captain's given the Word (I have this intelligence with utter certainty through My Spies) that no ship's officer shall dance with Miss FitzSnugglie until he's danced at least two dances with other partners—and I am not an "other partner," because the proscription, since leaving Mars, has been extended to me."

HITMAN: *(Continued.)* Proscription? Some kind of Mars crap.

He puts the book back in the case. He is quite bored. He gets up out of the chair and starts pacing. He goes to the bookcase—there seems to be nothing else to do. This time he looks at the titles of the books in the bookcase.

Yep. No Dostoevsky. *(Then he chooses a book. He mutters its title.)* "Dress for Success." Hmm.

(He reads.)
"Assuming that your basic suit wardrobe is the usual mix of grays, blues and browns, I suggest the following as a basic shirt wardrobe, given that the appropriate shades of color are chosen for each suit:
　　One dressy, solid-white broadcloth, to be worn regularly.
　　One dressy, solid-white broadcloth, to be kept in a plastic bag, clean, ironed and always ready for emergencies."

I ought to get this book. Over four million sold.

He puts it back on the shelf. Pause. After a while footsteps are again heard coming up the stairs. The footsteps get closer. This time the HITMAN *turns off the lamp on top of the bookcase. There is the sound of a key in a lock. The* HITMAN *takes out his gun. We hear the second lock to the door turn. The* HITMAN *hides in a dark corner. We hear the door open.* DMITRI *enters.* DMITRI *enters. He notices something is different about his apartment. Before he can do anything, the* HITMAN *grabs him by the ear.*

HITMAN: Not a peep out of you. Come into my parlor said the you-know-what to the fly. We've got some business, my friend.

DMITRI: No, no, no. Not me.

HITMAN: Yes, you.

DMITRI: There's been a mistake.

HITMAN: No mistake. Dmitri. See, I know your name. It's a Russian name isn't it?

DMITRI: It can be.

HITMAN: Yeah, it's Russian. Like Dostoevsky. That's Russian, isn't it.

DMITRI: Sounds like it.

HITMAN: Well, it is. Dostoevsky. "Crime and Punishment"—it's a great novel. "The Gambler." That's another one of his. *(Pause.)* You've got to pay up.

DMITRI: I don't know what you mean.

HITMAN: You know. *(Pause.)* A moral man, that Dostoevsky. Always looking for answers to the problems of existence. Yet he couldn't keep away from the casinos. *(Pause.)* You don't watch TV?

DMITRI: No, I don't have one.

HITMAN: You've got these books, though. 'They just for show? They don't have any continuity to 'em. Maybe you got the whole lot in a garage sale. But no Dostoevsky, huh? You know he got sentenced to death by the czarist court. For being a revolutionary. He and his buddies were marched out in front of the firing squad. At the last minute someone comes riding in with a pardon. The whole bunch of them had their sentences commuted. Just a few years in Siberia. Well, they got the daylights scared out of 'em, that's all. The authorities needed these brilliant young people for the future, these budding treasures of Russia. Do you want to live like Dostoevsky?

DMITRI: *(Not understanding.)* Excuse me?

> *Pause. The* HITMAN *lets go of* DMITRI'S *ear.* DMITRI *massages it. The* HITMAN *lifts his gun and paces*

HITMAN: I know your job stinks. Nobody really wants to be a waiter. *(Pause.)* You've been so negative. Even suicidal at times. I'll help you to the other side.

DMITRI: I don't need any help, thank you.

HITMAN: But it's why I'm here.

DMITRI: Life gets to me sometimes and I've said some things.

HITMAN: Things you shouldn't have said. We all say things. I say: you have to find your way. But that's not for me to tell you now, since you're going to die.

DMITRI: No, no. Wait.

HITMAN: The waiting's over.

DMITRI: Come on. *(Pause.)* Please.

HITMAN: That word doesn't pull any weight any more.

DMITRI: *(Pause.)* Man. My whole life is flickering before my eyes.

HITMAN: Stop with the clichés.

DMITRI: Can you... at least give me one wish before I die?

HITMAN: I said, stop it. And this isn't some kind of fable. *(Pause.)* What would your wish be?

DMITRI: Well, my whole life, but actually my whole day is what's coming to mind over and over again. My whole day's summed up by a... joke... that each day is told with me in the middle of it. It's all so stupid. There's nothing noble in it. Free me from it so I can die clean.

HITMAN: You're stalling.

DMITRI: I'm not. I'm just asking for one last favor. Look. This joke of a life of mine... It's not that I want to wallow in it. It's just what's been passing as life for me. Help me, please. Just one favor.

HITMAN: You are wallowing. *(Pause.)* You know, you really should have a better collection of books.

DMITRI: You're right. They're not me. I'm too caught up in my own problems. I need your assistance, your advice. Then my books'd be more interesting.

HITMAN: Yeah, sure. *(Pause.)* You're going to die.

DMITRI: Then help me to die properly.

HITMAN: What's in it for me?

DMITRI: A compliant victim who promises not to scream and leave too much blood. This'll make it easier for you.

HITMAN: I don't need things to be easier.

DMITRI: Everybody does. You're no exception. Come on. Just you play the customer, okay? I'm the waiter, like I normally am. This'll help me and you. I promise. Let me go through this one more time, and then, I'm yours. Come over here.

HITMAN: *(Waving his gun.)* Okay, I'll do this because I don't want no mess.

DMITRI *guides him over to restaurant table that is on the other side of the stage*

DMITRI: You've got to sit down.

HITMAN: No funny business. *(He sits down and puts his gun away.)*

DMITRI: All right. I'm not going anywhere. I'm just finding my apron.

DMITRI *disappears for a moment. He comes back tying on an apron. He walks up to the table where the Hitman is seated. Their little restaurant scene begins:*

HITMAN: Waiter. What's this fly doing in my soup?

DMITRI: I believe he's doing the backstroke, sir.

HITMAN: Please remove it.

DMITRI: I can't, sir.

HITMAN: Why?

DMITRI: Maybe he's enjoying himself.

HITMAN: He? And how do you know it's a he?

DMITRI: A guess.

HITMAN: Well, I don't care if it's a he or a she. Just take the soup away.

DMITRI: I can't do that, sir.

HITMAN: Why not?

DMITRI: Soup comes with the meal. If there's a fly in the soup that's just the way it is.

HITMAN: What kind of restaurant is this?

DMITRI: Italian, sir.

HITMAN: Nothing of this kind would ever be tolerated in Rome.

DMITRI: Italy's a lot more than Rome, sir. We've never taken the minestrone away in this restaurant before the customer has at least tasted it.

HITMAN: This is a special case

DMITRI: You might be surprised how much it isn't.

HITMAN: Good God!

DMITRI: We can't take your soup away. Minestrone is good for the digestion. We can't have people leaving here with upset stomachs.

HITMAN: I'm only talking about my stomach, not people's stomachs.

DMITRI: If we take your soup away we'd have to take away all the customers' soup. We can't set a precedent. It won't do. People leaving here with indigestion.

HITMAN: But there's a fly in the soup! And flies carry germs.

DMITRI: I'm only trying to be fair. You know, the fly doesn't have it so good. If, for example, the fly yells out, "Throw me a piece of thread, so I can climb out of here before I drown," I'd have to say, no. Because if I placed a thread in the soup this time for him, I'd have to place a thread in another bowl of soup for another fly. You see, it just isn't right to set a...

HITMAN: Precedent.

DMITRI: Right. The next thing you know, we've got flies buzzing all around the establishment. No, no. It's not fair to the courageous single fly who makes it this far in life. It's not fair to the customer who expects a certain ambiance in our restaurant.

HITMAN: I want to see your manager.

DMITRI: Sorry, that's not possible, sir. If you see the manger then all the customers have to see the manager. And that's not fair to the manager who has many things on her mind.

HITMAN: *(Getting up from the table.)* Thank you for your time.

DMITRI: Are you paying by cash or by credit card?

HITMAN: For what?

DMITRI: I'm here to serve you. You're not happy with the service?

HITMAN: Yes.

DMITRI: You must be happy. Our manager insists. Is there anything I can do to apologize? A free desert, perhaps?

HITMAN: You can give me a free desert? Wouldn't that be setting a dangerous precedent?

DMITRI: Well, I've got that to factor in, but I don't want to lose my job, do I? (DMITRI *takes the "customer" by the collar and tries to sit him back down at the table. The* HITMAN *is not happy with being manhandled.*) I don't want to make you pay by threatening violence. If I did that I'd have to threaten all our customers with violence.

HITMAN: You wouldn't be setting a precedent by letting me go right now. I hear a police siren in the distance. Perhaps they're headed in this direction.

DMITRI *lets go of the* HITMAN.

DMITRI: They'll never stop here. They're fully paid off this month. (*Pause.*) Please, order the most expensive thing on the menu.

HITMAN: For free?

DMITRI: Of course not. Damn it, we need to make a living! It isn't easy to earn a position as one of the best restaurants in the city.

HITMAN: You just lost that position. I'm a food critic for the New York Times.

DMITRI *moves away with respect.*

DMITRI: Why didn't you say so? I'll take the soup away at once.

HITMAN: What about the possibility of indigestion?

DMITRI: It's worth the risk.

HITMAN: What if I told you I was the food critic for the Hackensack Weekly Register.

DMITRI: I would have to show you the door.

HITMAN: So you do have a prejudicial system here.

DMITRI: You can only expect so much from those who work with food. (*Pause.*) Sir, you are an extortionist. You think that because you'll write a positive review of this restaurant—if you're a writer at all—that you'll be given a free meal? Hah! (*Pause.*) All right. I'm finishing for the day. I'm taking off my apron. (*He takes off his apron. He holds it in his hand.*) Could I have my tip now?

HITMAN: No.

DMITRI: It's customary to tip at least fifteen percent.

HITMAN: I haven't bought anything.

DMITRI: So you want special treatment? I may have a rare blood disease and I don't go around asking to be treated differently. So why should you deserve to be a special case?

The HITMAN *gets up from his chair and ends the scene.*

HITMAN: Okay, enough of this crap! I'm not sure how much this has to do with your rotten life. (*He takes out his gun and points it at* DMITRI.) Time to meet your maker.

DMITRI: No, I'm not completely ready yet.
It's so impossible. You have a dream when you're a kid. The dream stays with you. You want to make it happen. But no one's on your side. You need money to make anything happen. I don't care what they say: there's no job—not even that of a waiter, I have discovered—where you can get money without collaborating with a way of life that I personally despise.

DMITRI: *(Continued.)* You heard it: there's a whole list of do's and don't. A whole sickening pecking order. Freedom—that's the biggest lie in the world. It isn't possible to avoid the stupid, stupid life we're given. Isn't there anyway to carve out your own path? There's got to be a way. *(Pause.)* But I think of the girl next door. She's got a degree in geography from a well-known university. She's an interesting person, but she's gone all the time now. 'Cause she has to be *practical.* She's got a job so she can live. It's not related at all to geography. She's a flight attendant. It's just like being a full-time waiter, only your restaurant's going five hundred miles an hour.

HITMAN: At least you get to travel.

DMITRI: You don't understand.

HITMAN: No? *(Pause.)* Don't tell me how difficult it is. I've been there.
>
> Many stood in my way:
>
> Time-clock card punchers.
> Shoulder-hunching donut munchers.
> Cigarette smokers in coats of leather—
> Most looking worse for the weather.
>
> Yeah, women in trousers
> Competing with computer browsers
> And silly robots with Scandinavian waves in their
>   hair.
> Yeah I played the man and the mandolin,
> Under a blue cloud,
> Sidestepping big bumbling bears.
>
> Oh, do you know the pain of a divorcée looking for
>   God,
> Or the rage of a bitch with a shaved head eating
>   antacids?
> Have you had to suffer the mocker of capitalism who
> was born to money,

HITMAN: *(Continued.)*
>Has your distress ever been ignored by a union
>seamstress?
>
>Have you had to deal with the lover of beauty—
>Who loves only dead beauty?
>I have.
>
>The list goes on.
>There's the fellow rat who stabbed me in the back,
>A wife beater, an insecure orchestra leader—
>
>There's nothing special about your case.
>Most of us have it tough.
>You have to fight.
>It's war, man, war.
>No one's there to help you.
>So many things will keep you from your
>>*self-realization*—
>
>Yeah there's a big word for you.

DMITRI: You think you've paid your dues. To me it just looks like you've found the perfect job for somebody whose soul's been destroyed by his experience of life. You work harassing and even killing others. You call that self-realization?

HITMAN: *(Shrugging off the criticism.)* Yeah, well. *(Pause.)* It's about that time.

>*Music. The* HITMAN *aims and fires his gun. Only water comes out of the gun. Music ends.*

What? Have I been playing a joke on you?

DMITRI: This water is my tears.
>Tears of worry, anger and frustration.
>The tears of somebody who
>Can't take it any longer.
>But I'll wipe away these tears.

DMITRI: *(Continued.)*
> I'll go beyond'em.
> Trying not to be bitter.
> Knowing that fortune visits the fortunate,
> And that those who are fortunate rarely see it that
> way.

HITMAN: You lost me on that last part.

DMITRI *feels transformed.*

DMITRI: I'm feeling better. It's obvious that I'm gonna have to start building something. Something that works like the planet Jupiter. You know, Jupiter's there and it draws off all the comets and aster-oids that would otherwise slam into earth. Yes, that's what I've got to do. Build my own Jupiter to protect myself.

HITMAN: You just care about yourself.

DMITRI: Can't you be a little sympathetic to what I'm trying to say?

HITMAN: *(Pause.)* Are you going to thank me? I've just saved your life. No without causing some pain. You may have some scars from it.

DMITRI: Scars that will cause certain neuroses to rear up from time to time?

HITMAN: Yeah. Like casino gambling.

DMITRI: Yes. *(He thinks otherwise.)* No. *(He doesn't understand.)* What?

HITMAN: It's was one of Dostoevsky's faults. 'Came from his scars. Remember: roulette's a waste. The only thing worth playing is black jack. It's the only game were the odds are slightly on the side of the player, not the house.

DMITRI: I don't know how I'm going to get the money to build what I need to build.

HITMAN: Your Jupiter?

DMITRI: Yes.

HITMAN: Does it always cost money?

DMITRI: Money makes the world go round.

HITMAN: I suggest you steal the money. It's the easiest way.

DMITRI: That's fine advice.

HITMAN: If you get caught, there'll be a jail cell where at least you'll be fed.

DMITRI: Oh, no. I'm slipping. I'm going back to where I was a few minutes ago. The water, the tears, they're wearing off. What can I do? You've done your job now. You can go.

HITMAN: I could. Yeah, I've got the freedom you don't have.

DMITRI: I'm so happy for you. But I can go, too. (DMITRI *attempts to walk out, but his foot gets caught on the rug, he stumbles and falls flat on his face.*)

HITMAN: (*Laughing.*) Now that's funny!

DMITRI: Wow! You're really a dark planetary influence.

HITMAN: Funny. Very funny. Let me see if I can do that. (*Gets ready to do "the trick" that* DMITRI *just did with falling.*)

DMITRI: Let's just say you tried already and it wasn't funny at all. I need a breath of fresh air.

HITMAN: I know the feeling. In my younger days...

DMITRI: Yeah, let me hear your reminisces. I'll stay and listen to them all night long.

HITMAN: You will?

DMITRI: Yes, I will. *(Pause.)* See you later. (DMITRI *walks out.*)

HITMAN: Liar.

Lights out.

End of Play.

THE GLASS CEILING

a one-act play

Characters

CATHY   *Female. 20s-50s.*

SONIA   *Female, 30s-60s.*

TAMELA   *Female, 20s to 30s., capable of being masculine.*

Place: A psychologist's office, San Francisco.
Time: Present.

Notes

Depending on how old Cathy is, the "results" of this play will differ. Sonia and Tamela are sensitive, creative women and they are not themselves in an arrested state of psycho-spiritual development as Cathy is. The play speaks to impersonation—and by extension, theater—as a powerful means for self-discovery.

There's a little bit of the Marx Brothers in an early exchange between Sonia and Cathy in "If this were a meritocracy..." and an exchange right near the end between Sonia and Tamela in "We Swiss are known for our cheese...".

A reading of the play was directed by Petra Ulrych in Denver, Colorado on August 2, 2001. Laura Cuetara and Fanny Andrade joined her in presenting the play. Dramaturg: Walter Teres.

The Glass Ceiling

In the room where psychologist Dr. Sonia Westin sees her patients. A chair, a couch, a small desk with a chair behind it. Lights up. CATHY *and* SONIA *are sitting, talking.*

CATHY: Because I'm a woman, Doctor, I was passed over for promotion.

SONIA: You can't think like that. If you believe that we can never make any progress. In your mind, let's walk through where you work. There are spaces and places for you and your co-workers. Walls and halls. Partitions. You have your own cubicle. There's the desk, your papers. Your boss of course has a corner office with plenty of windows. He has to worry about the glare of the sun on his computer screen. That's one thing you don't have to worry about.

CATHY: Very true.

SONIA: See, there's something you have that he doesn't.

CATHY: Yes, I'm totally shut off from nature.

SONIA: You have only a small space so you can't clutter anything up. Everything in your cubbyhole is neatly ordered.

CATHY: Yes.

SONIA: You can always find anything there. No wasted time. You're efficient. This makes you very happy.

CATHY: No, I'm not happy. That's why I'm seeing you. I work long hours in a stifling environment.

SONIA: You must find a friend somehow in this environment.

CATHY: I bought a plant.

SONIA: That's good.

CATHY: An ivy plant.

SONIA: Oh, nice.

CATHY: But now I've got a plastic one. The ivy plant died. And I'm going to die too right there in my cubicle. My only hope was to get the promotion and get an office that has a window.

SONIA: Your *only* hope? Aren't you exaggerating? Do the windows in the office actually open? No. How much closer to nature would you really be?

CATHY: Are we focusing on my job or nature?

SONIA: Your job. But there are other horrible things in life. For instance, the fact that there's a television installed in every house, every waiting room—even in health clubs, for God's sake. Yes, it's awful! Don't you agree? At least we don't have a TV in our waiting room. See, we improve our world, little by little, first starting with our own backyard, so to speak.

CATHY: Well, I don't have a backyard, dammit. I've got a tiny little friggin' space.

SONIA: Now, now. You're upset. Sex is often unrewarding in the workplace.

CATHY: Do you speak from experience, Doctor?

SONIA: You can call me Sonia. *(Pause.)* Let's analyze this outburst of yours. You know, using an obscenity only sends up a red flag and tells the world that you're frustrated and probably depressed.

CATHY: I *am* depressed.

SONIA: But should the world know? Don't you want privacy?

CATHY: Listen, I don't use obscenities in public.

SONIA: Good, the kind of language you used is not exactly "ladies' language".

CATHY: We don't live in the world of our grandmothers.

SONIA: But we still live mostly in a man's world. And they don't want to hear such talk from a woman.

CATHY: You're being rather conservative.

SONIA: I'm only trying to see it from a man's point of view. A lady in business shouldn't be heard using that kind of language if she wants to succeed.

CATHY: Are you blaming me for not getting the promotion?

SONIA: You should examine your own actions to see if they may have contributed to your being turned down for the job.

CATHY: No one's ever heard me swear in the office.

SONIA: But maybe outside the office?

CATHY: I don't see anybody from the office outside the office.

SONIA: Ahh! So we get to an important point. You don't mix with your co-workers outside the job?

CATHY: Never.

SONIA: And you expect to be promoted?

CATHY: I'm excellent at what I do. Practically no one knows the company's inner workings as well as I do. And I know their sales base, too. If this were a meritocracy I would be president of the whole thing.

SONIA: If America were a meritocracy we'd never have the presidents that we've had who undermine democracy.

CATHY: If this were a meritocracy...

SONIA: ...I'd be president.

CATHY: Passed over for promotion again! *(Pause.)* No one deserved to be promoted more than I. I've given the company all that I've had.

SONIA: Except your free time.

CATHY: Dammit, it's my time.

SONIA: I think you have a very deep problem. With your job, with your anger. With your life, really.

CATHY: *(Seething.)* Professionally speaking, no one else holds a candle to me.

SONIA: Yet you still get burned. Look. Why don't you make a fresh start. You could change your job.

CATHY: Easier said than done. The only jobs available are worse than what I've got already. Long hours and terrible pay. And in my profession, foreigners'll put up with that crap. I won't.

SONIA: No, Cathy, don't get angry. You'll get even more depressed. We must assume that foreigners will do a lot of things we won't.

CATHY: I don't know why I came to you. You don't make me feel any better at all.

SONIA: I'm not here to agree with you. I'm here to put you on the path to self-fulfillment. In a job market where they have to hire foreigners because there are not enough American citizens to do the job, you are so pathetic that you can't get a promotion. Let me bring in my assistant. She knows what you're going through.

CATHY: Do you really think a third person is necessary?

SONIA: Yes.

> SONIA *goes to the door, opens it. A woman,* TAMELA, *is there. She has a shaman's stick by her side and slung on her shoulder is a bag filled with various shamanic items*

SONIA: She's a former patient of mine. She's a specialist in role-playing. She's got a few gender issues. Specifically, she's nervous about being stuck at the moment on two males as her role models. But she's got other things up her sleeve, you'll see.

> TAMELA *speaks with a low voice.*

TAMELA: Hello, my name is Tamela. But in this office I'm usually either Theophrastus Bombast von Hohenheim or Sun Sze-Mo. When I'm not working for Sonia, I'm the director of a small museum here in San Francisco and if you, being from Silicon Valley, and being rich, would care to make a donation to the museum, I'd be happy to accept. (*Pause.*) It's always best to get charity out of the way right at the start.

CATHY: You seem to making an assumption about me that's incorrect.

TAMELA: What assumption?

CATHY: That I'm rich.

TAMELA: You're not rich?

CATHY: No.

TAMELA: Then what are you traveling into the city for to see one of the most expensive therapists in the Bay Area?

CATHY: I don't need to explain to you.

SONIA: Now, Cathy, you should explain. She's your therapist, like I am. And we are expensive.

CATHY: I do what I think is best for me.

TAMELA: You'd be filthy rich if you cooked at home. They pay you enough at your job. Yuppies waste all the wealth of this country by spending it in restaurants.

CATHY: But that's good for restauranteurs.

TAMELA: Poor yuppies. Take my advice. Cook at home. There're fewer parasites in the food.

CATHY: I didn't come here to be insulted.

SONIA: Quite right. My assistant's techniques aren't always soothing—whether she's playing the role of Theophratus Bombast or she's playing Sun Sze-Mo. The first person was of unorthodox but sound methods. The second person was a little quieter.

CATHY: These names mean nothing to me.

SONIA: It's only important that they mean something to Tamela.

TAMELA: Bombast von Hohenheim renamed himself as Paracelsus. Do you recognize that name?

CATHY: Not really.

TAMELA: He said this:
> "He who knows nothing, loves nothing.
> He who can do nothing understands nothing.
> He who understands nothing is worthless.

TAMELA: *(Continued.)*
> But he who understands also loves, notices, and
> sees..."

SONIA: That's very good.

TAMELA: Paracelsus had his bombastic moments. I'll try to remain subdued.

CATHY: You've haven't been very subtle so far.

TAMELA: You have a problem with your over-self. Your spirit is sick and it's affecting your body.

CATHY: I wouldn't say my spirit is sick.

TAMELA: *Something* of you is having trouble in your fragmented, material world.

CATHY: Why kind of museum do you run, anyway?

SONIA: It's called the Museum of Medicine and World Culture. Don't get Bombast von Hohenheim off the track or she goes completely ballistic.

TAMELA: I was born in Switzerland. In 1493.

CATHY: You don't look your age.

SONIA: Cathy, she's playing her role.

CATHY: So?

TAMELA: *(Shaking her stick at her.)* Ah hah! You've proved that have no interest in any information except that which immediately concerns yourself. Sonia, what have you found as the particulars of her case?

SONIA: Hasn't hit rock bottom yet. She's an asocial misfit who's unwilling and unable to mix with her co-workers after-hours. She deservedly was passed over for a promotion. She nurses the delusion that she was passed over for a promotion solely because she's a woman.

TAMELA: She's a fool. (*Pause. Now, to* CATHY.) Sorry, you're a fool. (*Pause.*) Guess who wrote a book about germs in 8th century China?

CATHY: I have no idea.

TAMELA: I did. In my book I connected germs with the cosmos.

CATHY: Congratulations.

SONIA: She's now Sun Sze-Mo, the great Chinese writer and thinker.

TAMELA: Thank you. Everything is interconnected in the cosmos, don't you agree?

CATHY: I might.

TAMELA: But you don't really live that way. You're disconnected from the universe. This is the root of your problem.

CATHY: No, the root of my problem is that I've lived to see the day that some jerk has gotten the job that I should have. And it's very, very upsetting.

TAMELA: This jerk was a man—

CATHY: Precisely.

TAMELA: All right, then. I will speak to you as Hohenheim the Healer rather than Sun Sze-Mo the thinker.

CATHY: Whatever works for you.

TAMELA: Do you by chance have a brother?

CATHY: As a matter of fact, I do.

TAMELA: As part of our role-playing therapy here I assign you the role of your brother. Who is your brother?

CATHY: His name is Joe. But he likes to be called "Gone Fishin'"

TAMELA: And why is that?

CATHY: Because he doesn't like to work. He'd rather be out fishing.

TAMELA: Interesting.

CATHY: He's not the one under consideration here.

TAMELA: But he is. Because you're him now.

CATHY: I don't know how this has anything to do with me.

TAMELA: You'll see. *(Pause. She begins to ask "the brother" questions.)* Now, Gone Fishin', what kind of fish do you like to catch?

CATHY: Any kind.

   Pause. TAMELA *thinks for a moment.*

TAMELA: Would you say you are often tired?

CATHY: No.

TAMELA: And why is that?

CATHY: Because I don't work very hard.

TAMELA: Are you often depressed?

CATHY: No. I really was only once.

   Pause. TAMELA *thinks.*

TAMELA: What was the highest paying job you ever had?

CATHY: I worked for a pharmaceutical company deep in the jungles of the Amazon.

TAMELA: Do you still work for this company?

CATHY: Of course not, there was too much work there.

TAMELA: What do you do now?

CATHY: When I'm not fishing?

TAMELA: Yes.

CATHY: I play the guitar and write songs.

TAMELA: Ah-hah. But you can't possibly support yourself by playing the guitar and writing songs.

CATHY: No, I can't.

TAMELA: Then what do you do?

CATHY: I take people to the center of the earth.

TAMELA: You must be joking.

CATHY: It's a bit of joke. I give tours of subterranean caverns.

TAMELA: Is there any other kind of cavern?

CATHY: Not to my knowledge.

TAMELA: Does your sister Cathy think you are weird?

CATHY: I hope not.

SONIA: I think you can give a better answer than that.

TAMELA: Does Cathy think you're weird?

CATHY: Yes, a little bit.

TAMELA *is happy with this answer.*

TAMELA: Fine, fine. *(Pause.)* Do people at the caverns call you Gone Fishin' or Joe?

CATHY: Only a couple of people that work there who are close to me call me by my nickname.

TAMELA: Good. Do the caverns contain any water in them?

CATHY: Yes.

TAMELA: But no fish?

CATHY: No.

TAMELA: So the water is rather extraordinary. Do you know the writings of Hildegard von Bingen?

CATHY: No.

TAMELA: Are you aware of the writings of Carl Jung?

CATHY: Vaguely.

TAMELA: Do you associate your work in the caverns with the creative process?

CATHY: Yes.

TAMELA: Have you ever heard of Max Ernst?

CATHY: No. But I did make a collage as a child.

TAMELA: Hmm. Why do you associate your work in the caverns with the creative process?

CATHY: Because when I'm beneath the surface of the earth I start to grasp the notion of the collective unconscious. I feel free and creative in the dream-like environment.

TAMELA: What does your sister think about all this?

CATHY: She doesn't have a clue.

TAMELA: That's a problem. You know it's taken a long time for beings to evolve from non-thinking germs into beings that can have even the dimmest kind of reflective life.

CATHY: Have you shifted into being Sun Sze-Mo now?

TAMELA: *(Ignoring the question.)* Where does a poem come from?

CATHY: We all want to create things.

TAMELA: That's why you'd rather write songs than work in the caverns?

CATHY: I'd rather go fishing.

TAMELA: Does working in the caverns inform your writing of songs?

CATHY: I'd still rather go fishing.

TAMELA: There seems to be a stubborn streak in the members of your family. Note that, Doctor.

SONIA: Yes.

TAMELA: Are you aware of the noosphere?

CATHY: What's that?

SONIA: It's not *bio*sphere—that's the earth-skin made up of living things.

TAMELA: The noosphere is the earth's thinking-skin. It is a spiritual and philosophical realm.

CATHY: But where's that leave the caverns?

TAMELA: They can still function as metaphors. *(Pause.)* Okay, I'm through with your brother for the moment. What have we learned from this?

CATHY: *(Herself again.)* Nothing.

TAMELA: You're a very superficial person, you know.

CATHY: How can you say that?

TAMELA: Because your brother is so deep.

SONIA: Men are deep and worthy of our respect.

CATHY: I never said they weren't. What I'm saying is that men have an advantage over women in our society and I've been a victim of this.

TAMELA: But it's quite possible that men are deeper than women, and more deserving of reward in society because of this. *(Pause.)* You are a conformist.

CATHY: Well, I have a job, and I don't go around preferring to be called Gone Fishin' by my friends.

TAMELA: But you don't really have too many friends, do you?

CATHY: Not really. There isn't time.

TAMELA: And you're not originally from Silicon Valley.

CATHY: Of course not. Almost nobody is.

TAMELA: You're a lonely person.

CATHY: If you asked me that earlier I could have told you. But you prefer to show off with your weird questions. I can't believe the amount of money I'm paying to talk to somebody who's an imposter.

TAMELA: Yes, I am this or that other person. I told you from the start. (*Pause.*) Do I detect some hostility in your voice?

CATHY: I've been jealous of my brother my whole life.

TAMELA: You want to tell Bombast von Hohenheim about it?

CATHY: I already told him and maybe even that guy Sun Sze-Mo about it.

TAMELA: Tell me what your brother did in South America when he was working for the drug company.

CATHY: He chased little buggers out of the rainforest so they could farm the land for new drugs.

TAMELA: You seem happy to say that.

CATHY: Yes. He got pretty depressed then. It's about the only time in his life that he ever committed a big sin.

TAMELA: But isn't working to kill harmful germs a service to mankind?

CATHY: Not if you're removing people from their own homes.

TAMELA: So it made you feel good to see your brother conforming and doing something awful.

CATHY: Yes.

TAMELA: But ultimately he saw the error of his ways. Was it then that he desired to be known to people as Gone Fishin'?

CATHY: I think so.

TAMELA: Do you find your job morally repugnant?

CATHY: No, we don't hurt anybody.

TAMELA: But you seem to have been hurt.

CATHY: Yes—by sexism.

Pause. TAMELA *thinks.*

TAMELA: Do you know how to dance?

CATHY: Yes, of course.

TAMELA: I'm not talking about *(With disdain.)* rock'n'roll dancing.

CATHY: I can do a few dances, like ballroom dancing, if that's what you mean.

TAMELA: Actually, I'm talking about dancing like an Amazon. Sonia, if you could just stand aside. Cathy and I are going to dance.

SONIA *moves over a little bit.*

CATHY: *(To* TAMELA.*)* What?

TAMELA: Yes, dance.

CATHY: You know something about the dances of the Amazon Indians?

TAMELA: Did your brother already show you?

CATHY: I don't think he learned to dance down there.

TAMELA: It's his loss. (*Pause.*) Before I came to Sonia for therapy I was student of anthropology and archeology. I went to the fabled land of the Amazons, which is not in Brazil, but closer to the Mediterranean Sea. My work on the ancient Amazons—you know they were female warriors—was highly stressful. In fact, I got downright depressed. Because it was obvious that so much of the evidence had been *intentionally* destroyed. But I did learn how to dance their dances by deciphering a number of priceless clay tablets. It was only during my therapy with Dr. Westin that I realized that this ancient dancing could be a healing tool. Cathy, let's be feminine together.

> CATHY *does not respond.* TAMELA *takes off her shoulder bag and limbers up.*

TAMELA: (*Letting her in on a secret.*) It was through dancing that the Museum for Health and World Culture was born.

CATHY: Oh.

TAMELA: I'm taking you on a spirit quest. Let's go, Amazon-style, to the center of the earth! When you answered me in the role of your brother, you told me that he takes people to the center of the earth. That's where we'll go. We'll bring you closer to your brother.

CATHY: But I didn't come here to get closer to my brother.

TAMELA: No, that's where you're mistaken. This is where your problem is. It's with men. And it starts with your brother.

CATHY: Maybe it starts with my father.

SONIA: Cathy, we're not Freudians here.

TAMELA: Okay. Close your eyes first.

> CATHY *closes her eyes.*

TAMELA: *(Continued.)*

    We're living in the future.
    A confusing future where people sometimes
    Don't know who they are.
    It's the future where intelligence lives outside our
        bodies in machines.
    And these machines aren't even like
    Beings from another time and place.
    The intelligence outside our bodies
    Is not the intelligence we have known inside our
        bodies in the past.
    The intelligence outside our bodies
    Is coordinated by power and money and loves telling
        lies.
    Not fun, game-like lies.
    But lies that rip our souls out.
    True intelligence is acquired without aid of
        machines,
    True intelligence is found with our bodies.
    It is facilitated by various means,
    Including role-playing,
    We step, as it were, into other peoples' shoes.
    We've done this already, haven't we?

CATHY: Yes.

TAMELA: So it's on to the next step.

    Easily we are separated from the center.
    Machines, TV's, computers... they're good at making
        this happen.
    If we don't re-connect to the center,
    We are condemned to all kinds of foolish thoughts.
    What germ smiles to see these foolish thoughts being
        spread into infinity?
    The germ which is the idea that we're mere fragments
    Suspended in the soup of chaos.

TAMELA: *(Continued.)*
> What does this germ have in common with
> machines?
> Many things.
> And one thing is they both do not breathe oxygen.
> Breathe in now, breath out.

They both breathe in and out once.

> Our blue and white planet is not the center of the
> universe.
> We've known that for some time.
> But we don't have to overreact once we learn this
> information.
> Cathy, now use our bodies to re-connect. Let's
> Dance our way down to the important stuff.
> Keep your eyes closed. Now give me your hand.

Pause. TAMELA *leads* CATHY *in a dance: various broad movements, nothing formulaic. Towards the end of the dance they speak:*

TAMELA: You're there now. The center of the earth. Do you feel it?

CATHY: Not especially.

TAMELA: You're stupid, then.

CATHY: Hey wait a minute!

TAMELA: Don't open your eyes.

CATHY: I'm going to open my eyes if you continue to abuse me!

TAMELA: Do you know that Bombast von Hohenheim maintained that wounds would heal naturally if kept clean and drained?

CATHY: So what?

TAMELA: We are cleaning and draining.

CATHY: Yeah right. I don't understand why you have to play people who lived centuries ago.

TAMELA: We mix you up to get you off-balance, open you up. It's an old technique. So many of the wise have used it with great success.

CATHY *stops dancing and opens her eyes.*

CATHY: Okay. This is enough! You know about the glass ceiling. Women can only advance so far in business. They can't break through the glass above, where they can see that there are men making all the real decisions. Your therapy is too far out for me. I should have picked a more traditional therapist.

TAMELA: You want traditional therapy?! No problem.

She sets down her shaman's stick if she is holding it. She takes a mask out of her bag and holds it in front of her face while she chants at a higher pitch than that of her normal speaking voice:

> Retain your good root and curse not the snake.
> There are but brief hours in these argued days
> Where peace is real and pain subsides.
>
> Raise ye, raise ye.
>
> Rich fields are those that join with sky.

CATHY: No, that won't work either.

SONIA: You have to loosen up. This is one of your problems, dear. Look how your brother and people around him have loosened up. They call him Gone Fishin'. He works as little as possible. It sounds to me like he's happy. And you are not happy.

CATHY: Do you think a woman could go around being called Gone Fishin'? No, only a man can get away with doing something like that.

SONIA: I think you should choose a nickname for yourself. Just like your brother.

CATHY: I don't want to be like my brother.

SONIA: Don't you want to be happy like your brother?

CATHY: Well, I'd like to be happy, yeah.

SONIA: Then pick a new name for yourself.

CATHY: It isn't as easy as that.

SONIA: It's a start. Look what Tamela's done. She's chosen Bombast von Hohenheim and see what wonders it works.

CATHY: She hasn't worked wonders for me.

SONIA: I disagree. Much has been accomplished. We have established that 1) you work hard and have no creative outlet, 2) you're jealous of your brother, 3) a life of conformity exerts great stress upon you, so, 4) you blame sexism for not getting a promotion.

CATHY: But I tell you, number four is true. It's true!

SONIA: You must choose another name.

CATHY: Have you chosen another name for yourself? Sonia sounds pretty real to me.

SONIA: I have chosen a name for myself. But only my husband calls me it when we're in bed.

CATHY: Listen, I'll show you I'm not imagining things when it comes to not getting that promotion. Do you have an internet connection?

SONIA: Well, we thought long and hard about whether to have a computer here. Yes, we're connected.

CATHY: Good. It won't take a second.

SONIA: What you do want to do?

CATHY: Access my e-mail.

SONIA: And?

CATHY: I sent myself a copy of the memo that shows what I'm talking about is true. It concerns the promotion of the man to the position that rightfully should have been mine.

SONIA: And you got a copy of this e-mail by...?

CATHY: Hacking into my boss's e-mail.

SONIA: That's not so good. And the memo said...?

CATHY: It said that all things being equal they were going to give the position to Arjuna Krishna Gupta, instead of me, because he had a family to support and I didn't. What do you say to that, huh?

TAMELA: I say a busy mind can be at odds with healing.

SONIA: I think you should pick a new name for yourself before it's too late.

CATHY: I can print out the memo—

SONIA: That's not necessary.

TAMELA: Have you ever read Aristotle's book, "Ethics?"

CATHY: No.

TAMELA: Neither have I.

SONIA: I haven't either. But still I know the difference between right and wrong.

CATHY: You're both ganging up on me. Look, I only hacked in there to confirm my suspicions and they were confirmed.

SONIA: I don't need to tell you that a person who doesn't respect confidentially in the workplace might not be the best candidate for promotion.

CATHY: You don't need to tell me, but you are telling me.

TAMELA: It's a psychologist's trick of rhetoric. She used it on me all the time.

SONIA: Now let me see here. What would be a good name for Cathy to get a new start with her life?

TAMELA: My vote goes to "Amazon dancer".

SONIA: I think she might call herself simply "Jewel" because much of what she's been up to lately seems to have so little luster.

TAMELA: You can play either one of these people. Either one will inform your true self and help to heal your spirit.

CATHY: There's less a problem here with spirit and more of one with politics and society in general.

Pause. TAMELA *is unhappy with* CATHY.

TAMELA: I need you to be your brother again. Are you game?

SONIA: We've still a few more minutes.

CATHY: Well, whatever.

TAMELA: You'd rather go fishing than do anything else in the world?

CATHY *plays her brother now.*

CATHY: I never said that.

TAMELA: Oh. Going fishing's preferable to work, but there are other things besides fishing that you enjoy?

CATHY: Of course.

TAMELA: What do you enjoy?

CATHY: I like to dream.

TAMELA: Dream of what?

CATHY: The usual stuff. A summer's day. A breeze in the trees. The smell of the leaves. A kiss on the cheek from out of nowhere.

TAMELA: Do you ever think about your family?

CATHY: I'm single.

TAMELA: I mean the family you grew up in.

CATHY: Yes.

TAMELA: Do you ever think about your sister, Cathy?

CATHY: Sure. I like to see her. But she keeps to herself. Then again, she can get very intense, you know, when she is around. That drives me a little crazy.

TAMELA: Ah-huh. Do you think there's any chance that she ever may be a little more open and less intense?

CATHY: I don't know. It's up to her. There's only so much that anyone else can do.

TAMELA: Right. I'm through with your brother now. Thank you, Cathy.

SONIA: So what have we learned here?

CATHY: *(Herself again.)* That I have a serious emotional problem.

SONIA: And how can we deal with this problem?

CATHY: By getting even with that bastard who got my job.

SONIA: You're not thinking straight. Have you thought of a name?

CATHY: Absolutely not.

TAMELA: The only name she can think of is Arjuna Krishna Gupta.

SONIA: That will not do. *(Pause. To CATHY.)* If you want to move up the ranks in business then more and more is going to be demanded of you. You're not ready for that yet. Because you cannot be trusted. Here we lie to one another, take on names and roles and coax our demons out. Cathy, you have the chance with us to do something about your problems. *(Pause.)* Sorry, time's up. You decide whether you're going to come back.

CATHY: *(Pause.)* Well, all right.

SONIA: Good-bye.

TAMELA: *(Hard.)* Auf Wiedersehn.

 CATHY *picks up her handbag and goes. Pause.*

SONIA: It's tough being a woman in a businessman's world.

TAMELA: But we don't let it drive us crazy. We can make it into a business*woman's* world, too.

SONIA: Don't misunderstand me. Men *are* in the wrong—often. But in a therapeutic setting complaining doesn't get us very far. For us, the emphasis is more on *action*, though we will never deprecate reactions—they are natural, real, and true. *(Pause.)* Our kind of therapy works best when it's not an option to blame somebody else.

TAMELA: But it's an option to be somebody else.

SONIA: Who would you like to be now?

TAMELA: My name is Bombast von Hohenheim. Known also as Paracelsus.

They laugh.

SONIA: Bombast, for short—I like that. So tell me, what's the largest city in Switzerland?

TAMELA: It isn't Geneva or Basel like when I was a child.

SONIA: But you like Basel, don't you?

TAMELA: They have more museums there per capita, than any other place in the world.

SONIA: Why's that important to you?

TAMELA: It's not important to me. But it's important to Tamela.

SONIA: And who is Tamela?

TAMELA: Your assistant who happens to run the brand new *under-funded* Museum of Medicine and World Culture here in San Francisco.

SONIA: Why does this Tamela sometimes call herself Sun Sze-Mo?

TAMELA: It works for her.

SONIA: He's the germ-guy. Right. *(Pause.)* How healthy are your countrymen, if I may ask?

TAMELA: It depends—but we Swiss are known for our cheese.

SONIA: And the Matterhorn.

TAMELA: And goats.

SONIA: And Heidi.

TAMELA: And chocolate!

SONIA: And army knives.

TAMELA: And remaining neutral during the wars...

SONIA: ...but financing them all!

TAMELA: *(Looking in her shaman's bag:)* Do you want a cowbell?

SONIA: No, but I'll take that. *(She points to the shaman's stick.)*

> TAMELA *hands* SONIA *her shaman's stick.* TAMELA *holds her mask out in front of her face.* SONIA *shakes the stick in rhythm while she and* TAMELA *chant and dance together.*

TAMELA and SONIA:
> Retain your good root and curse not the snake.
> There are but brief hours in these argued days
> Where peace is real and pain subsides.
>
> Raise ye, raise ye.
>
> Rich fields are those that join with sky.

They continue to dance. The lights fade out.

End of Play.

MAD COW DISEASE IN AMERICA

a one-act solo play

The Character

CITIZEN   *Male or Female adult.*

Place: Somewhere in the U.S.
Time: Present.

Notes

To entertain and to provoke thought, surrealism in general, and this piece in particular, use paranoid-obsessive speechmaking, automatic writing, combinations of mundane and unusual subject matter, and surprising contexts. What is the most common thing here that is out of joint? The old folk songs. They will likely be unfamiliar to the reader. It is unfortunate that these cannot be heard in the mind of the reader because the counterpoint between what is traditional/beautiful and what is new/diseased will not be so vivid to them.

In performance this drama, with its initial jarring effects, will gradually give shape to very interesting unified whole. For the Citizen, America is the lover that s/he is disappointed with. This is conveyed obliquely by the use of the love songs in the beginning and the end. All the other songs (except for the next-to-the-last song) have humorous, odd, and ironic connections to the rest of the text.

This is a dramatic collage that allows for a certain amount of freedom, so I do not want to give too many stage directions. I will say however that delivering the lines with an almost naïve incredulity comes in handy from time to time. But having said that, I must also say that it benefits the drama at times for the actor to swagger through some of the material, sometimes being rather cocky about it.

If the Citizen is played by a woman there will be a few slight changes necessary to the script. All of the songs, except for the last song, can be found in the *Burl Ives Song Book* first published in 1953. Many libraries still have this book. The last song, "Charlie Brooks", which was slightly rewritten for this play, is also a traditional song in the public domain. I found it in an old *Song Dex* songbook.

Incidentally, at present about one-third of cattle feed producers fail government inspections that are designed to keep mad cow disease from American cattle. Mad cow disease has also recently shown up in Japan.

The piece was first presented by Bill Dunn in Paris, France on March 25, 2001. Dramaturg: Walter Teres.

Mad Cow Disease in America

The play takes place on an almost bare stage. In the darkness the CITIZEN
*sings the first and sixth verses from the American traditional song, "I'm Sad and
I'm Lonely":*

> I'm sad and I'm lonely,
> My heart it will break,
> For my sweetheart loves another;
> Oh, I wish I was dead.
>
> I'm troubled, yes, I'm troubled,
> I'm troubled in my mind,
> If this trouble don't kill me,
> I'll live a long time.

*We hear a collage of voices. The overlapping voices in the sound collage say:
"They're lying. They're lying to us again. They're lying to us. They're lying., etc."
The voices die down and end. It is still dark.*

CITIZEN: Rib steak. Rump steak. New York Cut. Eye steak.
Hamburger.
    Me? My name? I'm a citizen. That's all you need to know—

Lights up. The CITIZEN *sits in a corner of the playing area with an
American flag draped around him. There is a burlap bag next to him. On
the stage is also an easel. On this easel is a placard. The placard reads,
"Actually, he's the last independent American rancher."*

CITIZEN: *(Continued.)* —except the fact that I get upset when I hear people saying that the *first case* of mad cow disease in America might be in Gonzales, Texas where there was a quarantine of cattle in January of 2001. They imposed the quarantine 'cause of concern that the cows'd been fed some feed containing the ground up-bones and organs of other cattle.

The CITIZEN gets up off the floor. He takes off the flag and places it in the burlap bag .

But no, Nebraska comes before that.

The CITIZEN sings the third verse from the traditional song, "Little Mohee":

> She said, "My pappy's a chieftain and ruler be he;
> I'm his only daughter and my name is Mohee."
> I answered and told her that it never could be,
> 'Cause I had my own sweetheart in my own country.

The song ends.

1877. Fort Robinson, Nebraska. Crazy Horse, Oglala Sioux Chief, who's been under military arrest for some two years, is escorted to a cabin where he's to spend the upcoming winter. Just before he enters the cabin, a soldier accompanying him drives a bayonet into his breast. The soldier is not prosecuted. This assassination would be the only well-known incident to take place in the town of Fort Robinson until the year 1998. In this year, in Fort Robinson, the first known evidence in America of mad cow disease occurs. No people were infected.

Pause. We hear spacey music—like that heard during a planetarium show. The CITIZEN continues while the music plays.

The Currier farm lies down a road just off Nebraska state route 39, not far from the White River. In the early fall, it's always hard to get much done on the farm. The climate and the soil composition of the area is the reason. The climate is mostly dry, except in the winter when it snows and in September when it rains. The soil contains a great deal of clay. And in the autumn, when the temperature's cool and it rains, the soil turns into something the locals call *gumbo*. Not the chicken gumbo soup of Louisiana. This is something entirely different. Now this sticky gumbo makes it difficult to move at all if you happen to find yourself in it. You get paralyzed if you're not careful. And you think a snowstorm can be bad! You get all the mud slapped up and sticking on the bottom of your truck so your wheels can't turn. You could just as well be trying to drive over a road of newly poured cement in a freshly-made adobe house.

The planetarium-type music fades out.

There are a lot of dirt roads in the Fort Robinson area, but not near plenty enough to get around on farm property with its wide-open grazing areas. You have to drive off-road at times. The gumbo gets four feet deep in some places and takes on the character of quicksand.

Now, it was in the fall of 1998 that the first case of mad cow disease in America was confirmed. How did this come about? The cattle near Fort Robinson did something crazy. In a distant section of the Currier farm they went into the gumbo which they normally have a sense to avoid. When the cows were dead, their brain tissue was sent in for analysis. They did not have rabies. But there was proof of mad cow disease in one of them. How was it that the story never found its way into the press? Well, first the gumbo slowed everything down. It took a while to haul the cows out of the mud and get the tissue samples sent to Lincoln, Nebraska, the capital of the state. By that time it was Christmas and the folks at the lab were on vacation. They got back and finally got to testing. When they found out they had a case of mad cow disease on their hands, they kept it real quiet. They concluded on their own that this was a bizarre, spontaneous outbreak of BSE, the scientific name for mad cow disease, 'cause it happened only in that one cow, and the odds of spontaneous BSE had recently been calculated at one in 960,000 cows. Apparently the other cattle that died stuck in the gumbo were cows that wandered there out of curiosity. It seems they wondered what was up with the diseased cow and went to check her out. Anybody who knows cattle knows what I mean.

Pause.

CITIZEN: *(Continued.)*

The scientists in Nebraska figured that mad cow would pop up like this from time to time. They just were victims of that one-in-a-million occurrence of the disease. There are more than two million cattle in Nebraska. Probably at the other end of the state there was another case of the disease that'd go unnoticed. But maybe it would be noticed. The thing now was, scientists were just starting to be able to test for mad cow. In fact, it was only 16 months since the state of Nebraska had got their first test "kits" for the disease. The officials in the state capital were positive that that cow in Fort Robinson couldn't have eaten feed made with cattle by-products. Because this kind of feed isn't marketed in the U.S.

The great problem with the disease is when it's *not* spontaneously occurring, but when it is *spread.* Mad cow is transmitted when cows eat feed that contains tissue from infected dead cattle. Humans get the human form of mad cow disease when they eat the meat of infected cattle. In Europe, the problem started when cows were given feed that was not wholly of vegetable and mineral origins. Ultimately 80 people in England and the mass destruction of millions of cattle occurred. Now, some people, when they first hear of "BSE" being used instead of the words "mad cow disease" think that somehow the "B" of "BSE" stands for British something or other. Actually, BSE, is an abbreviation of bovine spongiform encephalopathy; to get more technical and more human at the same time, when BSE happens in humans it changes its name to "new variant Creutzfeld-Jakob," or vCJ, for short.

More planetarium-type music fades in.

The whole science of mad cow is exasperating. We don't really know where the mutant protein that causes the disease comes from. Yes, *mutant protein.* Vaguely like a virus, this mutant protein is not part of the evolutionary apparatus we see in action among the mammals, fish, reptiles, what-have-you, here on our planet. This leads many scientists to conjecture that this mutant protein, or *prion* must come from outer space.

He changes the placard on the easel. The new placard reads, "Ultimately everything comes from outer space:". *After the audience has had time to read this he changes the placard. The new placard reads,* "try to tell this to a fundamentalist." *The planetarium-type music continues.*

Prions breathe no air. Yet they are animated. They are opportunistic hellions, microscopic entities with a concept of existence that surely is not our concept of life. We don't know much about prions but we do know that we can't cook them out of food, and that they eat us alive.

The planetarium-type music ends.

Rib steak. Rump steak. Ground Round. Chuck.

Pause.

The next case of mad cow disease in America was discovered 5 months after the deaths of the Nebraska cow. This brings us roughly to March, 1999. The disease was found again in the heartland of America, in another big cattle-state, in Kansas. Not far from the town of Russell, Kansas. The town itself is known as the birthplace of senator Bob Dole, who ran for the U.S. presidency on the Republican ticket in 1996 and lost. This is also the birthplace of U.S. senator Arlen Spector, another Republican, who now operates out of Pennsylvania. There must be something in the water of Russell, Kansas for lightening to strike there twice like this.

The CITIZEN *sings the first verse from the song* "The Young Man Who Wouldn't Hoe Corn":

> I'll sing you a song—and it's not very long,
> About a young man who wouldn't hoe corn.
> The reason why—I can't tell,
> For this young man was always well.

The music fades.

CITIZEN: *(Continued.)* Well, Kansas is a huge state for beef. Signs proclaim that one farmer in Kansas feeds beef to 384 Americans per day. That's a lot of meat. That's a lot of souls of defenseless cattle floating around in heaven. When it became apparent to state officials who were testing the brains of two head of cattle who had died mysteriously in the Big Sky area of Russell, Kansas that they had a *couple* of cases of mad cow disease on their hands, these officials went into a top secret mode. It might as well have been the first atomic bomb that they had in their possession. You couldn't explain the business away as a spontaneous occurrence of the disease. They were into new territory. Like when scientists found the brain-wasting disease called *kuru* in Papua, New Guinea, in the nineteen-fifties. The disease was not spontaneous. In New Guinea, they found the tribe was eating the brains of their dead relatives. In Russell, Kansas, *something* was transmitting the disease. But the officials in Kansas undertook no investigation into how the two cows became infected. They sent out an advisory, which had been sent out before, that cattle should only be fed American cattle feed. That was it and life moved on.

More planetarium-type music plays in the background. The CITIZEN *continues.*

It has been observed in European patients who've contracted new variant Creutzfeld-Jakob, or vCJ, that the mutant protein works by slowly eating a hole in the brain until the brain can no longer function and the patient dies. As with viruses, antibiotics are useless. Those with vCJ can expect to experience a painful 12-month decline during which synthetic opiates—or opiates themselves—are administered to alleviate the suffering.

The planetarium-type music fades out. Pause. The Citizens sings from the folk version of "Old Dan Tucker":

> Went to town the other night
> To hear a noise and see a fight.
> All the people's was jumpin' around and said,
> "Old Dan Tucker's a-comin' to town."

Hey, get out of the way for Old Dan Tucker,
Too late to get his supper.
Supper's over, dinner's cookin',
Old Dan Tucker just stand there lookin'.

The song ends.

At the same time that the outbreak was discovered in Kansas, we now know that there also was an outbreak occurring in Texas. Of course, Texas nearly borders on Nebraska, and would touch that state if not for the tiny sliver of Oklahoma in the Panhandle region. Whether or not this has anything to do in a causal sense, is open for speculation.

Pause.

The mad cow disease in Texas that appeared in March of 1999 involved not only the death of cattle but the death of two school children who'd eaten beef for lunch or dinner one day much earlier in their all-too-short lives.

The deaths of the children followed the deaths of the cows, which, of course, is usually the case. Thankfully each of the children's illnesses was brief. Each died within the new moon. Their lungs gave out before their brains did. They were still incubating new variant Creutzfeld-Jakob when nosocomial pneumonia, that is, pneumonia that they caught in the hospital, struck them down. Oh—we shouldn't blame the hospital too much. This happens in all of them. The Germans are only being sensible when they call their hospitals *Krankenhäuser,* which means sick houses.

The CITIZEN *takes a cowboy hat out of the burlap bag. He puts it on.*

The Texas officials were aware of what the cows died of, courtesy of those brand new mad cow disease test kits provided by a giant multi-national company that shall remain unnamed. They were very busy officials who were still trying to disseminate the literature from the Los Alamos Education Group that describes the food irradiation process as safe and highly effective. They'd also been occupied with that uproar over genetically modified corn that had

CITIZEN: *(Continued.)* prompted the recall of millions of taco shells. Well, the Texans had hoped that the suspicious cows had succumbed to pollution from a nearby plastics factory or oil refinery. But of course the cows died outside Waco, Texas—and there are no oil refineries in that area. Anybody who is familiar with this unstable area—it lies on the Belcones Fault—knows that cattle are about the only thing you can do with the land there.

Pause.

Now the children were first sent to the hospital after showing persistent flu-like symptoms. At first the parents of each of the two kids thought the children caught colds because of freakish weather. In this region temperatures in summer may reach the 100s and stay in the 100s for two weeks at a time. At any period of time, and this includes even August, the Waco region may get north Canadian air that comes down the Great Plains. The result can be an ice storm. Though the effects of global warming are quite obvious in Texas, it is these spells of chilly weather that tend to make central Texans complain more about the cold than the heat. Because of these temperature swings, absenteeism in the schools due to illness is greater in Texas than in any other state in the United States. This is part of the reason why Texas ranks at the bottom of the country in the quality of its public secondary schools.

He changes the placard on the easel. The new placard reads, "In real life I'm a schoolteacher."

The CITIZEN *has changed the song, "The Sow Took the Measles" to "The Cow Took the Measles" and sings:*

> How do you think I began in the world?
> I got me a cow and sev'ral other things.
> The cow took the measles and she died in the spring.
>
> What do you think I made of her hide?
> The very best saddle that you ever did ride.
> Saddle or bridle or any such thing,
> The cow took the measles and she died in the spring.

What do you think I made of her nose?
The very best thimble that ever sewed clothes.
Thimble or thread any such thing,
The cow took the measles and she died in the spring.

For a while there grew suspicions that these unusually sick Texas children each had died from what is known as legionnaire's disease, because nobody wanted to accept the fact that the children actually died from pneumonia, which more often attacks the elderly. Of course, the oddity that dragged these kids down and sort of made them older than their years was the mad cow prion. How did it come to pass that the children were tested for this prion?

Just like the Department of Agriculture, the State Health Department of Texas was also now in possession of a new kit that tested for the new brain-wasting diseases. It just so happened that tissue and brain samples from the school children were there in Austin, Texas when a lab technician decided to have a go with the brand new test—which was provided gratis by a pharmaceutical company, in hopes that the state would buy more. To the technician's surprise, really a seismic shock, of course, the tests turned up positive. The test was repeated four times. Each time the test showed positive. A call was put into Basel, Switzerland where the tests came from. There could be no doubt about it. The tests were not defective, the children who had died from pneumonia were also infected with new variant Creutzfeld-Jakob.

I do not know what the Texas officials exactly thought when they uncovered mad cow disease in both the cows and the children. But they probably thought, "Damn these testing kits! Before we had them there was no reason to worry. Before these kits came there was no such thing as mad cow disease, except in Europe!"

We all know the diet of American school children is less than perfect. High in fat and cholesterol. High in sugar. High in beef that is often rife with E. coli and other contaminants. Some attribute the diet of American children to the frustration of the McDonald brothers of Pasadena, California.

He changes the placard on the easel. The new placard reads, "Any extra weight that I'm packing is because". *After the audience has had time to read this he changes the placard. The new placard reads,* "I have a Russian-American wife who likes to cook for me." *The* CITIZEN *continues:*

These McDonalds ran a drive-in restaurant more than a half a century ago. They became dissatisfied with their employees, who were high schoolers—and with their clientele, who were also high schoolers. The brothers were tired of the constant turnover of carhops, dishwashers and short-order cooks, tired of replacing the dishes and silverware that their teenagers either stole or broke. Their solution was to streamline their operation and make foods, like fried foods, that could be wrapped in paper, not served with a fork and a plate. Because the McDonald's food was turned out by assembly line, the food cost less and could be sold for less. Thus a very happy meal for all was created.

We all know the story of fast-food restaurants and how they've prospered. What most of us do not know is how hard they make it for the independent farmer and rancher to survive, and how they foster the increase of bacteria and will be one day, if they are not already, the conduit for an epidemic of the human form of mad cow disease in America.

He takes off his cowboy hat and puts it back in the burlap bag. A high-pitched alarm tone starts beeping softly.

Prions. If only they were a little more like the germs we know. We've got a handle on the bacteria. There's soaps, sprays, dishwashing detergents, lotions, bandages, toothbrushes, toothpaste that contain chemicals to fight them. In England they have plastic food storage containers that are impregnated with antibacterial chemicals. In Japan they have chopsticks, telephones, pens, bicycle handles, tambourines and origami paper treated with bacteria-killing compounds. This is all fine and dandy but it's not going to stop the prions.

The alarm tone fades out.

You know, India—a country which everyone thinks of as extremely poor and ridden with earthquakes—is perhaps the safest country in this new century. Why? The Hindus don't eat cattle. India's not like the West where beef is king. It's not like America where the hamburger is the sky and the french fry is the earth. And thinking of potatoes we should remember what happened in Ireland when the potato blight hit that country.

If there is a silver lining to any cloud that hangs over mad cow disease it is that we as human beings can get along perfectly without a shred of beef. But of course this isn't what the American West wants to hear, with its mythology of the cowboy, the horse, the rope, the lasso, *(Miming the lassoing of a calf.)* the lil' doggie.

Cattle driving music—from some movie—is heard. The CITIZEN *continues.*

The powers in the American West hate even the mention that someone may be allergic to dairy products or beef, which sometimes has as much to do with the hormones that they give to cattle, as much as anything else. Yes, their lobbyists for the Yi-ha West work overtime so that nobody hears the fact that cattle are totally inefficient food sources, consuming 250 times the energy that they deliver back to human beings in the form of meat and milk.

The music ends. The CITIZEN *puts on the cowboy hat again.*

But back to the state of Texas where the first human deaths of mad cow are known. Texas deserves special attention not only because of its "first" in the detection of the dreaded human European disease, or so we thought, European, but also Texas deserves special attention due to its leading the nation in its number of human executions. Everybody knows the majority of Texans support the death penalty. Though it's been shown that such a penalty falls disproportionately upon black men, and is also meted out upon innocent men from time to time, this doesn't seem to matter much to either the people or the officials of the State of Texas. One gets the impression that Texans simply can't cope with problems that are long and drawn out, or problems that may somehow fly in the face of their expectations, intuitions and institutions.

He changes the placard on the easel. The new placard reads, "The U.S. Constitution & the U.N. Charter of Human Rights". *After the audience has had time to read this he changes the placard. The new placard reads,* "are not all that respected in Texas."

CITIZEN: *(Continued.)* But Texans aren't the only stupid people. There are those from other parts of the country, like that overpaid idiot on national TV, who jeered at an escaped convict for wanting his "five minutes of fame" before he gave himself up. The prisoner, a Texan, was giving himself up for the rest of his life. He only wanted five minutes to speak about pain on television. We cannot be healthy if we don't want to hear about pain. Thankfully, the prisoner got his demand. He said,

"The Texas system of justice is as corrupt as the prisoners it keeps behind bars. If you're going to do something about us, well, do something about that system too. The reason why I'm finally turning myself in tonight is not from fear—because I've been set to die ever since I escaped 40 days ago. No, I'm stepping out of these doors with the sole purpose of honoring the person I love, my wife, and to keep my voice in the media. I am going to start writing. My wife and I are both going to do it. We're going to holler. We're going to try to get something changed."

This is from a man, Donald Newbury, who got 99 years for a robbery of $68—where nobody was hurt. Yes, he was a habitual offender, he was stupid, but there are signs that he's wising up. That's what I'm talking about, *wising up.* Criticize Mr. Newbury for a lot of things, but lay off him for wanting to have his say.

I believe the TV airwaves are the people's. It's only that the rich and powerful have bamboozled us, and snatched them from us. A way to show that these airwaves belong to us is to wave a gun, force our way onto the air. I guess the place that's left for those of us who don't wave guns and who want to speak is a street corner—where all the passersby are racing past, or a theater—where hardly any people ever come in to see what's going on.

Sausage! T-bone. Swiss steak. Filet Mignon. Cheeseburger. First invented in Denver in 1944 by Lewis Ballast.

Pause.

Cows. *(The sound of cows mooing is heard.)* We're supposed to be more intelligent than they are. So intelligent that we can slaughter them and eat them.

The CITIZEN *motions like a orchestra conductor and the mooing of the cows grows softer and then is ended. Pause.*

Who knows? Maybe the reason for America's urge toward self-destruction and destruction of the world is because slow-acting prions are eating away at the brains of those we have in power. This isn't a glib suggestion. It provides an interesting answer for the decline of culture in our country and the obsession of the Republicans to invent yet another new national nuclear missile defense system. Sometimes medical science provides *the* explanation, The Truth.

Perhaps, as mad cow disease settles into our land, there'll be a few uninfected people who can be counted on to lead us out of the disaster we've made for ourselves. Oh, wouldn't the organized religions just hate this! It would endanger their authority.

On the other hand, they might call such uninfected people prophets, and say their appearance in the United States was foretold in scripture. That's one way for them to carry on.

Changing his tone, the CITIZEN *urges the audience to fight against the forces that would damage America:*

Carry on. Carry On!

He changes the placard on the easel. The new placard reads: "Have A Nice Day." There is a happy face underneath the phrase. The CITIZEN *sings the first verse of the eighteenth century song, "Free America", but slower than march tempo:*

CITIZEN: *(Singing.)*

> Born from a world of tyrants, beneath the western
>   sky,
> We'll form a new dominion, a land of liberty.
> The world shall own we're masters here, then hasten
>   on the day;
> Oppose, oppose, oppose, oppose, for North
>   Americay.

The Citizen then swings into a couple of verses (re-written here) from the traditional song, "Charlie Brooks":

> Miss Adair, since I left the city,
> I've got these thoughts on my mind.
> Pray do not think me faithless
> Nor deem me the least unkind.

> Miss Adair, I'm needin' the distance
> From some of the things you do.
> If you would curb your excesses
> I'd never think of leavin' you.

The music fades here. The CITIZEN has already picked up and the flag. He leaves while the music fades. Lights out.

End of Play.

THE SWIMMING POOLS OF PARIS

a play in two acts

Remembering
Eugène Ionesco (1909-1994)

Characters

DONALD   *Male. 40. Handsome.*

TOMMY/FELICITÉ   *Female. 30-50. (This actress plays
                          the 30 year old gay male, TOMMY and
                          FELICITÉ, MARIE's mother. FELICITÉ
                          has a French accent.)*

CAROLINE/MARIE   *Female. 30. Pretty. Thin.*

CARL/GASTON   *Male, 60. CARL has a Northern European accent.
                          GASTON has a French accent.*

*Place: Act I, stage is almost bare. Act II, a middle class home (living room)
in the Paris suburbs.*

Time: Present.

Notes

   Donald, attractive user and maneuverer, tries to manipulate those
around him—and the audience, too, especially in the first half of the
play when he tells the sad story of Caroline. Once getting the audience's

empathy, he's off and running. A nearly bare stage in the first half of the play is meant to tell us that there has been barely anything going on in Donald's life for quite some time. The bare stage is a great help to Act One's memory play whose events occur in a number of places in the past and whose people are long and gone.

In the first half Donald must slip effortlessly between talking with the audience and acting in scene with the other characters. Time has given him some distance to the man he once was; Donald plays his earlier self with sympathy but with some restraint. The other characters are not so restrained. They act fairly realistically.

In Act One, the four actors are always onstage. They use gestures to signify their entrances and exits. The audience needs to be gripped by the tale being told. However, there are intermittent recitations of "Three swimming pools in the eleventh arrondissement," and the like. What are these? These ritualistic intrusions are relief to the comedy/drama, just as we see comic relief or intrusions in Elizabethan tragedy. During this pause in the play's linear trajectory the audience is entertained in fresh manner; perhaps during this time they may also consider the play's various ideas at a little distance. Another type of distancing comes to flower in the second act of the play when three of the actors (not Donald) each play different roles.

The Swimming Pools of Paris changes in tone and texture in the second act. It is as drastic a change as watching a film go from black and white to color. To signify that Donald has finally found a real home, there is now an apartment represented upon the stage: a sofa, a coffee table, chairs, etc. and a living, breathing family.

One parallel between Donald's life and my own as a playwright, has been beneficial contact with Paris and Parisian culture—and for me, Parisian culture includes Eugène Ionesco. Ionesco's plays and criticism have had a tremendous influence upon my playwriting. Refiguring something remarkable seen in the ancient world as an absurd but exciting *new* something (like the ancient three noses used in *Jack, Or The Submission*) is a conceit/technique used by Ionesco which inspires me. My treatment here of the "wounded man" theme from cave art comes from this approach.

When the actors are in character in the second half, in France, they will be acting in a different style than in the first half—no surprise here, they are in a different country!

Petra Ulrych directed a reading of *The Swimming Pools of Paris* on August 2, 2001, in Denver, Colorado. Dan Hiester, Laura Cuetara and Fred Lewis played the three other characters. Dramaturg for the play: Walter Teres.

The Swimming Pools of Paris

ACT I

A fairly bare stage. We see a couple of chairs. Off to one side there is a crate that will be unpacked, also there is a portable radio. A hammer with a claw is on the floor next to the unopened crate.

Lights up. DONALD *speaks to the audience.* CAROLINE, TOMMY, *and at more of a distance,* CARL *(in a suit and tie) stand by.*

DONALD: Staying on the surface of things means stagnation. You're kidding yourself if you think you can have a life with little or no reflection. I was one of those guys who looked in the mirror and didn't see past the skin on my nose—for years! All that changed when I broke my arm and leg on a Manhattan street and was forced to stay in a hospital room for days on end.

As I lay there recovering I realized that I had only one story of any importance in my life. The only story I had until I got to France.

Pause.

Eighteen years ago. New York. I'd just returned to the 'City from Florida where I'd spent four months away from Caroline. She was back in the hospital. It was November, Tommy was almost thirty. Caroline was in a wheelchair.

CAROLINE *sits down.*

DONALD: *(Continued.)* Pretty freaky for a twenty-seven year old girl, but she was weak. When I got there Tommy was offering her Evian water. She turned her nose up at it. Caroline asked him what she was doing there in the hospital. Tommy said,

DONALD and TOMMY: (DONALD *speaks softer than* TOMMY *does here.*) It's just the flu.

DONALD: Yeah, I was hanging outside their room listening to the conversation before going in. Tommy told her she'd been in the hospital for three weeks after she asked him how long she'd been there. Then I heard her ask Tommy:

CAROLINE: Where's Donald?

DONALD: That's me.

TOMMY: *(To* CAROLINE.) Don't ask, dear. It gets you upset whenever I say I don't know.

CAROLINE: But you must know. Everybody knows except me.

TOMMY: *(Sits down in a chair next to* CAROLINE. *Finally he says:)* Donald's somewhere in Florida.

CAROLINE: I know that. But where in Florida?

TOMMY: That I don't know.

CAROLINE: Does he have enough money?

TOMMY: I don't know.

CAROLINE: Is my father coming?

TOMMY: Sometime.

CAROLINE: Where's Donald?

TOMMY: He's in Florida. You asked me that before.

CAROLINE: Did I? *(Pause. She is delirious.)* I was coming home in a cab. I went by the gallery. I started crying. I realized I was loved so much. You love me. That's part of it, but...

TOMMY: God's love.

CAROLINE: That's right. *(Pause.)* I was coming home in the cab. I passed by the gallery. I began to cry. I realized so much. *(Pause.)* What have you got there?

DONALD: Tommy didn't have anything there that I could see. He just lied to her flat out.

TOMMY: It's a picture of Donald. In his new apartment. He's wearing the beautiful coat you gave him.

CAROLINE: *(Pause.)* Isn't it silly of Daddy to try to marry me off to people that don't understand? (CAROLINE *coughs lightly.*)

TOMMY: You're cold. Let me get a blanket.

DONALD: She closed her eyes. I came in while he was putting the blanket over her. I noticed how painfully thin she was. She was sort of asleep. *(To* TOMMY, *softly.)* Hi, Tom.

TOMMY: *(Angered, but softly.)* Where d'you come from?

DONALD: *(Softly.)* Come over here.

TOMMY *gets up.* DONALD *takes him over to one side.*

DONALD: *(Softly.)* Carl's been in touch. He located me two days ago. 'Was wasted when he phoned. 'Kept on telling me that he loved me and that I shouldn't kill him.

TOMMY: What?

DONALD: That's what I threatened to do when I last saw him—if he ever let anything bad happen to Caroline.

TOMMY: You don't threaten to kill people, Donald.

DONALD: Look, I was angry. *(Pause.)* He told me she was in here. Can I have a few words with her, please?

TOMMY *hesitates, but then consents.*

TOMMY: All right.

DONALD: So he goes halfway out of the room.

TOMMY'S *gestures signal that he leaves.*

I sit in the chair next to Caroline and whisper her name. *(Pause.)* She comes to.

CAROLINE: Donald? *(Pause.)* You look so handsome and well.

DONALD: Are you surprised?

CAROLINE: Oh, no. I see you every day.

DONALD: *(To the audience.)* Right. Oh, God. It was terrible.

CAROLINE: "I never loved you. I don't know what love is."

DONALD: *(To the audience.)* She was quoting from the letter I sent to her the last day I was in town.

CAROLINE: "Between your life and mine, I have to choose mine."

DONALD: That was the cruelest thing I've ever said. But I was made to say it.

CAROLINE: "I have to leave."

DONALD: Yeah, I had to leave all right. Or the cops were going to bust me.

CAROLINE: But you didn't ever leave me. *(Pause.)* Everything's growing into God.

DONALD: Excuse me, Caroline?

CAROLINE: It's like the tide's in. Covering me.

DONALD: I didn't want to take that kind of talk too seriously. I pretended she was talking about her blanket and I fixed it for her.

CAROLINE: Our love... *(She sighs weakly.)* My life has been... *(Pause.)* It's good now.

She looks away from DONALD *and stares elsewhere.*

DONALD: *(Alarmed.)* Are you all right?

CAROLINE *regains some self-possession.*

CAROLINE: I must look frightful to you. *(Pause.)* I remember... when you snubbed me. At the gallery. I had to come back. You were irresistible.

DONALD: I'm sorry. Look, I'd just come to New York. For the first time. Everything was so new to me.

CAROLINE: I only hated you that day. *(Pause.)* The next week I was strong all over again.

DONALD: Caroline, listen. Everything I said in the letter... it wasn't true. I was made to write it. Otherwise Carl was going to do something to me. I was wrong to leave you here.

CAROLINE: We're together now. *(Pause.)* My father won't cause trouble. He wants me to live.

DONALD: We all do.

CAROLINE: I'm going to live. You make me so happy. *(Pain crosses her face.)* My body hurts. *(Pause.)* I need to walk. It's getting hot. I need to feel the breeze... *(Pause. She starts to fade.)* Don't forget me. You're all I've had.

DONALD: *(To the audience.)* And saying that, she kind of fell asleep. Her face and her neck: words can't describe how emaciated she was. After about a minute and a half. I saw her quiver. I got a funny feeling. Not a good feeling at all. I looked at her. She was still. I didn't know where Tommy was, I thought he was listening in from right outside the door.

He touches CAROLINE.

Come on, Caroline, wake up.

He touches her head.

You don't have a fever. *(Pause.)* Oh, no! Oh, no. *(He shakes his head "no".* Then, to the audience:) Suddenly Tommy appears from out of nowhere. *(To* TOMMY, *with great emotion.)* She's dead, Tommy. And I killed her!

TOMMY: *(He's drained at this point.)* So.

DONALD: I killed her. I thought it was over—me ruining other people's lives. Well, it isn't over. Now I kill people. I killed the one I love, Tommy. I killed her. *(He cries.)* Tell Carl I won't kill him. One murder's enough for me.

TOMMY: Donald, will you get a hold of yourself! This is a hospital. Show some consideration for others.

DONALD: *(Crying.)* Caroline, no!

TOMMY *has a change of heart and pities* DONALD, *but speaks with a "stiff upper lip."*

TOMMY: You poor boy.

Pause.

DONALD: *(To the audience.)* Well, Tommy didn't have to let me be alone with Caroline. He could've said no. It would have been horrible not to have seen her. I'm not sure if Caroline was ever clear that I was really in the same room with her. Her anorexia had gotten so bad. There's only so much doctors can do when somebody doesn't eat.

Being with Caroline—it was the first time I felt fully human. You see, it was the love we had that made me feel part of the human race.

Pause.

We met at an art opening that Tommy took me to. It was at Carl's gallery.

CAROLINE *gets up from her chair. The time is months before she dies.*

CAROLINE: I just finished with classes at the Cordon Bleu in Paris. I have a stack of recipes that I'm dying to do. I hope Tommy and you will come for dinner sometime. I live off Madison Avenue. *(Pause.)* You don't say much.

DONALD: I'm listening. To your voice.

CAROLINE: Where are you from? I didn't hear anything about you coming from Shaker Heights in Cleveland, did I?

DONALD: No.

CAROLINE: I had a roommate from Vassar who was from there. She was into mulled wine. (DONALD *does not understand.*) That's when you heat it up. Mind if I? (CAROLINE *holds* DONALD's *arm while she breathes in and then exhales. Then she lets go of him.*) I've been tired. *(Pause.)* Where'd *you* go to school?

DONALD: Palm Beach High, miss.

95

LANCE TAIT

Uncomfortable pause.

CAROLINE: And college?

DONALD: Actually, one man I knew tried to get me to go to one of his *beauty* colleges.

CAROLINE *is taken aback, but intrigued.*

CAROLINE: What's that? I don't know if I quite understand.

DONALD: To get trained to be a hairdresser.

CAROLINE: You would have been delightful as a hairdresser. All the women would have been at your feet.

DONALD: And men too. I told him what he could do with his beauty colleges and to drop me off right there.

CAROLINE: You were in his car?

DONALD: I was... uh... hitchhiking.

CAROLINE: People still do that?

DONALD: Yes, miss. *(Pause.)* But Tommy says I can get into the community college down by Battery Park when I've saved up the money.

CAROLINE: What will you study?

DONALD: Accounting.

CAROLINE: You don't look like the accountant type.

DONALD: Tom says there's always work for accountants.

CAROLINE: I caution you not to take other people's advice, even the advice of dear friends of mine. Maybe you should go into film. NYU's got a great department.

DONALD: I don't know anything about film.

CAROLINE: That's why you go to school. *(Pause.)* First you could start in front of the camera—then you could finish out your life behind the camera.

DONALD: *(Laughing.)* You've got it all planned for me. Just like that man.

CAROLINE: What man?

DONALD: The man with the string of beauty colleges.

CAROLINE: Oh, I don't mean to be so... advising. *(Shocked.)* I've just been talking like my father. That's horrible!

DONALD: What's your dad do?

CAROLINE: He manages money. His own. The art thing is just his playground.

DONALD: Must be nice to be rich.

CAROLINE: Buckets of fun. What's your father do?

DONALD: He took off.

Uneasy pause.

CAROLINE: Maybe tonight after the opening ends—we could go down to Tribeca. There's a restaurant—I guarantee, you've never seen the likes of it before. My treat.

Pause. TOMMY'S *gestures signal his entrance.*

CAROLINE: *(To* TOMMY.*)* Tommy, where have you been?

TOMMY: I was on the other side of the room.

CAROLINE: No, I mean since I've been back. We used to see one another for days on end before I left. You're nowhere to be found these days. Is this *(She means Donald.)* the reason why you've been so scarce? We've had a delightful conversation. He comes from Palm Beach.

TOMMY: *(To DONALD.)* What did you tell her?

DONALD: I did live in Palm Beach once.

CAROLINE: He's agreed to come over to dinner sometime.

TOMMY *glares at* DONALD.

DONALD: I didn't exactly say yes.

TOMMY: *(To CAROLINE.)* You look thinner than before you left for Paris. Oh, there's Carl.

CARL *comes closer to the others. He speaks with a North European accent.*

CARL: I hope you're all enjoying yourselves.

CAROLINE: Well, I'll be seeing you just a little later, bye.

CAROLINE's *gestures signal her exit.*

DONALD: *(To the audience.)* Funny to think that this took place almost twenty years ago. That's when it began. The only closeness I'd ever known.

DONALD *looks on.*

TOMMY: He's new in town.

CARL: Are you sleeping with him?

TOMMY: Yes. I'm helping him out. Do you still need a receptionist for the gallery? He needs a job.

CARL: He's a handsome boy.

TOMMY: He'll be good public relations.

CARL: I'll think about it.

Pause.

DONALD: So I get a job at the gallery and it's months before I make the connection between Caroline and Carl. Tommy keeps me in the dark. He wants me all for himself. He's protective of his position in "high society" if you want to call it that. Caroline is as secretive as she is thin. I almost don't notice either. Women are way too complex for me. Caroline comes to visit me a few days after I get my job in the gallery. I hadn't been to her house for dinner yet. Though she doesn't know me well, she says that everyone's boring except me.

CAROLINE: It must be a big change from living in Florida. (*Pause.*) I hope your plans come together like you want them to.

DONALD: I'm still too young to have plans, maybe. But I feel old sometimes. Like I've been through a lot and it's time to start something new.

CAROLINE: I know what you mean.

DONALD: Do you?

CAROLINE: New York, Paris, back to New York. I've been like a gypsy for the last four years since I dropped out of school.

DONALD: Paris must have been cool.

CAROLINE: I got so horribly fat and ugly when I was there. It was a combination of the French food and eating it so late in the evening. You put on weight when you eat so late.

DONALD: You look fine now.

CAROLINE: I'm burnt out. Nothing seems new anymore. That is, except you. We should be friends. Perhaps we have lots in common.

DONALD: And not so much in common.

CAROLINE: How do you know?

DONALD: It's not a good idea to be talking so much here.

CAROLINE: The gallery's empty.

DONALD: But Carl'll come in soon and see me talking with somebody.

CAROLINE: Maybe I'm asking you about which painting I should buy.

DONALD: Look, I'd rather not have Carl see you here with me.

CAROLINE: Really? Why?

DONALD: You've got to go, okay. (*We hear a door slam. Protesting, nervous:*) I've only been here for a little while.

CAROLINE: Well, if that's the way you want it, I'll say good-bye, but not adieu.

    CAROLINE *gestures leaving. Pause.*

DONALD: Okay, so she left. And it was good, too that she left right then.

CARL: You didn't pull the blinds all the way back. I want the people to be able to see *something* from the street.

DONALD: I'll get it right away.

CARL: It's too late in the day to bother now.

DONALD: It won't happen again.

Pause.

You look handsome today.

Carl *is surprised.*

CARL: Do I?

DONALD: Very suave.

CARL: Well, thank you.

DONALD: Your suit is sharp.

CARL: I'll tell my tailor.

DONALD: I used to have clothes I really liked. A couple of psychedelic shirts, made out of silk. A pair of dress pants made from such thin material—they got worn out. I wonder what they were made of.

CARL: I'm sure my tailor would know.

DONALD: I bet he would. *(Pause.)* Carl, this is the nicest job I've ever had. I'm so glad Tommy introduced us.

CARL: It seems to be going all right with you so far.

DONALD: I'll be working here days and going to college at night.

CARL: You'll be able to handle both?

DONALD: Since I'm not in community college yet, maybe you could train me more for the art business. So when you go to Europe you won't have to worry about what might be going on around here while you're gone.

CARL: It's an idea.

DONALD: Where'd you get your tie?

CARL: Oh, this—it's...

DONALD: It's pretty cool. (*Pause.*) Living at Tommy's is cramped. It makes me feel like I got a tie around my neck when I don't. I never knew apartments here could be so tiny.

CARL: They are small.

DONALD: You've got an apartment as big as an airplane hanger, don't you?

CARL: Who told you that?

DONALD: Tommy.

CARL: He exaggerates considerably. But, ah... some of the artworks that I can't sell—I have room enough to keep them in my apartment.

DONALD: I'd like to see them sometime.

CARL: Sure.

DONALD: How about tonight?

Pause. CARL *thinks.*

CARL: All right.

DONALD: I don't have to be at Tommy's till later.

CARL: (*Pause.*) Tommy never buys anything from me.

DONALD: He doesn't have the money. But it's nice you keep him as a friend.

CARL: I like him. I've helped him out in a tight spot.

DONALD: Maybe he'll do the same for you someday.

CARL: He'll never buy anything from me. Neither will you. But you can be bought.

DONALD: Not me, Carl. I'm free as a bird.

CARL: What does Tommy say to that?

DONALD: Tommy. Sits at home. Goes out one night a week.

CARL: He used to go out more.

DONALD: He says he doesn't feel like it anymore. New York's exciting.

CARL: It can be.

DONALD: I'm going to buy some clothes and hit the town when I get my first paycheck. Maybe I can use your tailor.

CARL *laughs.*

CARL: You'll never be able to afford him.

DONALD: With what I have on now I feel like a poor farmer. Or, to be honest, I feel kind of naked.

CARL: Naked?

DONALD: Kind of.

Pause.

CARL: Would you like to stop off for dinner with me at Four Seasons on the way home?

DONALD: Sure.

CARL: They'll provide you with a jacket. *(Pause.)* About your clothes. Maybe we can work something out with my tailor.

DONALD: Sounds fine by me, Carl. *(Pause. To the audience.)* Well, that was that. *(Pause.)* In a few days, Caroline comes back to the gallery.

CAROLINE: I'm not afraid of you like I'm afraid of one-hundred percent of the men I meet.

DONALD: Oh, yeah?

CAROLINE: I'm not afraid of you like I am of other men.

DONALD: *(To the audience.)* Is this one of those girls who makes friends with gay men because they're safe? Anyway, I was glad I was in New York. Traveling with a better class of people than I ever had before.

For six weeks Caroline comes to the gallery when she knows Carl's not going to be there. Never once gets me over for dinner at her place. I always wriggle out of it. She found out the news pretty quickly when I moved out of Tommy's place and into Carl's apartment. She and I develop a strange closeness. I liked her. It took stupid me quite a while to notice that she was wasting away. Her trick was to talk about giving a dinner. She also let herself be seen around food—she'd come into the gallery with a sandwich that she'd just ordered from the deli. She never ate it, though. At home she ate just enough salad to get the strength to get around town. She believed that love would save her from her problems. And that this love would come from me.

Well, Carl was gone for a week. I went back to his apartment each day after work and started feeling lonely. On the fifth day of Carl being gone, on a whim—and I thought it would do her good—I invited Caroline over to Carl's apartment to have supper with me. I couldn't cook much. But I knew how to make a salad and how to bake potatoes in an oven!

CAROLINE: I came over here because I want you to make love to me, Donald, not because I want a meal.

DONALD *is startled.*

CAROLINE: *(Continued.)* I'm sorry. You didn't hear that. I'm being a bad girl.

DONALD: It's just that since Carl's in Europe I thought it would be nice to get together.

CAROLINE: And it is. You're trying to feed me, like others have tried to. But let's not talk about eating. There are so many other things, Donald. You know, I'm very particular in my choice of men. This was people's major criticism of me when I was in Paris.

DONALD: I know I'm not good enough for you.

CAROLINE: You're self-conscious. I like that. I might not be good enough for you. Do you like girls as thin as me?

DONALD: You're a lovely girl.

CAROLINE: Lovely? No one's ever said that to me before. "Pretty", maybe. Or "beautiful". But "lovely" sounds so... *(She looks at him wistfully).* I know you're not saying it just to get me into bed. Will you kiss me though, please?

DONALD: I couldn't do that.

CAROLINE: Because you're in Carl's house?

DONALD: He's sort of my meal ticket.

CAROLINE: Dear, we have more in common than you think. You know, I live off my father.

DONALD: Yeah, wherever he is.

CAROLINE: My fairy godfather lives right here in New York. It's a lot better when I don't see him. There's a lot less pressure that way. *(Pause.)* You know, Donald. I'm flattered that you seem to care about me. You are kind of answering my prayers.

Pause.

DONALD: *(To the audience.)* She didn't eat anything that night. Instead we talked. *(To* CAROLINE.*)* But the sun is not a planet. It's on fire.

CAROLINE: In astrology, it's a planet. The moon is too.

DONALD: Do you expect me to believe that the position of the planets at the time of my birth is somehow going to predict my life?

CAROLINE: It is. Absolutely.

DONALD: But everybody that's born at the same time around the world that I'm born—they can't possibly have the same life as I'm going to have.

CAROLINE: Of course not. They're born in different locations on the planet. You have to factor that in.

DONALD: It's complicated.

CAROLINE: Yeah. That's why the newspaper stuff isn't right very often.

DONALD: What does it mean, "the Age of Aquarius."

CAROLINE: It means we're going to be in that constellation soon. And that society is going to become more intelligent and be able to accomplish amazing things.

DONALD: Sounds like a variation on heaven.

CAROLINE: Only it's going to be here on earth.

Pause. CARL *exits the stage.*

DONALD: *(To the audience.)* I hadn't talked much about things outside the physical realm with anybody much in my life. How interesting it was that women can jump from one extreme to another with the bat of an eye. One minute they're concerned with the moistness of their eyes and the next they're worried about Neptune transiting their seventh house. There's a whole lot of stuff in between.

Anyway... *(Pause.)* Phone call from Tommy to me:

DONALD: Yes, I know she's sick.

TOMMY: Sicker than you think.

DONALD: She'll get better. She's a smart girl.

TOMMY: That has nothing to do with it.

DONALD: Why do you put her down?

TOMMY: I'm not putting her down.

DONALD: You're no help. You're a wimp. You don't make her eat.

TOMMY: See if you can do that and all is forgiven. You'd better watch it or I'll tell Carl you had her over to his place.

DONALD: Go ahead. See what I care.

TOMMY: You'll be out on the street.

DONALD: That's what you think.

TOMMY: Some day your luck is going to run out. Anyway, what are you doing? For God's sake, she's a *girl.*

DONALD: It's been men, men, men since I got here.

TOMMY: So you're checking out what's on the other side of the fence?

DONALD: It *is* interesting that she's a woman. Women have different things to say than men do.

TOMMY: *(Mocking him.)* Hello? *(Briefest of pauses.)* Where have you been?

DONALD: In the gay world, where everything's so happy.

TOMMY: You're such a little shit.

DONALD: And so he hung up the phone.

> DONALD *goes over to the portable radio that is nearby the unpacked crate. He turns the radio on. The music is loud. He starts to open the crate—the crate has a piece of sculpture inside it. The music plays while* DONALD *works. Before too long* CARL *walks in carrying two presents.*

CARL: Donald, I know the gallery's closed. But isn't the music a little loud?

DONALD: Oh, you're back. *(He switches off the music.)* You're early.

CARL: Really, Donald. I bought you a present in Berlin. Two presents. You damned boy. I'm not early. I had to come back today for a physical. You know that. You have my schedule. The doctor says I'm fine.

DONALD: Wow. Let me see the presents.

> CARL *offers him the presents.*

CARL: Yes, open them.

> DONALD *takes one of the gifts and starts to open it.*

Why don't we go to a screening tonight? I know the director.

> DONALD *drops the gift box on the floor and he holds up the shirt that was inside.*

DONALD: *(Looking at it.)* The cut doesn't look right.

CARL: Oh, wear it tonight.

DONALD: The shirt's too prissy. (CARL *is unhappy. He holds the other gift.)* Carl, uhm, I need to get away.

CARL: Away? I've just come back into town.

DONALD: Here. *(He gives the shirt back to* CARL.) Keep the other present, too. I don't want either one of them. If I didn't know any better I'd think all Europeans do is mope around if they can't get anybody to jerk them off in the morning. *(Pause.)* I'm going to get out of town for the weekend.

CARL: But the new show starts next week. We've got an opening to prepare for. This is your first exhibition as my assistant.

DONALD: I don't want to be exhibited.

CARL: Donald, what is wrong?

DONALD: I'm taking your car. For the weekend. I'll be back Sunday night.

> Pause. During DONALD's *next speech* CARL *picks up the box from the floor and puts the presents over by the crate that* DONALD *opened.*

DONALD: *(To the audience.)* Well, how do you like that? Hey, and the last thing I wanted to do was see a movie by a friend of his. One thing that I discovered about myself when hanging around Carl was that I was unfazed by celebrities. I don't know why. Maybe it was because the first one I met with Carl was Andy Warhol. Or as a few friends would call him, "Andy Arsehole." Looking at pale Andy made my flesh crawl. He had these asinine silences that he would put on, in order to appear intelligent. He was a con-artist, not an artist. It takes one to know one.

Pause. All actors fix their attention upon DONALD *for a moment until he says:*

DONALD: *(Continued.)* One.

*In the following, "*CARL *actor", for example, means that the actor that plays* CARL *is not in character—though some of* CARL's *characteristics might be still be there—for example, the accent that the actor has worked so hard to perfect.*

TOMMY actor: There's one swimming pool in the fourth arrondissement of Paris.

CAROLINE actor: Two in the fifth.

TOMMY actor: One in the sixth arrondissement.

CARL actor: A couple in the ninth.

TOMMY actor: A couple in the tenth.

CAROLINE actor: Three of them in the eleventh.

TOMMY actor: A couple in the fourteenth.

CARL actor: Three in the thirteenth arrondissement.

CAROLINE actor: Two in the twelfth.

Pause.

DONALD: You swim, your neck's like the prow of ship. You may even feel young once again for a moment, as you work down your lane. *(Pause.)* Young ones. In and out of the water.
(If not to the audience before, certainly now:) Well, I'd look in the mirror in New York and say: I'm not old old. But more and more I'd noticed that people didn't notice. There were those who asked me point blank—I didn't lie. When they found out how old I really was they'd inevitably ask more. People want to know what you've done,

DONALD: *(Continued.)* where you've been, when you're forty-one.

I said I'd been living in Manhattan—that's what I've done with my life. Manhattan's got a lot. It's fabulous to live there. But I knew they knew I'd been wasting my life going from dull, to boring, to meaningless jobs. Eating in restaurants. Then 'time for bed. *(Pause.)* I had become a terribly uninteresting person.

After the accident, when I could walk with crutches, I went over to hear a concert in Damrosch Park. When it was over I passed by the fountain in the middle of Lincoln Center. I thought back to Florida. And the stories you hear in school about Ponce de Leon exploring Florida in search of the Fountain of Youth and never finding it. I'd been relying on my youthful looks and life just passed me by.

Pause.

So I took Carl's car for the weekend and spent the time in upstate New York. I bring his car back Tuesday night. There's this big party at Carl's gallery. The one I was supposed to help him get ready for.

We hear some party music.

TOMMY: How dare Donald not to show up!

CAROLINE: He's never coming back.

TOMMY: We should charge him with auto theft. He's not fit to be out on the streets.

CAROLINE: He needed to get away. I hope he's not blaming me for anything. I think I'm going to start to cry, Tommy.

TOMMY: Now, Glenda, the Good Witch of the North says, don't.

DONALD: *(To the audience.)* Oh, I forgot to tell you. The party at Carl's—most of the people are dressed up in masquerade. Tommy's the Good Witch from the Wizard of Oz. Caroline is dressed up as a butterfly.

CAROLINE: I hope he doesn't have someone else upstate.

Tommy: *(Muttering.)* I wouldn't put it past him.

CAROLINE: What?

TOMMY: I said, he wouldn't pull a fast one like that.

DONALD: *(To the audience.)* Anyway it goes on like that until Carl comes in.

CARL: The opening's a stunning success. Thank you for your help, Tommy.

TOMMY: Well, I only had to give up a whole weekend of proofreading to take over for Donald.

CARL: Good evening, Caroline. What a gorgeous costume.

CAROLINE: You look very nice as well.

CARL: Here, have some grapes.

TOMMY: *(To* CAROLINE.*)* He's Bacchus. The god of wine—

CAROLINE: No thank you, Carl. The idea of thick rubbery marbles sliding down a human throat is absolutely repulsive to us butterflies. I'm going to freshen up. Excuse me.

    CAROLINE's *gestures tell us that she goes.*

TOMMY: Bye, dear.

CARL: All the gallery people look wonderful. See there: it's Madonna. She's divine.

TOMMY: She's commercial.

CARL: She'll probably wind up owning a record company.

TOMMY: Who's she sleeping with tonight?

CARL: Somebody that Donna Summer is not. We'll be in Vanity Fair with this party! Steve Martin is not in town but Billy Murray is here. I thought Lori Anderson was coming.

TOMMY: She's here. She's screwing Superman.

CARL: Chris Reeve's here?

TOMMY: No, Chris *Walken*. (TOMMY *mimics* CARL.) I always get those two uebermen confused.

CARL is not particularly happy about being made fun of. He points to someone in the crowd.

CARL: That was horrible what happened in Nicaragua. Bianca. Bianca Jagger—it's wonderful what she's being doing for those kids there. Cement prices are going to go up. I must call my broker. (*He shakes his head in sorrow.*) That earthquake. (*Pause.*) Speaking of things breaking—what do you think of Julian Schnabel's plates?

TOMMY: Some people are so gullible. They'll buy anything.

CARL: We should get Judy Chicago to make the plates and Julian to break them!

DONALD: So then I arrive. Thankfully, Carl is off somewhere and it even takes a minute before I run into Tommy.

TOMMY: What do you think you're doing?

DONALD: Sorry, I didn't have the time to get dressed up.

TOMMY: That's not what I'm talking about.

DONALD: I tried to get here on time.

TOMMY: God, showing up in jeans!

DONALD: I thought we we're talking about dressing up.

TOMMY: It's not everyday that Carl has an opening for an exhibition with costumes.

DONALD: You people are always in costumes.
  (To the audience.) I see Caroline and I start to feel really bad. She looks very nervous. She's been crying. She comes over the minute she sees me. I smile at her and touch her costume.
  (To CAROLINE.*)* Nice wings. Let's fly to heaven on them.

CAROLINE: Thank God, you're all right.

DONALD: *(To the audience.)* Then she almost faints. I grab her and hold her up. (DONALD *touches* CAROLINE's *arm.)* Are you okay?
  (To the audience.) She was sort of okay. As okay as can be expected.
  As soon as I could, I asked her for the keys to her apartment. I didn't want to stay over at Carl's. *(Pause.)* Carl looked like he'd done ten lines of the white stuff—he was so out of it.

  The party music fades out.

I go stay at Caroline's for two days. Thursday night, Carl comes over and I find out what a fool I'd been. Amazing how so many people could pull the wool over my eyes.

CAROLINE: Stay. You two boys be friends.

TOMMY: No, I've got to go.

CAROLINE: Stay and play the piano.

TOMMY: And serenade you both?

CAROLINE: It's a Bösendorfer. I bought it because you think they're nicer than Steinways.

TOMMY: Have a wonderful supper.

DONALD: *(To the audience.)* So Tommy leaves.

Pause.

CAROLINE: I've started to eat a little rich food since the doctor's been here.

DONALD: What kind?

CAROLINE: Excuse me?

DONALD: What kind of rich food?
CAROLINE: Does it matter?

DONALD: Yes, I'd like to know.

CAROLINE: I had cream sauce, with spinach pasta, as I recall.

DONALD: *(To the audience.)* This from a person who barely put salad in her mouth. *(Pause.)* In a few minutes Carl buzzes from downstairs and demands to be let in. Caroline buzzes him up. Carl's in the apartment, he looks at me and says simply:

CARL: How long's this been going on?

DONALD: *(To the audience.)* Carl is drunk.

CARL: *(Drunk.)* I've been gambling. Drinking and gambling. Drove down to Atlantic City early this morning. All the casinos are the same. I've got no luck today. Tried to play black jack. Forgot how to count to twenty-one. No one knows how upset I've been. *(Pause.)* All the cards are lying face up now. I curse the day you both met at my gallery. *(To DONALD.)* You've gone to Woman, Donald. I never thought you would go to Woman. You're... not that way, I thought.

DONALD: Please leave.

CARL: You're good at secrets, Donald. But in some ways, I'm better. I've been to Atlantic City. Managed to stay on the road all the way back to Manhattan.

CAROLINE: You should go home to sleep.

CARL: You can't go over to Woman. You're just like me! Don't you know? Man is created either this way or that.

CAROLINE: I don't think that's necessarily so. You know yourself...

CARL: *(Loudly.)* Quiet!

CAROLINE: I should leave the room.

CARL: Stay!

DONALD: You're making us all uncomfortable.

CARL *laughs.*

CARL: *(To* DONALD.) You belong with me. *(Pause.)* It was such a bad day in Atlantic City. Nobody knew me. They treated me like a common... gambler!

CAROLINE: I'm going to be in the bedroom.

CAROLINE *turns away from the two momentarily to signal her exit. Pause.*

CARL: I won't allow this.

DONALD: You're drunk. You should go home.

CARL: You tell me what I am? Where I should go? *(He laughs.)* Drunk? Well, perhaps you can tuck me into bed. Help me out of my clothes, you snake.

DONALD: No. Don't make a scene.

CARL: The curtain is already up. *(Pause.)* You shall write her a letter now. Telling her that it's all over between you two.

DONALD: A letter?

CARL: That's right. Quaint, yeah? That way she'll have it in writing. You'll tell her that you don't love her. That you don't want her to imagine that you love her.

DONALD: I don't have to do what you want me to do. I'm as free (CARL *joins in to say with* DONALD:) as a bird.

CARL: How much do you want? A thousand? Five thousand? What's your price?

DONALD: You're out of your mind.

CARL: You must have a price.

DONALD: You're drunk and out of your mind.

CARL: You don't have a price? If you don't do as I say, her father'll take all her money away from her.

DONALD: So you've even got something going with her father.

CARL: You silly, silly boy. There are reasons not to tell people. Professional reasons. I don't want to be questioned by any more people than those who already know. So any new people that I meet are not to know. I can't be pestered time and time again about something over which I have no control.

DONALD: I don't understand.

CARL: Yes, I'm better at secrets than you. You will write the letter, exactly as I tell you.

DONALD: No I won't.

CARL: Yes, you will, you fool. You see, Donald, *(Pause.)* Caroline... is my daughter.

Pause.

DONALD: If I stop talking to her and anything happens to her because of it, I'll kill you. Honest, I will.

(To the audience.) Damn all these people! Damn them all, except Caroline. Them and their secrets, their lies! Yeah, the fewer people that knew Carl was Caroline's dad, the fewer people that knew that Carl was gay, the fewer people that knew he was drunk or coked up most of the time! Oh, and he would never have to explain that Caroline's mother cracked up and died when she was a child.

(Pause.) Well, Carl left the apartment. I didn't write the letter. Not that night.

The next day I went over to Carl's, got my stuff. Carl came up with the idea that it was better for her recovery if I was in Florida. We came up with a lame excuse for me: college.

Carl bought me a bus ticket and said once I was down there he'd send me seven-hundred fifty bucks to start life over in the Sunshine State. He cooked up another reason to keep me in Florida: if he saw me back in town he'd press charges against me for stealing the lunch money he always gave me out of petty cash.

(Pause.) But I did go back to New York after a while. *(Under his breath, meaning* CARL:*)* That bastard. *(Pause, resuming:)* And, after Caroline, died, I stayed there. There wouldn't ever be any going back to Florida. No, after New York everything else is too provincial. Hey, I finally got my own place in Manhattan after bumming around for a couple of years. My apartment was not too far from the Twenty-third Street "Y."

Pause.

It's not the physical thing that gets you when you're laid up. Hospital. Artificial. Cold white. Institution. Nothing to do but let your mind dangle.

A drug kicks in. You break away from gravity. No one rushes you—that's bad. You look up at the ceiling. Explore it like babies explore floors. You shiver. You come down. Was it my fault? Bamm. Your mind goes blank. No, not blank—it's more like a hundred empty white foam cups are trying to cram themselves into your head. I came to on the street. I smelled New York City. Naked pavement. Brown and black filthy. City of my dreams.

Pause.

Caroline once said there was only one place better than New York. (*Pause.*) Her apartment in Paris had been on Rue des Archives. She used to brag about hanging around in the Marais—she'd give me a wink and tell me that the gays always had a knack for locating themselves in the most picturesque parts of any town. When she talked about Paris she might as well have been talking about the moon.

Pause.

"Take it," I said, when my lawyer called from his Brooklyn office to tell me he'd just negotiated an insurance settlement for eighty thousand dollars. I'd made up my mind: I was going to visit Paris. Do something different for a change. Hey, I didn't know any French but I figured if a kid could learn it, than I could at least learn some of it.

Pause.

Paris. When I arrived, Caroline's spirit hovered nearby. This was not necessarily a good thing. I couldn't go on thinking about her so much. Sure, there was lots to do. I had counted on seeing the museums, the monuments. But I hadn't counted on there being so many people in Paris who seemed to have nothing to do but socialize. Americans—there's like a quarter of a million of them living in Paris. Plus a million other foreigners. Then you've got the French. It's pretty hard not to get invited somewhere for tea or dinner or just a party. It was livelier in Paris than anywhere else I'd been before. This really was the "joy of life." It was a surprise, and there was some getting used to the new situation. Meanwhile I decided on a slower way to get to know Paris. I went to the pools. Various swimming pools. A three month pass is cheap.

Pause.

I have this thing for swimming. It brings me closer to other human beings. It's a phony kind of closeness, I know. The kind of closeness you feel when you look to see how well the clothes fit a man or woman riding on the metro. But all the same, it's a closeness

DONALD: *(Continued.)* that produces a calm in me.

I see the swimmers in the pool: there's no worry, no secrets on their minds. They cut their accented paths through the waves. They're strong as oak. Under the glassy water they go, turning, coming smoothly up to start a new lap with feet skilled and graceful, flanks thick and concentrating on the task to be done. *(A frank admission:)* It's the nakedness of the scene that attracts, comforts me.

(Pause.) Well, when I wasn't swimming, I did slowly become involved in the Paris scene—and by that I mean also that I started to talk to French people, not just the English-speaking ex-patriots. The whole situation was fascinating, really. The surprising thing was that people in Paris found me... intriguing!

CAROLINE actor: We French people now have a thirty-five hour work week.

DONALD: That's incredible. How did *that* happen?

CAROLINE actor: The government made it a law.

DONALD: Unbelievable. I've wasted a good deal of my life working fifty hours a week. To pay the rent in New York.

CAROLINE actor: You have to work that hard to live in New York?

DONALD: You'd better believe it. And for all your troubles you get two weeks of vacation a year.

CAROLINE actor: Two weeks? We get six.

DONALD: I think I'm going to live here for the rest of my life. I love France.

(To the audience.) Those last words are work like magic around Paris. I wasn't lying—I did like France very much. And the more I got to talking, the more I heard myself saying some rather interesting things.

DONALD: *(To the* CAROLINE *actor.)* You know, the wealth in the United States is disgusting.

CAROLINE actor: Yes, I know, I know.

DONALD: I'm not interested in being rich, only happy. The rich people I've known have been boring. The more money you get, the more money you want. I'm from Florida, originally. I can't go down there any more. It upsets me too much to see the sick treadmill they're on.

CAROLINE actor: Yes, it's terrible. And to think that the Americans lead the world. It's repugnant.

DONALD: There are a few good things about the United States. Like the weather—it's really enjoyable if you don't happen to get shot by some nut who owns a handgun.

(*To the audience.*) I came to Paris to stay for two weeks. But now it's been two years.

Actors, as previously:

CAROLINE actor: Three swimming pools in the eleventh arrondissement.

TOMMY actor: Two in the twelfth.

CARL actor: Two in the first.

TOMMY actor: *Seven* in the fifteenth!

CAROLINE actor: In the sixteenth there are a couple.

TOMMY actor: In the seventeenth there are a couple.

CARL actor: In the eighteenth there are three.

DONALD: In the twentieth there is one. And if you get bored with the thirty-eight swimming pools I know of, there's sure to be some others. I didn't even go to a dozen pools.

DONALD: (*Continued.*) Ah, the pools did help me get my arms and legs in full working order. France in general worked quickly to get me out of the ridiculous swamp my life had become in the 'States. Eighteen years of stagnation. Rip Van Donald. Donald Van Winkle. Well, I didn't rush to make up for lost time in Paris. I was in too great a state of culture shock for that.

There was one swimming pool where my tour of the pools stopped. One day I met a girl at the swimming pool on avenue Gambetta in the twentieth arrondissement. I'd regained more than a little self-confidence from a few months of mixing with the French.

Hey, I wasn't being gratuitously harsh on America when I said I was annoyed by its materialism and lifestyles. I was venting. So what if all my venting makes me Mister Interesting to the French? I can live with that.

Lights out.

End of Act I

ACT II

In the front room of the LaSalle apartment in the suburbs outside Paris. A table is in front of a sofa. There is tallish standing plant. Two straight-back chairs are in the room. So is a vase of flowers.

Lights up. Donald introduces Marie, who is played by the same actor that plays Caroline.

DONALD: This is Marie.

MARIE *waves a little wave to the audience.*

I met her at the Georges Vallerey swimming pool on avenue Gambetta. This is the first time I ever met her parents, Gaston and Felicité LaSalle.

GASTON *enters.*

GASTON: Marie, why don't you go into the kitchen and help your mother with the dinner while I talk to your friend? (*To* DONALD.) I've heard you're an extremely interesting man.

MARIE *exits.*

DONALD: I still can't get over how it's possible that life can change so drastically from being near-hell to being something much, much better. It's almost absurd, the incongruity of it...

GASTON: We French are connoisseurs of the absurd and of incongruity. Tell me, is it true that you fled the disgusting parts of America—I don't mean the slums, but the vulgar rich areas—to come to France to get a better balance in your life?

DONALD: You've been talking to Marie about me.

GASTON: And is it true that you once met Andy Warhol?

DONALD: I don't like to name-drop. But his name came up when Marie and I visited the Musée d'Orsay together.

GASTON: I don't like Warhol. American trash. No offense.

DONALD: No offense taken.

GASTON: He wasn't a true artist.

DONALD: He didn't paint nudes like all the great French painters do.

GASTON: "Art is anything you can get away with." Did he say that?

DONALD: Yes.

GASTON: Sacrilege. He's spread his disease even to France. No wonder people are getting more stupid. There are no good artists out there to lead us to higher ideals. *(Pause.)* Marie can't hold back with her chatter about you. I think she loves you.

DONALD: Love has been a rare thing for me.

GASTON: Has it now? Do you want to tell me about it?

DONALD: I rather not talk on such a serious note.

GASTON: *(Surveying* DONALD.*)* But how could such a theme be painful for you to talk about? What happened? I don't mean to pry. You're such a young man.

DONALD: Not really. To be honest, I'm forty-one now.

GASTON: You look so young!

DONALD: Maybe it's because I haven't done much with my life so far.

GASTON: Oh, that's not true. (*Pause.*) Your age won't matter to Marie. She's thirty-one herself.

DONALD: Uh-huh.

GASTON: You and my daughter have the same age difference as me and my wife!

DONALD: Really, you're ten years older than your wife?

GASTON: You flatter me!

DONALD: I love France!

GASTON: You're really wanting me to like you, aren't you? Not all Americans are as friendly as you, I bet. You and Marie met at the pool, right? Near where she works—

DONALD: Yeah, avenue Gambetta. It's convenient to be a foreigner. You can break the ice with anyone just by pretending you don't understand what the situation is.

GASTON: You're very sly. But frank. I appreciate that.

DONALD: I was attracted to your daughter. All's fair under those conditions.

GASTON: I *adore* you, Donald, if I may call you Donald. Now, avenue Gambetta is in the 20th arrondissement. How did you wind up there?

DONALD: By chance. In the beginning I thought I might start with the first arrondissement and work my way up. Good thing I didn't.

GASTON: What makes you say that?

DONALD: If I'd done things differently I might never have met the mermaid that lives here.

GASTON: Of course. *(Pause.)* It's fate, my boy.

DONALD: I do care about your daughter. More than I have cared about anyone in many, many years. *(Pause.)* I guess women today aren't as interested in astrology as they were some years back.

GASTON: I don't understand.

DONALD: I thought women were generally interested in astrology.

GASTON: Remember, Marie is French. Life is more fun for us than those who live in English-speaking countries. Thus we have far less interest in the supernatural.
(Pause. Eyeing him.) A good looking boy like you must have gotten the spear in quite a few times in the past. Had many girlfriends in your life?

DONALD: Not really.

GASTON: One or two?

DONALD: Let's just say I've had girlfriends.

GASTON: And ah,...boyfriends?

DONALD: Actually, some, yes.

GASTON: You're not saying you're gay are you!? *(Almost warning him.)* Remember, you are one or the other.

DONALD: It was in the past.

GASTON: Everything's in the past. It's a dream to think that it could be in the future.

DONALD: You French are so abstract.

GASTON: We enjoy that.

DONALD: I'm trying to enjoy life now.

GASTON: You didn't before?

DONALD: Not like the French.

GASTON: Too many hang-ups? With girls or boys?

DONALD: Maybe with myself.

GASTON: We French don't see psychiatrists as often as you do. But we do have crazy people here.

DONALD: It seems to me that France is one the sanest places on earth.

GASTON: I know this country better than you.

DONALD: Of course you do.

Pause.

GASTON: So you've done it with other men? (*A look of disgust crosses his face but it soon turns to a smile.* GASTON *playfully gives* DONALD *a punch on the shoulder.*) I was a sailor once. I know what it's all about. Been there. Done that.

DONALD: You're very open-minded.

GASTON: Sometimes. But I don't remember what exactly brought you to Paris.

DONALD: A girlfriend used to talk and talk about Paris.

GASTON: A girlfriend. Is she your girlfriend back home?

DONALD: No, actually, the girl's dead.

GASTON: That's good. I mean, that's not so good.

DONALD: Yes, and life was terrible for me after she died. For quite a while. Now things are looking up.

GASTON: It sounds like a very manic life you've had. Bad first, then not so bad.

DONALD: Better that way than good, then bad.

GASTON: My daughter—she has not had it so good.

DONALD: Really? She's never told me.

GASTON: No, no. She has grave defects. I'm sorry, but I must be open with you. Poor thing. Sweet thing. (*Pause.*) Can we talk on a serious note?

DONALD: If you feel you have to.

GASTON: No, I can't do this. I can't.

DONALD: Okay. Don't.

GASTON: But I must.

DONALD: Don't bend yourself out of shape if you don't want to.

GASTON: Oh, God, I must.

DONALD: Then do it. Don't worry. What's up?

GASTON: I can't tell you. (*Shakes his head "no".*) Absolutely not.

DONALD: What could be so bad that you can't tell me?

GASTON: (*In agony.*) But you see she needs to get married! There's no other way for her or for us. We can't be looking after her any more.

DONALD: She's living here because there's an extra room.

GASTON: I'm not talking about rooms! Her mother and I—we need a younger family—the next generation—to look after us in our old age. It's the French way.

DONALD: In the U.S. we just throw the old people in old folks' homes. *(Pause.)* Now, don't be worried about Marie. Tell me what you feel I ought to know.

GASTON: You're a nice man. But how nice are you? Would you be willing to put up with her handicap?

DONALD: What handicap? I see her in the swimming pool and she does just fine.

GASTON: But don't you know—she was married once before. She's been divorced!

DONALD: Is this some kind of Catholic thing? I'm not Catholic. Divorce doesn't bother me.

GASTON: Fabulous! I mean, that's okay. *(Worried.)* Donald, you don't think you'd ever divorce?

DONALD: I would hope not. It sounds like a terrible, terrible thing to do.

GASTON: That's good, very good. Would you like an hors d'oeuvre?

DONALD: How much longer before dinner?

GASTON: I don't know. Maybe an hour.

DONALD: *(Surprised.)* An hour? Yeah, I guess I'll have one.

GASTON: It's goat's stomach.

DONALD: Oh.

GASTON: It smells a little.

DONALD: Oh, well, down the hatch!

DONALD *eats it. There is an uncomfortable look on his face.*

GASTON: Are you all right?

DONALD: *(Gulping.)* I hope so.

GASTON: Listen, there's one more thing.

DONALD: I'm all set with hors d'oeuvres for the moment, thank you.

GASTON: It's about Marie.

DONALD: What is it?

GASTON: *(Seized by fear.)* No, I can't tell you.

DONALD: You can tell me. We've both got open minds here. Was she once a lesbian?

GASTON: No, no, no. Look. My daughter's been divorced and there's a reason for it.

DONALD: There usually is.

GASTON: But it was her fault.

DONALD: Nobody's perfect. There are times in my life that I've been no angel.

GASTON: But you see, this is something she couldn't help.

DONALD: Well, then, if she couldn't help it, it's not her fault.

GASTON: But it *is* her fault. Her biological fault.

DONALD: You're being abstract again.

GASTON: We French can't avoid it.

DONALD: So what's the problem? Tell me, straight out, Monsieur.

GASTON: Call me Gaston, please. Now I will tell you this even though it petrifies me to say it: her husband divorced her because the doctors found out she's unable to have children.

DONALD: Big deal. Who cares? God, I'd prefer not to have children. I have enough problems of my own.

GASTON, *overjoyed, embraces* DONALD *and kisses him on both cheeks.*

GASTON: Oh, my dear, my dear! Though this is the first time we've met I'll tell flat out: Marie is yours. I give you her hand in marriage.

DONALD: Thank you. She and I haven't really gotten that far yet.

GASTON: And there's more. A dowry.

DONALD: What's that?

GASTON: A custom we have. Not everyone still practices it. A dowry means that I'm to give you money when you marry Marie. To offset any inconvenience she might be to your new life.

MARIE *walks in.*

MARIE: Are the two of you getting acquainted? Father, would you like another aperitif?

GASTON: Isn't she sensitive? *(He smiles.)* Don't ask me what I would like. First tend to our special guest.

MARIE: Would you like anything, Donald?

DONALD: Just hearing you ask me if I want anything sounds so pleasant to me.

MARIE: That's very sweet.

FELICITÉ enters with a tray of food.

MARIE: *(To* DONALD.*)* Oh, Donald, did papa tell you? We've had the butcher slaughter a calf in your honor.

DONALD: You didn't need to go to any trouble just for me.

FELICITÉ: It was no problem at all. In Europe, you know, we still hang on to some of the old ways.

She sets the tray down.

GASTON: Not only the bread is fresh here in France!

DONALD: I love this country! I guess this means we'll be having veal later.

FELICITÉ: If that's all right with you. But first, for more hors d'oeuvres, we have a small assortment. Crab puffs. And my original creation, these—

GASTON holds up a specimen of his wife's creation for all to see.

GASTON: What we have here is smoked cheese alternating on the skewer with halves of Brussels sprouts which have been sautéed with butter and curry powder. Delicious.

MARIE: They are, actually.

GASTON: Felicité is a genius.

FELICITÉ: Nouvelle cuisine.

MARIE: *(To* DONALD.*)* You're not hungry?

DONALD: Almost.

MARIE: So you want to wait a moment?

DONALD: They look delicious. I will have some. *(Pause.)* It's just that my appetite... I didn't go swimming today. That always helps me to work up an appetite.

GASTON: We have aperitifs, these are what the French use to stimulate the appetite.

MARIE: Maybe playing a game would help Donald work his up. Have you heard of the game called "French Colonial Torture"?

DONALD: Is the game anything like the game we call American Globalization?

GASTON *jams his hands together in glee.*

GASTON: Oh, you two are positively *made* for each other!

FÉLICITÉ: Having a similar sense of humor is all-important. But of course, happiness, as the philosopher says, is the feeling that power is growing, and that resistance is being overcome. But there are two of you. Wouldn't one expect that at times one of you would be resistant to the other?

MARIE: Mother, Americans are not as inclined to abstract discussion as we are. And don't go suggesting problems before they've started.

DONALD: Madame LaSalle, I'm sure you and your husband have had your disagreements.

GASTON: Yes, but we've worked such things out on the springs.

DONALD: I'm sorry, I don't understand.

GASTON: The bed springs, my son!

FÉLICITÉ: Don't make him blush.

GASTON: Felice, I think *he* could tell you some things that might make you blush.

MARIE: I'll have one of mother's creations.

She takes one and eats.

GASTON: Isn't she lovely when she eats.

They all wait until she finishes eating.

MARIE: Maman, Donald has never traveled in Europe and soon we thought we might like to go somewhere together.

FELICITÉ: That's a good idea. You know Europe extends all the way through Turkey now.

MARIE: It'll be a good test for our relationship.

FELICITÉ: Perhaps one is not necessary. I hope you don't think I'm being outrageous by suggesting this analogy: but I picture our Marie as a wondrous, French, feminine, receptive black hole of fantastic density, hugely compressed. I picture Donald as a bright, New World star, capable of great masculine explosive energy. I see any resistance that were to come between you to be completely superintegrated when either of you moves a centimeter in either person's direction.

GASTON: Are you suggesting that there is a synergy between them?

FELICITÉ: I am.

GASTON: Wow. But isn't this a bit self-centered? I mean, the world is a tangle of evil where A) anything that can be exploited will be, B) nothing is real until turned into a commodity, and C) a thing's worth is what the public will pay. Shouldn't we be doing something about these things?

DONALD *steps out of the discussion.*

DONALD: *(To the audience.)* Well, what can I say? Vital discussions. Such an amazing change from my previous life.

MARIE:
>Your bad times—they're over.
>You were young then.
>But now you're *healthier*.

DONALD: Oh, I want you.

MARIE: Yes, and I want you. Let's go swimming.

DONALD: Yes, let's.

MARIE: Is it too soon to think about getting married?

DONALD: Taking the plunge? Let's go swimming and think about getting married. If we get married why not do it in a swimming pool?

MARIE: I want you.

DONALD: I want you too.

MARIE: I want to get married in a swimming pool.

DONALD: Which one?

FÉLICITÉ actor: There's that one in the fourth.

GASTON actor: Or that one in the sixth.

MARIE: Why shouldn't we get married where we met, in the Georges Vallerey pool in the 20th.

DONALD: *(As if to say, "How stupid of me.")* Yeah, that's the thing to do.

MARIE: But they'd never let us do it there.

Back in the scene, all actors in character now.

FELICITÉ: It's too bad that you two couldn't visit the caverns of Lascaux. But they're shut off to the tourists. All you can see now is what's there in the visitor's center. Do you like cave art, Donald?

DONALD: I don't know any of it.

FELICITÉ: They have a number of famous paintings there. They're about 15,000 years old.

DONALD: Older than Adam and Eve.

GASTON: That's what I find interesting too.

FELICITÉ: And the animals are superbly drawn, but the humans— they're just represented as stick figures.

GASTON: What does this mean, Marie? You know. You took a class in anthropology at the university. (*To* DONALD, *winking*.) The paintings have a lot to do with the *hunt*.

MARIE: Quit trying to show off as a family, everybody. Donald does-n't care how stupid or intelligent we are.

DONALD: I certainly do. One of the reasons why I enjoy being in France so much is that people here don't talk as much superficial nonsense as they do in America.

GASTON: Oh, how we love you. Are you sure you won't have some Alsatian beer? We have an old family goblet that we can put it in for you.

DONALD: No, thank you. But I think I'll try one of your skewers now.

He takes one of the skewers. He takes a bite.

GASTON: You don't have to eat standing up.

FELICITÉ: Yes, won't you sit down?

FELICITÉ *gestures to the sofa.* DONALD *chews in order to finish his mouthful.*

FELICITÉ: *(Continued.)* Look at him. Such a handsome man when he's eating.

GASTON: How lucky we are to have a daughter who knows how to swim. *(To* FELICITÉ.) See, darling, I always told you it was important for our child to learn how to swim.

FELICITÉ: And to play a musical instrument as well.

GASTON: Swimming has saved our lives on dry land. Could music do such a thing in the water?

DONALD: I'm sorry, but I'd be more comfortable in a regular chair.

GASTON: Well, then, Marie, pull a chair up for our guest. My wife and I will sit down in the sofa. We're to be all on the same level in this house. Come, dear.

DONALD: It tastes very good.

> DONALD *happily takes another bite.* FELICITÉ *and* GASTON *sit down on the sofa.* MARIE *pulls up the chair for* DONALD. *She positions the chair near the tall plant. Unfortunately,* DONALD *miscalculates where* MARIE *is placing the chair, or* MARIE *is not looking at* DONALD *as he bends his legs to sit down. The result is that* DONALD *falls down on his butt. As* DONALD *loses balance on the way down his hand loses control of the skewer. It gets half-embedded—or so it appears—in his side.* DONALD *lets out a strange groan.*

MARIE: I'm sorry, Donald. Are you okay? (DONALD *mumbles something.*) Yes, you can wait, until your mouth's no longer full.

GASTON: Are you all right?

MARIE: He's still chewing.

FELICITÉ: So polite.

They wait until he swallows his food.

DONALD: Ow.

MARIE: Here, I'll help you up.

DONALD: First, take this.

> DONALD *hands* MARIE *the skewer that he pulls from his side. In a couple of seconds* MARIE *notices his side.*

MARIE: But Donald, you're bleeding.

GASTON: What?

> GASTON *rises from the sofa.* MARIE *touches* DONALD'*s side and he lets out a pained cry.*

DONALD: Ouch.

> *He loses his balance and falls to the ground.* MARIE *points to the wound.*

MARIE: Right there, in your side.

FELICITÉ: Oh, Gaston.

MARIE: The skewer must have stabbed him.

> DONALD *gets up off the ground and sits in the chair.* GASTON *attends to him. The standing plant is positioned between the sofa and the chair. As* FELICITÉ *leaves the sofa to go over to* DONALD *she accidentally moves into the plant and the plant comes crashing down on* DONALD. GASTON *stands the plant back up.*

GASTON: Don't sit. Lie down. We'll have to examine you. If it's a puncture wound you'll need special attention.

DONALD: I think I'm all right.

MARIE *attempts to give* DONALD *a light kiss but they bump heads.*

GASTON: Please, do me a favor, and just lie down.

DONALD: I was probably only grazed.

MARIE: Do as Daddy says, it'll be okay.

GASTON: First aid in the Navy. You can't imagine the bizarre accidents one has aboard a ship. The tossing of the sea and all that dangerous metalwork.

DONALD *complies and lies down on the floor, face up.*

Marie, you go get a sponge and some bandages. Felicité, you go get my clothing. (MARIE *and* FELICITÉ *start to leave.*) Wait, Marie. Give me the skewer. I need it to compare it to the wound. (MARIE *gives him the skewer.* GASTON, *to* DONALD:) No, Donald. I want you to lie down on your stomach. We wouldn't want the blood to settle into your kidneys.

MARIE *and* FELICITÉ *exit.*

DONALD: Really, I'm all right.

GASTON: No, no, no— (GASTON *raises* DONALD'S *shirt and sees the wound.*) There, I see it. How long's it been since your last tetanus injection?

DONALD: No idea.

GASTON *places the skewer up against the wound.*

GASTON: You feel a little pinch?

DONALD: Yes, what are you doing?

GASTON: It's a puncture wound, for sure. (*He puts down the skewer.*) Yes, well, you've punctured our girl. And now we've punctured you back.

DONALD: Excuse me?

GASTON: You don't see what I mean?

DONALD: Not exactly.

GASTON: You soon will. Now be sure not to cough. That is very bad for someone in your condition. It's a good thing there were no barbs in that skewer. You've never insulted our girl have you? I bet you think you haven't.

DONALD: What on earth are you talking about?

GASTON: I'm just trying to reckon to what lengths we may have to go.

MARIE *comes back in.*

DONALD: Marie, darling. Did you get the bandage?

MARIE: And a sponge. (*She bends down and looks at the wound.*) But it doesn't seem to be bleeding much.

GASTON: But you never know what may happen once the moon comes up tonight. *Dumque nimis crucior satis alto vulnere lesus.*

DONALD: (*Suppressing most of his outrage.*) Marie, is it okay if I get up?

GASTON: Marie, give me the bandage and sponge.

She gives them to him. He sets them aside.

There, we may need them later.

DONALD: But why not now?

FELICITÉ *enters with* GASTON's *ritual clothing. It consists of a gold T-shirt and a white cassock that will reach just below his knees.*

GASTON: You stay there, my fine androgyne. Of course this could never happen with you when you were with boys. You feel pain now, but think how lucky you are to be complete and part of the mysteries of food and blood.

FELICITÉ: And sex, too, that's part of it.

GASTON: *(To* FELICITÉ.) Absolutely, my dear bison woman.

MARIE: Father, remember he's from Florida originally and he doesn't always understand European ways.

GASTON: These are not only European, they are world-wide, anywhere where technology has not transgressed the natural order.

> *Leuis exsurgit zephirus*
> *et sol procedit tepidus,*
> *iam terra sinus aperit,*
> *dulcore suo difluit.*

DONALD: Marie, you told me that everything was so Americanized here.

MARIE: To a certain extent.

FELICITÉ: Gaston, are you ready for your inner robe?

GASTON: If the man-horse agrees to lie there. As still as a hunter in wait.

MARIE: He'll cooperate. He's an easy-going guy.

DONALD: I guess there's not much else to do in the suburbs on a Sunday afternoon.

GASTON *takes off his shirt and puts on the gold T-shirt brought in by* FELICITÉ.

MARIE: We could go to a film later.

DONALD: I might like that.

MARIE: They're having a Buñuel retrospective the Studio Giles Coeur.

DONALD: Great.

GASTON: Thus I put on the inner robe.

> *Ver purpuratum exiit,*
> *ornatus suos induit,*
> *aspergit terram floribus,*
> *ligna siluarum frondibus.*

DONALD: That's not even French! Hey, one language at a time! Starting a life over in a new country is hard enough with one foreign language.

MARIE: Relax, Donald, he's just reaching out to you as a fellow human being.

GASTON: I'm ready for my outer, and final, robe now.

FELICITÉ *hands him the white cassock.* GASTON *puts it on.*

DONALD: We could call a doctor.

FELICITÉ:

> *Struunt lustra quadrupedes,*
> *et dulces nidos uolucres*
> *inter ligna florentia*
> *sua decantant gaudia.*

DONALD: Oh, no, not you, too!

GASTON: Thus I put on the outer robe.

MARIE: By the way, you're supposed to hold a flower while he ministers to you.

MARIE *goes over to a vase of flowers and takes out a flower.*

GASTON: You may roll over and lie on your back now. You shall look up and see a bird upon a staff.

DONALD: What about the blood flowing into my kidneys?

GASTON: That will not happen any more.

MARIE *gives* DONALD *the flower and he holds it.*

DONALD: And I thought you were fairly normal middleclass.

GASTON: We are. Donald, the wound wounds you individually, it's also an opening to the Great Opening. All this should strike at your conscience for what you've done with our Marie.

DONALD: The only thing I've done is make her happy.

GASTON: Yes, now it's time for the man to choose Woman and marry her.

DONALD: But...

GASTON: Only then will the wound heal.

DONALD: But...

GASTON: The civil service can come later. *Necesse est enim sit alterum de duobus.* But first we have to get on with the ceremony.

DONALD: Aren't we going to have veal soon?

GASTON: Afterwards. Now may we be guided by blood and spear, by food and flower, to our manifest good. We throw off the impulsive, we enter gloriously, having endured. We near the forces which promise us that resistance between hunter and prey is resolved in union.

DONALD: I thought I'd seen everything in New York.

FELICITÉ: I thought I'd seen everything until Gaston and I stumbled into a circumcision party in European Turkey. The thirteen year-old boy was lying on a cot much the same way that you're lying there right now. Except he wasn't getting married.

DONALD: Don't I have any say in this? Does Marie have any say in this?

FELICITÉ: It was many people gathering to share one common emotion.

DONALD: Great.

MARIE: (*Trying in part to excuse her family's conduct.*) The family impulse—the collective impulse—is very strong here in France.

GASTON: Out of consideration that much of what I would normally do would only go in one ear and out the other for you, I will make our ceremony shorter.

DONALD: Thank you. But I just want to hear something more from Marie before you continue. Marie, ...oh, man, I don't know what to say. You know that I like you. It's more or less shaping up to be a great love. So marriage is an idea that's not too far out. Okay?

MARIE: I was so glad you came up to me at the pool. You don't know happy you've made me. When you went with me to see the Gustave Moreau house... It was wonderful, wasn't it? We'll never be able to afford a house like that of course, especially in the 9th arrondissement. We don't need that kind of space, there's just the two of us. It's a good idea to get married.

MARIE: *(Continued.)* Neither one of us would get on each others' nerves because, well, you have your interests—which consist of cultivating a better knowledge of the world around you—and I have my interests which overlap with yours because I feel that I'm open to anything, except of course, a life of crime. Oh, and I have to say this: I don't care how old you are, I will always find you terribly handsome.

DONALD: And I will find you always beautiful, I'm sure. *(To* GASTON.*)* Now, *that's* simple.

GASTON: But it's not enough. If I'm going to give you a dowry I want a little satisfaction of my own. I couldn't sleep at night if I thought you two were only having a physical relationship—you both knowing full well that there are to be no children coming from it.

MARIE: Father, what did you tell him? *(To* DONALD.*)* He lies.

GASTON: All this talk about being handsome and beautiful! Superficial! That's what the likes of Elvis Presley and the culture of rock and roll have done to people.

DONALD: I think I might actually agree with you on that last point.

GASTON: This is why we need to bring you into the fold—properly! *(Pause.)* The battle has been waged. The skewer *(He looks down at the skewer.)* has played its part. The realm of the flesh has been visited and *(He looks meaningfully at* MARIE *and* DONALD.*)* you are to be transhumanized.
   We live on earth in order to obtain experience that will exempt us from future incarnation as beasts and malcontents. Blessed by virtue and perhaps even thoughts of the sublime, what could be wished or wanted more than that? Donald, take my daughter's hand. Both of you hold the flower together.

MARIE *bends down. She and* DONALD *take each others' hand. They hold the flower between the two of them.*

GASTON: (*Continued.*) We reciprocate through blood and flesh and renew with the flower. The fatal doom of death is a ridiculous concept to us, because death for us is only another modality of existence, a modality that we do not wish to dwell on at this time because we have enough to be occupied with in our present modality.

As striving souls against regression we are not complete until we are united in the Absolute. Holding this flower and gathering 'round we sensitize ourselves with all our hearts and highest hopes, to the Divine that reaches into our souls with a loving spirit. May we widen our circle so that we may embrace the world. In the name of the Wisdom, and of the Justice, and one Eternal Spirit, and in the Wound that brings us together.

> DONALD *releases the flower and* MARIE'S *hand. He gets up and nods a thank you to* GASTON *and* FELICITÉ. *These last two move and stand apart from* DONALD *and* MARIE. MARIE *stands not too far from* DONALD. *He addresses the audience:*

DONALD: Okay, that was the ceremony in the short version. I'm not one to laugh in the face of those who are concerned about their daughter, and other people, being happy.

We had a pleasant dinner shortly after Gaston completed the ritual. The pain in my side was gone. For just a moment I pretended to dicker with Gaston over the amount of the dowry. I had, and I have, a lot to learn from the French. They are not to be underestimated as a race of people. As the past two years have gone by my respect for Gaston and Felicité has only grown.

Since getting married to Marie I have known a fullness to my life that I have never known before.

> FELICITÉ *comes in with a basket of bread—a sliced-up loaf of fresh bread is inside. She puts the basket down after clearing the table.* DONALD *picks up a small slice of bread. To* MARIE:

DONALD: See this piece of bread. This is the kitchen of our new house.

MARIE: *(Choosing another piece of bread.)* And this piece of bread is our bedroom.

DONALD: *(He picks up another piece of bread.)* And this piece will be the front door, which, I'm going to eat right now and that means... what does it mean? It means, I've come in the door to find you home and I can't believe you're there. You're a magical shape that I can't believe is solid and real. Not only are you just there, but you're not indifferent to me. You want me. And we're going to have plenty of fun together before the evening is over.

(To the audience.) All right. So things turned out well for me. After those eighteen years of stagnation. How fascinating it's become for me, settling down here in Paris with a girl who, like Caroline, has got a European father. Hey, just think, Carl was the one that was pushing me out and this guy's pulling me in.

Well, France is still a little strange. But that makes for fewer dull moments. *(Pause.)* I still swim. So does Marie. I may be swimming till my dying day.

GASTON actor: Three swimming pools in the eleventh.

DONALD: I'm glad I didn't get fixated on any of those in the eleventh, or those in the fifteenth...

MARIE: ...where there are an amazing number of them: *seven* swimming pools!

FELICITÉ actor: Only two in the sixteenth arrondissement.

DONALD: Just like in the fourteenth. And the first.
GASTON actor: Ah, that pool in the twentieth. Not far from the Théâtre de la Colline.

MARIE: On avenue Gambetta.

DONALD: It's a tragedy when you're in a rut and you don't even realize it. My way out was the accident. I've found myself in a fabulous
city with one great family. *(He thinks to himself, then:)* I've really grown.
The world's a chaotic, messy place. Sometimes dark, sad, sick—and
then, like in the eye of a hurricane, there's the still wondrous part.

Ah, sliding into the waters of life. You swim, your neck's like the
prow of a ship. You may even feel young once again for a moment, as
you work down your lane.

Lights fade out.

End of Act II

End of the Play.

A FAMILY PORTRAIT

a one act play

Characters

DAD   *Male. 30s-40s.*

SHIRLEY   *Female, his teenage daughter.*

MOM   *Female. Dad's wife. 30s-40s.*

BRAD   *Male, their son, slightly older than
                        Shirley.*

Place: In a family home.
Time: Present.

Notes

  Dad and Mom are progressive. Though they at times may appear to
be saying cold words to their children, they are warm to them. They
love them. This may be one reason why the actor who gives the introduction to the play (and who will later play Brad) says that this portrait
of the human species is "a little flattering at times."

  I don't know why some people don't "get" this play. Well, how often
do you hear a play (outside of nursery school television) about two,

three, and... four? The deep resonances of at least two and three surround us, so why not play with them? There is a question of how stylized each actor's performance should be. It seems to me that the kids—Shirley and Brad—are the straight characters in the comedy and Dad and Mom are not. If we must insist on the "purpose and points" of *A Family Portrait*, what are they? 1) That bad never disappears 2) That play, engagement, discussion and music make it possible to enjoy life.

A Family Portrait was first presented in a reading at Moving Parts in Paris, France, on March 25, 2001. Thanks there go to Stephanie Campion, Bill Dunn, Lori Lamb, Sheila Coren-Tissot and Olivier Raynal. The play is dedicated to Martin Lockley.

A Family Portrait

This play should be presented in a lobby of a theater, or can be presented in any other space except the inside of a theater.

The scene is set in the living room of a house. Furnishings can be minimal and suggestive. There is no special lighting. The play is presented in whatever light that is available.

The actor who will play BRAD *makes his announcement while* DAD *and his daughter* SHIRLEY *standby ready to begin the play proper.*

BRAD: *(Not in character.)* Hey, listen up. It seems this play isn't really a play—that's what a few angry people said in Paris when it was first done. Yep. They said that nothing happened in the drama. Well I guess our little show isn't good enough for a proper stage, that's why we're here. Why are we doing this play called "A Family Portrait"? Because we like it. It says something about the human condition. It's a portrait of our species, a little flattering at times, but why beat up on ourselves constantly? We'd like for other folks to appreciate the play, but we're not holding our breath. We've decided we're playing to the balcony. The cosmic balcony. I mean the one filled with space aliens. Beings that don't have any pre-conceptions about what a theater piece should be. Beings that are curious about us, but have so far not been able to get close enough to us to understand us. I'm sorry if any earthling critics will find what we do is undramatic. We've got no murder, rape, theft, accident or alcoholism here. We're just not in the mood to manipulate people's guts with that stuff. So without further ado, we present to you our *thing.*

The actor playing BRAD *exits.*

DAD: Shirley, your mother and I have discussed this. She thinks you're ready... Certain facts of life...

SHIRLEY: *(To herself.)* Oh, no!

DAD: They say a daughter's bond is stronger with her father than with her mother. *(Nervous cringe.)* Hmm. You're mature. I'm sure you can handle it. "Bring it out in the open," they say. Yeah. I don't want you to get into any trouble.

SHIRLEY: How would I get in trouble?

DAD: The innocent are easily corrupted.

SHIRLEY: I'm not completely sheltered, Dad. I know about it: foreplay, intercourse and orgasm.

DAD: The old three-stage rocket.

SHIRLEY: Excuse me?

DAD: See, you *don't* understand.

SHIRLEY: Dad, I do.

DAD: You said, "foreplay, intercourse, orgasm."

SHIRLEY: Yes, Dad.

DAD: Very good. That's a start, I mean, it's, after all, what you pick up on the street.

SHIRLEY: I didn't pick it up on the street.

DAD: It's only an expression, dear. Perhaps you picked it up in the locker room.

SHIRLEY: No.

DAD: You didn't pick it up anywhere else, did you? At some boy's house?

SHIRLEY: Dad, we have sex ed in school. And they tell us that sex means nothing to the human unless it's linked with love.

DAD: Fine. I respect the teachers. But there'll always be something left for the parents to explain. 'Cause the classics only go so far when it comes to child development. Take "The Iliad," for example. A great work, without equal. But it's so dependent upon war as a concept. Now, don't let me lose my train of thought. (*Pause. He's lost momentarily.*)

SHIRLEY: I think you want to explain something to me that the teachers can't.

DAD: Right. All creatures are made up of top, middle and bottom. And all tops—or heads—are made up of centers and tops and bottoms. It's complex. At the same time it's simple. Small, medium, and large; rodent, carnivore, and the hoofed animals.

SHIRLEY: I don't see how the last thing follows the others.

DAD: You will, you will.

SHIRLEY: We have science in school, Dad.

DAD: It is only one type of science. There are others.

SHIRLEY: Like biology, chemistry and physics.

DAD: That's three. (*To the audience.*) And *three* is very important.

SHIRLEY: Is that why you want me to apply to Trinity College?

DAD: A coincidence, perhaps.

  Pause.

SHIRLEY: But if there were a college by the name of Quadriatic University you probably wouldn't want me to apply.

DAD: Heavens no! *(Pause.)* Now, as I was saying, there are the primary colors of red, green and violet...

SHIRLEY: You never said that.

DAD: But I'm referring to threes, triads.

SHIRLEY: What about fours? The four seasons?

DAD: Spring and autumn are very alike, you know. Especially in the tropics.

SHIRLEY: We don't live in the tropics. And everything is one there. Every day has the same amount of light at the equator.

DAD: I'm not talking about the equator.

SHIRLEY: Okay, I understand. Like there are *three* states of matter: gas, liquid and solid.

DAD: Right.

SHIRLEY: Wrong. There's a fourth state of matter: plasma.

DAD: You're a very smart girl. But it still doesn't change the facts: *(Shows three fingers in succession.)* Lions and tigers and bears.

SHIRLEY: Groups of three.

DAD: Yes, darling.

SHIRLEY: I like categories of two. Like boy and girl.

DAD: You would at your age.

SHIRLEY: Black and white.

DAD: But there's gray. Look *(He touches his left shoulder, touches himself at mid-chest and then touches his right shoulder.)* One, two, three, you see, even though the body appears to be bi-modal, two is only the outside poles for three. We're tri-modal.

SHIRLEY: I think you're being kind of rigid.

DAD: Perhaps the same goes for you, as well. Right now you only want to get a job and save up enough money to buy a car. Am I correct?

SHIRLEY: Well, you're not buying me one.

MOM *enters, she carries some rolled-up plans.*

DAD: That's because you need to devote yourself to homework.

MOM: I hope I'm not interrupting any deep conversation.

SHIRLEY: No, it's just Daddy with his old threefold philosophy.

MOM: Sam, have you been repeating yourself again?

SHIRLEY: Only for the third time at least this week.

MOM: I know it's hard for a father to relate to a daughter at your age. It's easy to hit an impasse.
   Speaking of impasses, I've been thinking about how that which holds us back may be built into our bodies. Take the eyes of the human being, for example. Wouldn't it be more advantageous if we humans possessed a third eye, in the back of the head, so as to better see oncoming predators? I mean, two eyes are enough to see friends, because in general, friends aren't going to attack you. But what about those that want to harm us? Two eyes aren't enough. We're vulnerable. We have to be optimistic or we'll worry ourselves to death.

Pause.

DAD: Exactly. I love you. I love you even more because you think.

MOM: We all think. But most of us don't think for ourselves. We rarely make our own discoveries. We voice discoveries made by others like, "Life is a comedy for those who think, and a tragedy for those who feel."

DAD: And an opera for those that yearn.

MOM: Bingo! Now that's original.

SHIRLEY: If you don't mind I've got to do my homework.

DAD: Oh, what is it you're working on?

SHIRLEY: Well, I wanted to do something on Georgia O'Keeffe. Or Emma Goldman. But it's a project called "The Otherworld Journey and the Threefold Death."

DAD: Threefold never dies.

SHIRLEY: It's from Nikolai Tolstoi's book "The Quest for Merlin."

DAD: Well, go on your Otherworld journey then. But be sure to enjoy the rest of your childhood while you still can.

SHIRLEY *(Frustrated with him.)* Oh, Dad!

SHIRLEY *leaves. Pause.*

MOM: When there was time to learn, we all wasted it.

DAD: Yes, when we were young all we thought about was sex and cars. Now when we as adults try to find the time, it's no longer there. What strange, inadequate habits our culture has evolved. Life is truly an opera.

MOM: We must stop yearning for a better life. We have to *build* it. In the concrete. Now. I have some new plans.

DAD: Are you surprising me again? I'm all eyes and ears. All six of them if only nature had been so wise.

MOM: *(Sexy.)* I still find you sexy just the way you are.

Mom spreads out the plans.

MOM: Consciousness is not neutral. It knows direction, and this direction is away from pain. And we move in the direction of what's around us. So we aren't harmed by friction. Now, what's around us? Nature. We don't compete against it, we complement it. Look, I've come up with a fresh suggestion for the shape of our new home: a starfish shape.

DAD: *(Aghast.) Five* sections?

MOM: Is there anything wrong with that?

DAD: It's not three.

MOM: No, it isn't.

DAD: Not even two.

MOM: No.

DAD: But if you add two to three you get five.

MOM: Precisely.

DAD: But I don't exactly know what I mean by what I just said. It seems very complex.

MOM: Be optimistic about how I can make this interrelate.

DAD: Well, is this five plan somehow related to the sea?

MOM: What makes you say that?

DAD: You mentioned starfish. And starfish live in the sea. There's a lake nearby. It's not saltwater. Okay, I'm trying to figure this out.

MOM: Well, frankly, I thought a little contrast might be exciting.

DAD: But five! Five! *(Pause.)* And remember: we've talked about the *homeopathic* element. *(Lowers his voice.)* Because of you-know-who. To stimulate a negative part of our personalities *just a little bit* so as to fight the big bad negativity that threatens us all. Do your plans address the homeopathic element?

MOM: Yes, can't you see the *aggression* built into the form of a starfish on land!

DAD: Now I see it, yes I do! My God, you're brilliant.

MOM: That's enough for now.

She folds up the plans.

MOM: I wonder what we should have for dinner.

DAD: Is it my turn to cook or not?

MOM: Yours, I think.

DAD: Then we'll have my favorite. Noodles and eggs.

MOM: And broccoli.

DAD: Right-o. *(Pause.)* Maybe we should picture the house in terms of a *pentagonal* leaf. Leaves are not only living parts, whole trees can be grown from them.

MOM: That's very poetic, darling. There is the trajectory of life built right into that concept. Let me see the plans again.

She spreads out the plans once more.

DAD: I'll go start dinner.

He leaves.

MOM: A leaf. In terms of a leaf... Ah, the soul of a leaf... *(She drifts off in her imagination. Her reverie is destroyed by the blaring of loud music from the boom box of her son, BRAD, a slob with shaved head and arm tattoos, who enters carrying the boom box and shouts over the music.)*

BRAD: Hey, Mom. How's it goin'? Time for dinner yet?

MOM doesn't bother to shout. She just mouths her words and gestures to his radio.

MOM: Turn your radio down. (BRAD *switches the radio off. Mom speaks in her normal voice now.)* Thank you, Brad.

BRAD: What's that? Plans for another Euclidian dream house? As long as you're dealing with triangles, squares, pentagons you're perpetuating the same old crap.

MOM: I'm always open to constructive criticism.

BRAD: Well, I'm not into giving it. *(Pause.)* At least there's hope for you.

MOM: What do you mean, son?

BRAD: Your dream is to build another house. That means you want to stay put. That you don't want to be a nomad.

MOM: There's nothing wrong with nomads.

BRAD: Sure there is. They don't want to fit in. They want to live like animals. Stinking animals. They should be shot.

MOM: Excuse me?

BRAD: You heard what I said.

MOM: You should watch your mouth.

BRAD: I'm just rebelling. And that's natural for someone my age.

MOM: Well, you don't have to be so promiscuous about it.

BRAD: Oh, I wish there were elephants here. Because I'd like to shoot them too.

MOM: I really hope this is a phase.

She rolls up her plans for the house.

BRAD: You know, Hitler was a very misunderstood person. Isn't it easier on us all if we shut up and follow somebody who's got our best interests in mind?

MOM: *(Being very nice.)* Why don't you just shut up and follow your father and me?

BRAD: I don't mean that. I mean somebody with practical ideas. The only people that really understand Hitler are the Israelis. That's why they've got apartheid in Israel now.

MOM: What a stupid thing to say.

BRAD: I could say something intelligent like biological systems are governed by non-linear mechanisms. That means that triads and pairs are totally out of it. But I'll let you find that out for yourself. If you find out.

MOM: Oh, son, son. You need a job. A job that'll act like a drug on you. Don't tell your father I ever said such a thing.

BRAD: You guys are so nervous about doing everything the right way. Why bother? Look what happened from it all. Me.

MOM: Are you trying to get me depressed? Oh, boy.

BRAD: Can't I keep a gun in the house? You never know when an elephant might float by. *(He pretends to aim a rifle at an elephant and shoot...)* Kak-kak-kak-kak! Hah-hah!

SHIRLEY *enters.*

SHIRLEY: *(To* BRAD.*)* I thought you came in.

BRAD: Who else?, fat cow. What do you want?

SHIRLEY: One of your friends called. I was going to tell you who but now I won't.

BRAD: Who called?

SHIRLEY: One lousy turn deserves another.

SHIRLEY *leaves.*

BRAD: What did I do to you?

MOM: See where your behavior gets you? Nowhere.

BRAD: That's right, I'm a n i h i l i s t , Mom. And nowhere is everywhere.

MOM: Where did we go wrong with you?

BRAD: I got to start working out. There's a little bit of flab here. *(He grips part of his stomach.)*

MOM: Off in your own world. Is it this house? Wasn't there enough space for you here? We care that hens live in batteries, but we don't question the small size of our own bedrooms. Was it your school? I know the teachers there are good, they work for your sister. Is it the size or shape of the school? Is it society in general that's warped you?

BRAD: Something like that, Mom.

MOM: Oh, I'm so sorry.

BRAD: Okay, let's all be sorry. But let's not forget that dinner's on its way. *(He smells the dinner cooking in the kitchen.)* Noodles and broccoli. And fish.

MOM: No, eggs.

BRAD: What?

MOM: Eggs, not fish.

BRAD: But still broccoli. Always broccoli with Dad. Wouldn't want to get cancer, oh, no, no... Got to have broccoli, cauliflower, kohlrabi, Brussels sprouts!

MOM: Not all of us are bent on self-destruction. I hope one day you'll wake up and see that there are no kings, and that you're not in line to be a king, nor will you produce a line of kings. You are simply a man. And you will not live forever.

BRAD: Thanks for the lesson.

MOM: Excuse me. I'm going to play the piano for a few minutes before we eat.

She exits. We hear the sound of the first movement of the F major Mozart piano sonata. Before BRAD *speaks he lets out a big burp.*

BRAD: You know, I'm thinkin': if there's a disaster... and the world blows up... and leaves only my parents and my sister. There's enough there to start the human race over again. Obviously Dad has been fertile, and if Mom isn't anymore, then he can do it with Sis. I wouldn't touch her with a ten-foot pole.

Music continues. DAD *enters wearing an apron.*

DAD: I know what you've done. Every time Mother starts playing that music I know you've upset her.

DAD *raises his hand as if in preparation to strike* BRAD.

BRAD: But if you're thinking of punishing me, remember that using violence only shows you have a lot of aggression in you that you yourself don't know how to deal with.

DAD: On the contrary, punishing you is a way to make you learn that what you're doing is wrong.

BRAD: Sorry, but I don't make the connection between physical torture and education. And be careful, you may sprain your hand.

DAD: We have to discipline ourselves to live among others.

DAD *raises his hand again in preparation to strike* BRAD.

DAD: Oh, I can't do it. *(Pause.)* Oh, son, I try to think where we might have gone wrong. Maybe the reason is genetics. There are gaps in what I know about our family tree. *(Pause.)* How can you do this to me? I'm the one that feeds you eggs, noodles and broccoli.

BRAD: I'd rather have crispy mountain potatoes.

The music stops. MOM *walks in.*

MOM: It's true that without discipline we humans can't survive, welcome others and thrive. I think we should *fine* Brad for his actions. It should make him stop and think. Money seems to matter to him. The recording that he blasts in my face must cost some sort of money. If he hasn't stolen it.

DAD: Yes. Fine him. It's the good solid middle-class solution.

SHIRLEY *walks in.*

SHIRLEY: Brad doesn't have any money. So you can't fine him.

DAD: Then we'll make him work for money. We've got a new house that wants to be built.

MOM: We'll take the money we would have paid him for his work.

BRAD: What if I don't want to work?

DAD *whips out a knife from inside his apron and brandishes it.*

DAD: We'll make you work.

BRAD: *(Regarding the knife.)* Oh. Surprise, surprise.

SHIRLEY *(To* BRAD.) You're making it so hard on yourself.

BRAD: Force, it all comes down to force. Dad's got the knife and I don't.

DAD: Force is not what it's all about, son. It's all about the three-foldness around us. I wish you could see that. *(Pause.)* You know, in the first three weeks of your life we saw your unique personality—aspects of which we still fight over today. And on the third day there was that thing about having to surgically remove the little tail you had above your behind when you were born... or is that just a nightmare I had?

BRAD: How you suffer, old man.

DAD *puts away the knife.*

DAD: Please, set the table. It's just about time for supper. I'll go see if it's ready.

DAD *exits.*

SHIRLEY: But just before we eat... *(Pause. Then, to* MOM:*)* Mom, will you play that song, Satin Doll? I really like the Duke.

BRAD: *(Impolitely.)* The Duke.

SHIRLEY: Duke Ellington, then.

MOM: And Billy Strayhorn.

SHIRLEY: Yeah, what cool names. It doesn't take long to play. Will you, please?

MOM: Why, certainly, dear.

> MOM *exits and soon we hear "Satin Doll" played on a piano. Pause. Then:*

SHIRLEY: *(Holding up two fingers.)* Two things, Brad. Not three, as Daddy would say. Two. There is good and there is evil.

BRAD: Screw you.

> BRAD *leaves in a huff. The music continues. Pause.* DAD *comes back in. He goes over to his daughter and they dance to "Satin Doll" with great enjoyment. As they dance, the actor playing* DAD *says to the audience:*

DAD: *(Out of character.)* So that's our play.

SHIRLEY: *(Out of character.)* I hope somebody somewhere likes it.

End of Play.

SOMETHING SPECIAL

a play in two acts
with songs

Characters

LIEUTENANT	*Male, late 30s to 50.*
MARIANNE	*Female, 30s to 40s.*
CLAUDE	*Male, 30s to 50s.*
PAULINE	*Female, 20s to 50s.*
LISA/LISA ARNY	*Female, late 20s to 30s.*
HAZZITALL	*Male, 30s to 40s.*

Place: In and around a suburban house in the desert.
Time: End of the twentieth century.

Notes

Tom Hazzitall (has-it-all) loses his wife Lisa and then marries her mysterious double, Lisa Arny. An actor, especially in early rehearsals, may seek for clear psychological motivations in order to realize his or her role "truthfully" in this play. But it is recommended that the actor "surf" the language rather than focus on fine points of characterization. The quick, jagged rhythm of the play and the fantasy realm in which the play takes place discourages attempts by actors to be intensely realistic. It helps to keep in mind that the comedy "machine" here can't be stopped, even by death.

Something Special is split into a "mundane" half—the first half, and a "spiritual" half—the second. The play is not a musical per se, though short songs and incidental or background music are integral. If there were no music here, the later spiritual agony contained in the play would be no fun. Hazzitall never sings in the play, except in the last song.

For the characters inside the Hazzitall home in act II, the Kafkaesque clown, the Lieutenant, serves as a menacing link to the outside. The Lieutenant is physically large. The actor playing the part may be dressed in a body suit.

The *movement* and physical aspects of this play are to be undertaken with skill and care. Movement at times should not be rushed—in act II, for example, it can take Hazzitall (who suffers badly from eczema) a full minute to go up or down the stairs. "Adventurous" costuming and make-up are recommended. The music to the songs for this play, composed by the playwright, though not published here, is available from the playwright. A demo-tape of the songs, with orchestrations, also exists. The name "Bibo" (bee-boh) gets an accent on the first syllable. The name Arny could just as well be spelled Arni.

Michelle Powell was dramaturg. Danielle Villegas directed a reading of the play in Los Angeles in August 1997 and Ms. Powell directed a second reading of the play at the American Repertory Theatre at Harvard University, Cambridge, Massachusetts in October 1997. The play is dedicated to Jeanne Stebnisky.

Something Special

Prologue

A small neutral playing area, not the main playing area of the set. Before the lights come up a police siren is heard approaching from the distance.

Lights up. A writing table stands alone. A flashing light of a police car illuminates the stage. The siren blares to a stop. A large, hulking police LIEUTENANT *in a trench coat enters, sits down, takes a pen out and says aloud while he writes on a sheet of paper:*

LIEUTENANT: "To my... esteemed colleague: Looks like a lack of effort on the part of the criminal elements tonight. Was busy with the old cases. You know how that makes me feel. Signed, Your Lieutenant."

The LIEUTENANT *examines what he wrote, then:*

Oh, hang it!

Disgusted, he wads up the note just written and shoves it in his pocket. He writes the note again, taking pains with his handwriting.

"Esteemed colleague: Just the usual dried blood, nothing new. Stuck in here for the whole evening. Have a nice shift. Yours, the Lieutenant."

He looks over what he has written.

It'll have to do.

Lights out. End of Prologue.

ACT I

Scene 1

In the solarium of a house. The back wall of the room is mostly of glass window. The desert can be seen outside. The front door to the house, unseen, is not far away. A small set of stairs (three or four steps) leads out of the room and towards the front door.

Lights up. Very dim light. It is evening. A candle on a table is lit. Strange music and sounds are heard. LISA, MARIANNE, CLAUDE and PAULINE are seated at the table. They are in the middle of a séance.

PAULINE: *(In an Otherworldly voice.)*
> Thus I appear to you devoid of form
> A mere sound a scratch on the window pane
> A chatter of the wind against the reeds
> A beam of light given audible resonance.

LISA is awestruck by PAULINE'S power. PAULINE now speaks in the voice of a talk-show host on television.

Our next group of women have broken all three ankles. Because they were allowed to leave their homes.

CLAUDE: *(To MARIANNE.)* It's ectoplasmic television.

MARIANNE: What do you mean, Claude?

PAULINE: *(Abruptly, cutting off the others.)* How did you cope with not being able to stand?

Now PAULINE speaks in the voice of an interviewed person on TV.

PAULINE: *(Continued.)* I washed the floor on my knees. *(Back to her television show host voice.)* Thank you, dear. Sounds like you survived the accident. *(Voice of the one being interviewed.)* In order to heal you must swab.

MARIANNE: *(To* CLAUDE.*)* There's cleaning again.

CLAUDE: *(Carefully, to* MARIANNE.*)* Marianne, notice the ectoplasm from Pauline's daily life. And the psychoplasm from the other side. Together they make teleplasm. But television is intruding into the teleplasm.

PAULINE *goes on to the next "guest." In the TV host's voice:*

PAULINE: And you. It sounds like you need a repair manual for the VCR of your life. *(In the voice of the second interviewed guest.)* I came home. The bed covers smelled like a garden in southern France. I'm descended from a French Gaul goddess, so I should know.

LISA: Wow, Pauline, this is amazing.

MARIANNE: *(To* CLAUDE.*)* Why can't we ask her about the future?

CLAUDE: *(To* MARIANNE.*)* Honey, the spirit speaking through her is not finished yet.

PAULINE: *(In her original Otherworldly-type voice.)* My work never finishes. *(Pause.)* The future. Some say it is a crime against hope. We know that the future is death, my friends.

CLAUDE: But before we die. Important future events—so we can avoid disappointment. Disease.

PAULINE: Life is short and death is long. Lisa, you've always thought you would die before the age of thirty-five, is that correct?

LISA: I've had that feeling. Several times in my life.

PAULINE: You've mentioned such feelings to your cleaning lady, Pauline.

LISA: Yes, and Pauline is the woman through whom you're speaking right now.

PAULINE: It's a shame to feel that you are not long for the world.

Pause. PAULINE *clams up. Another pause.*

LISA: Yes... well, it's a shame—but is it true?

Long pause.

CLAUDE: I guess the voice is finished.

Pause.

PAULINE: *(Still in the Otherworldly voice.)* Don't be so sure.

CLAUDE: Sorry.

PAULINE: I'm surfing on a wave so blue. The color beggars my ability to tell you how blue it is.

LISA: Ahum... Did you finish about me?

PAULINE: Yes. But... *(In the voice of the television talk-show host.)* Next week my guests will be ghosts from French Guyana.

HAZZITALL *silently enters.*

PAULINE: See you next time.

HAZZITALL *turns on the lights. The eerie sounds and music stop.*

HAZZITALL: Lisa, can I have a word with you?

LISA: You've disturbed us, Tom.

HAZZITALL: *(To* LISA *only.)* You don't believe all this stuff do you? You're smarter than this. Why are you doing it?

LISA: This is our outlet for faith in a desert community.

HAZZITALL: They put people who do things like this on Xanfar.

CLAUDE: We should go.

LISA: No, Claude, wait.

> PAULINE *and* MARIANNE *burst into a song.* CLAUDE *joins soon afterwards.*

(Song #1: "Didn't Old Egypt Get Lost?")

PAULINE and MARIANNE: *(Sing.)*
>> Didn't old Egypt get lost,
>> Get lost, get lost—
>> Didn't old Egypt get lost
>> While he was looking 'round?
>>
>> He couldn't find young Moses

PAULINE, MARIANNE and CLAUDE:
>> Floating in the reeds.

PAULINE and MARIANNE:
>> He was blind to the sun.

PAULINE, MARIANNE and CLAUDE:
>> Everywhere he pleased.
>>
>> Didn't old Egypt get lost,
>> Get lost, get lost—
>> Didn't old Egypt get lost
>> While he was looking 'round?

PAULINE, MARIANNE and CLAUDE: *(Continue singing.)*
>Hark, hear the voices,
>The voices in the fray
>These are all the voices
>That God is wont to save.
>
>Didn't old Egypt get lost,
>Get lost, get lost—
>Didn't old Egypt get lost
>While he was looking 'round?

HAZZITALL: Lisa, can you call your meeting quits for now?

(Song #2: "We Will Die in the Field")

PAULINE, CLAUDE, MARIANNE: *(Sing.)*
>We will die in the field if we have to.
>We will sign in the cosmic choir.
>We will fight as long as we're here
>To freely conduct our pleasures.

HAZZITALL: Look, it's time for you to give my wife back to me. I don't mean she's my wife as in "wife and she's subordinate to her husband." Or "wife" as in "she has to do what I say." What I mean is... well, in other words, Lisa, please... enough, okay?

(Song #3: "Talk On, Tom")

PAULINE, CLAUDE, MARIANNE: *(Still singing.)*
>Talk on, Tom, talk on, Tom,
>You're the old sheep that knows the road.
>Talk on, Tom, talk on, Tom,
>We're the young lambs who have to find the way.

HAZZITALL: It's not that hard to get to the door.

PAULINE, CLAUDE, MARIANNE: *(Spoken, not sung.)* Oh. We're not wanted here by the "man of the house." We won't hang around then. He's grumpy.

HAZZITALL: Thank you. *(To* MARIANNE.*)* Let me help you with your shawl.

PAULINE *shoots a look at* MARIANNE.

(Song #4: "Don't Touch-a My Garment, Tempter")

PAULINE and MARIANNE: *(Singing again.)*
>Don't touch-a my garment, tempter,
>Tempter, tempter.
>Don't touch-a my garment, tempter,
>I'm a going home.

HAZZITALL: All right. I won't. Man!

PAULINE, CLAUDE *and* MARIANNE *gather their things and exit.* Lisa, *almost leaving the room, is stopped by* HAZZITALL.

How am I supposed to be comfortable around all this? Isn't it a tad extreme? I'm pretty easy-going. Don't you think it's time to stop indulging yourself in these ah...

LISA: A séance.

HAZZITALL: We bought a house in the desert. To escape the city. Now I feel civilization coming this way. It's not even the normal kind. You have too much time on your hands. People need tools to survive the system. Not conjuring.

I need a home that soothes me. I need an independent wife who has not gone completely out of control. Why can't you focus more on your job? And when you're here, we can enjoy our soothing home and the southwestern vista. *(Pause.)* We will practice silence.

LISA: Practicing silence is not the type of man I married.

HAZZITALL: Then you haven't ever really known me.

LISA: You should have some faith in what I know.

HAZZITALL: *(Apologetically.)* I do. *(Pause.)* Silence. And let's get around to fixing our desert garden that's full of rocks and only one flower.

LISA: I'm ready whenever you are.
   Remember when we took your car up the side of the mountain? The tan land was baking in the valley below. That's when we both knew we'd like to live out here. Clean, thin air. If equilibrium could have a smell, that's what it would have smelled like. You smelled it too.
   I felt what you felt. Tom, it wasn't the silence. The night before, we went dancing. The music was really loud. I was surprised you could take it. You danced for two hours straight.

HAZZITALL: My eczema put an end to that. The backs of my legs that time.

LISA: You have to admit you enjoy commotion now and then.

HAZZITALL: It upsets me. When it's a seance in our solarium.

   LISA *kisses* HAZZITALL *and he calms down.*

But no matter. We're alone.

LISA: Yeah, that's nice.

   Both HAZZITALL *and* LISA *smile at each other. Lights out. End of the scene.*

Scene 2

The solarium, as before. A day soon after the last scene. Lights up. LISA *is drying her hair with a towel.* PAULINE *cleans.*

PAULINE: How far did you jog today?

LISA: Three miles. *(Pause.)* It's great to have you living with us. I can't handle it all myself. Tom's working from the house more. He'll be busy. So I shouldn't talk to him. *(Pause.)* I imagine conversations with him. Ones where I say I don't know if we should be married anymore.

PAULINE: Why?

LISA: He tries to be interested. He asks me about my job at the card company. He only scratches the surface. Are we growing apart? Don't you think that we should be soul mates?

PAULINE: If you want.

LISA: I mean Tom and me. There's a "will" to diminish me, I think.

PAULINE: He's just envious of your flair for making friends. He hasn't made a lot of friends since he came out here.

LISA: No. It's a problem.

PAULINE: This may be what causes him to want to diminish you.

LISA: *(Pause.)* I can't ignore what I need. And what I need from my partner is to remain open to what I say. He doesn't have to think exactly the way I do. I don't want to admit that he's weak. In his character, I mean. It's a laziness, I guess. He has to put some effort into the relationship if he wants it to work.

PAULINE: Is your physical life with him all right?

LISA: Sometimes he avoids it. We both have fantasies about one another.

PAULINE: Kinky fantasies?

LISA: No.

PAULINE: Tell him. That you're having emerging shadows in your mind about your marriage.

LISA: Should I disturb him today?

PAULINE: You might have to.

LISA: He wasn't feeling very well. A new kind of pain seems to be building up inside him lately. *(Pause.)* My boss'll be here any minute. Is lunch ready?

PAULINE: All I have to do is put it on the table.

The doorbell rings.

LISA: Oh. It's Claude at the door. I'll get it. Call Tom. He said he'd join us for lunch.

Both exit. We hear PAULINE *calling* HAZZITALL. *After a moment,* LISA *and* CLAUDE *enter.*

LISA: Birthday cards, bingo cards, business cards. When will it end? And then there's perfumed cards.

CLAUDE: Yes. No matter what, we're always supposed to come out smelling like roses. *(Laughing.)* Oh, you're beautiful, Lisa. But then again, you were once a junior princess. Agriculture, wasn't it? Some ancient agricultural club in the American hinterlands. They chose you.

LISA: Farmers still exist in some places, Claude.

PAULINE *enters.*

PAULINE: Tom's coming right in.

LISA: *(To* CLAUDE.) Please sit down.

CLAUDE *sits down.* CLAUDE *sees* HAZZITALL *entering the room from the other end.*

CLAUDE: I'm glad we're able to see each other on a social level. Marianne and I had a wonderful time when we were over the other evening.

LISA: You'll both be over again soon, I hope.

HAZZITALL *approaches* CLAUDE *at the table.*

HAZZITALL: Hello, Claude. Regardless of what my wife thinks of you as a boss and a friend, I'm here to welcome you back to the old ranch, to say, "Hearty welcome".

LISA *is embarrassed and confused.* HAZZITALL *approaches* CLAUDE *as if ready to embrace him, but then he turns away from* CLAUDE.

CLAUDE: *(To* HAZZITALL.) Well, thank you.

HAZZITALL: Superstition. Rituals. It's all the rage. I do like a little mystery, of course, but what about something called science? Too boring for you?

LISA: It's time to eat, Tom.

PAULINE *brings in lunch.* HAZZITALL *sits down to lunch.*

We were just talking about work.

HAZZITALL: *(To* CLAUDE.) Your business of cards... Next time I need a new birthday card I hope I can get one for free.

CLAUDE: Of course.

LISA *sits down.*

HAZZITALL: I'm not just any lawyer, you know. If I work at times for next to nothing it's because I know justice won't be served otherwise.

CLAUDE: You're a rare bird in your profession.

HAZZITALL: It takes a lot of brains to figure that out, huh?

LISA *is astonished into silence by her husband's words.*

PAULINE: There's rye bread and wheat bread. It's chicken salad.

HAZZITALL: *(To* CLAUDE.) Lisa didn't tell me what brings you out here today.

CLAUDE: She and I are going to discuss staggered shifts for the employees.

HAZZITALL: Staggered shifts? You don't say? Don't you enjoy Marianne anymore?

CLAUDE: Marianne is all for the employees staggering their shifts.

LISA: Here Claude, you be the first. (LISA *helps* CLAUDE *with the fixings to make his sandwich.*)

HAZZITALL: The polite thing is to not expose the other person. To an embarrassing or demeaning situation.

CLAUDE: Excuse me?

LISA: *(To* HAZZITALL *only.*) You've been acting strange lately, but so far not this strange.

HAZZITALL: I think I'll make a sandwich.

HAZZITALL *serves himself, plunking two tablespoonfuls of chicken salad on a slice of wheat bread and putting a slice of rye over it to complete the sandwich. Pause.* CLAUDE *and* LISA *are silent, Then* LISA *speaks.*

LISA: *(To* CLAUDE.) If you want my opinion, there are enough of us so that someone will always be able to answer the phone. Like today. The office is running smoothly. Even though I've taken the day off. And you've come out to have lunch.

HAZZITALL: I've worked it out.

LISA: Worked what out?

HAZZITALL: Oh, cards, cards. The king of hearts. And for the future, there's Tarot cards! I've got a *report* card for you, Claude. I think your wife would like to see it, too.

CLAUDE: Tom, we don't do report cards.

HAZZITALL: But I do.

CLAUDE: There's just not enough profit doing business with schools.

Silence. PAULINE *enters momentarily and puts extra napkins on the table.*

LISA: Tom, if you're not feeling well you can eat in the other room.

HAZZITALL: *(Thinking* LISA *is trying to get rid of him.)* You should have some faith in me.

LISA: I do.

HAZZITALL: Not now.

LISA: You're not very sociable now.

PAULINE: He's not adapting to the desert situation at all.

PAULINE *exits.*

HAZZITALL: My business isn't much to brag about. There are a lot of lawyers who give the profession a bad name. But cards? Come on!

CLAUDE: You can criticize me and what I do in my spare time. But if you laugh at my business, we'll have to step outside to the patio.

HAZZITALL: You're some kind of smooth operator. (*Pain seizes him in the legs. The stress has been too much for him. He cries out.*) Ooww! (*Pause.*) Excuse me. I have to go.

> HAZZITALL *exits like a wounded animal.*

CLAUDE: What was that all about?

LISA: I'm sorry, Claude. He's not feeling well today.

CLAUDE: I can't come back here again, Lisa. I won't have my company insulted. What have I ever done to him?

LISA: Nothing.

CLAUDE: I thought I'd have a nice drive, I *did* have a nice drive, I thought I'd visit friends.

LISA: I hope you still accept me as your friend.

CLAUDE: Lisa, you're fine, don't worry. I can't stay in this house another second. I'm not angry. No, I'm not angry. Just disappointed. Not in you.

> CLAUDE *gets up from the table.*

LISA: Sorry. I really am. Don't go.

> LISA *follows* CLAUDE *offstage to the door.* HAZZITALL *limps in. In pain, he paces across the floor.* LISA *reenters.*

LISA: This is outrageous. What were you doing?

HAZZITALL: Staggered shifts!

LISA: Okay. Now I'm going to tell you. I had hoped to tell you when you were calm. It's something important.

HAZZITALL: You can't keep it secret forever.

LISA: I have reasonable complaints. You may not want to hear them. I've made a big mistake being married to you.

HAZZITALL: Your actions speak louder than those words ever can.

LISA: You're considerate about your down-on-the-heels clients. But you don't care about me. I'll be fixing up the basement. I'll move down there.

HAZZITALL: Why don't you just leave, move in with him?

LISA: You have no idea what's going on.

HAZZITALL: I do now. Just go altogether.

LISA: It's my house too. I didn't tell Claude this, but I'm taking a leave of absence from my job.

HAZZITALL: Where are you two going to do it then?

LISA: I need to reassess. Things.

> *The telephone rings.* HAZZITALL *goes silent. The phone rings another time.* HAZZITALL *answers the phone. The party on the other side hangs up immediately.*

HAZZITALL: Well, that must be Claude calling you.

LISA: He wouldn't have had time to get to a phone yet.

HAZZITALL: So you know exactly what he's doing?

LISA: I don't care. You're being ridiculous.

HAZZITALL: Then why are you so edgy?

LISA: I'm not.

LISA *turns and walks out.*

Lights out. End of the scene.

Entre Scene

In between scenes the actors hum the tune, "If I Was Sane It Would Drive Me Crazy."

Scene 3

The solarium. The next day. Lights up. LISA *has gathered* PAULINE *and* MARIANNE.

LISA: It's unusual. But it might work. Tom's got to learn what it's like to be wrongfully accused of fooling around. Both of you, I appreciate your help. Marianne, you know what to do now.

MARIANNE: What if he doesn't take the bait?

LISA: You just turn up the heat more.

MARIANNE: But isn't it dangerous?

LISA: It has to be dangerous. Or he won't feel guilty. Now, once you get him Pauline will walk in on you two. She'll really rub it into Tom. Pauline, you've got to make him think that God will punish him severely for what he's doing.

PAULINE: But Tom's a non-believer.

LISA: You've got to make him believe only for a few seconds.

PAULINE:

> I feel uneasy about this.
> Should I be part of this charade,
> To teach a man who's selfish to the point of jealousy?
> What right do I have to deceive another person?
> I know truth is what the world needs most.

LISA: If this is compromising, we'll do it without you. It's just that it'd be more effective if you came in like the Old Testament and let him have it.

MARIANNE: He's not interested in me.

LISA: You never know with men. Most aren't meant to be monogamous.

MARIANNE: My Claude is.

PAULINE: You're smart, Lisa. I'd never think of this. I don't know about coming in with the fire and brimstone speech.

LISA: Whatever you do needs to work. I can't appeal to his rational side.

MARIANNE: That's why everything's wrong in the world. It's too rational. You pick up the phone and half the time you hear a stream of binary numbers. And the government. It's growing. Out of control. Where's all the emotion?

PAULINE: Or faith?

LISA: That's why we're here. We use physical evidence. Something that his busy brain can grasp. Look, he's coming now. Pauline, scatter. Marianne, I'll stay here with you for a second. Then you'll be alone with him.

PAULINE *exits.* LISA *notices the necklace* MARIANNE *is wearing.*

LISA: I've never noticed that necklace before.

MARIANNE: I just started wearing it.

LISA: It's beautiful.

HAZZITALL *enters.*

HAZZITALL: A headline just caught my eye. "Milk and the multitudes." Overpopulation and the third world. The dilemma continues. I'm glad I have my work. How else could I get through. (*Noticing* MARIANNE.) Oh, hello.

LISA: Excuse me, dear. (*She exits discreetly.*)

MARIANNE: I hope you're feeling well today.

HAZZITALL: I'm all right.

MARIANNE: Sometimes what I read or see gets on my nerves. Like— I understand about milk and the multitudes.

HAZZITALL: The what?

MARIANNE: You were just saying, the world's population...

HAZZITALL: Oh, I was. Yes. But that's what you talk about when you have no time or power to do anything about it.

MARIANNE: How about talk like, "It's a beautiful day today."?

HAZZITALL: You can mean it or not.

MARIANNE: You can't change the weather. But you can change the conditions of the social atmosphere. (*Pause.*) Do you think I'm too clever as a woman?

HAZZITALL: I don't know you well enough.

MARIANNE: Neither do I. We have something we can agree on already. I'm still exploring. It's hard to analyze human impulses. Impulses by their very nature happen just like that. *(Pause.)* What would you say if I ran my fingers through your hair?

HAZZITALL: I would say, "where's my wife?"

MARIANNE: You would?

HAZZITALL: She has a right to know what's going on.

MARIANNE: That's logical. Isn't it nice to talk about things logically? The world may be overpopulated but that only increases our chances of meeting someone we can really talk to.

HAZZITALL: What are you talking about?

MARIANNE: You know—you lift me up. It takes a special kind of person to do that to me. You're a man of the world, a thinker, a doer. That oxygenates my blood. My muscles tense up—I mean in a good way. *(Seductively.)* Maybe you could help me relax them.

HAZZITALL: We've got a couple of books around the house—

MARIANNE: You could show them to me.

HAZZITALL *notices her strange necklace.*

HAZZITALL: Interesting necklace.

MARIANNE *avoids being thrown off by the remark.*

MARIANNE: I have a tense muscle right here.

MARIANNE *shows* HAZZITALL *one of her "muscles" when she bares the area near her navel.*

HAZZITALL: There aren't muscles there.

MARIANNE *closes her eyes and purses her lips, expecting to be kissed.*

What *is* this?

MARIANNE *stands, still expecting to be kissed.* LISA *walks in.*

LISA: Tom. What is happening here? *(To* MARIANNE.*)* And you, you poor innocent victim! *(To* HAZZITALL.*)* You're just awful. Don't you respect me at all? *(To* MARIANNE.*)* You... you inconsiderate hussy. *(*MARIANNE *puts down her blouse.* LISA, *to* HAZZITALL:*)* You should be ashamed. I've always been honest with you. I never expected this.

HAZZITALL: I didn't do anything.

LISA: You have the nerve to think that you were somehow more faithful than me.

PAULINE: *(Entering.)* Don't tell me. I can see what's going on. *(To* MARIANNE.*)* You poor child, you shameless hussy.*(To* HAZZITALL.*)* Tom, you made a vow to your wife. To have her and hold her.

> Dost thou know that the angels measure the
>   righteous,
> That they return after each age, with their cords?
> Behold, the ropes of the righteous are fastened on
>   high beams
> To the name of the Lord forever.
>
> Those that have constellated their stars in pagan
>   positions,
> Those that have made bodily that which should be
>   Platonic,
> They shall be plunged into a fire worse than the sun,
> No sound shall be emitted from their frosty ghosts.

PAULINE: *(Continued.)*
> Sinner, nowhere but near Satan's coast will you find
> So little faith and dis-sacrifices.
> Shunnest thou the path of deceit
> Shunnest thou that path O Man.

HAZZITALL: Am I being accused of something?

PAULINE: As heaven's my witness, I thought I would never live to see the day.

MARIANNE bursts into phony tears. PAULINE tries to comfort her.

There, there, we adults make mistakes from time to time.

LISA: *(Feigning discouragement)* I don't know what to do. Maybe it's my fault. *(Pause.)* For being a woman.

PAULINE: It's nothing you've done, dear. It's him. Don't shoulder responsibility when it isn't yours.

HAZZITALL: Enough, Pauline. *(To All.)* You're all possessed. Let's all go back to what we were doing before. I was on my way outside. To stretch. In the sun.

HAZZITALL leaves.

LISA: Passed right over him.

MARIANNE: It's not that easy to be a femme fatale. It's been years since I've been single.

LISA: We need new tactics. Retreat and reconsider.

Music starts up. LISA sings, accompanied vocally by PAULINE.

(Song #5: "Tried Something")

LISA, with PAULINE: *(Sing.)*
>Tried something, but was no use,
>Tried something to clear the junk from his mind.
>Tried something to clear the junk from his mind
>But it was no use, no use at all.
>
>Tried something and it didn't work
>Got shot down—it didn't work a bit.
>Feel incredibly dumb and really frustrated.
>What can be done to make him understand?
>
>Tried something, but was no use,
>Tried something to clear the junk from his mind.
>Tried something to clear the junk from his mind
>But it was no use, no use at all.
>Tried something to clear the junk from his mind.

Lights out. End of the scene.

Scene 4

In the solarium. Another day, soon after the last scene. Lights up.
MARIANNE *and* HAZZITALL.

MARIANNE: I hope you can forgive the past. I'm here because I—I need you.

HAZZITALL: That table may be curious about what you did. Probably more than me.

MARIANNE: I'm here to tell you something bizarre and unbelievable.

HAZZITALL: A surprise.

MARIANNE: I'm here because Claude needs a lawyer.

HAZZITALL: So—

MARIANNE: No one but you can understand him.

HAZZITALL: People understand well when money's added to the picture.

MARIANNE: No, I mean really understand. And then, give him excellent advice.

HAZZITALL: Who could be suing Claude for making his harmless, boring cards?

MARIANNE: It's not because of cards. The only way out for him is to take the Third Amendment.

HAZZITALL: If I recall, the Third Amendment concerns itself with quartering soldiers in private homes. Are you and Claude posing as soldiers in someone's home?

MARIANNE: No. It's not the Third Amendment I mean. He's in jail. Bail hasn't been set. He needs to take the Eighth Amendment.

HAZZITALL: Cruel and unusual punishment. Did he kill somebody?

MARIANNE: He didn't kill. He tortured.

HAZZITALL: Maybe he should take the Fifth.

MARIANNE: He's not doing too well.

HAZZITALL: He? Well, what about the victim?

MARIANNE: *(She shudders.)* The victim was an animal. He's in jail for cruelty to animals.

HAZZITALL: You don't go to jail with no bail for that.

MARIANNE: There's more.

HAZZITALL: There always is. He's one of *those* types. Feet on the escalator of spiraling guilt. How long has he had a problem with violence?

MARIANNE: His problems are spiritual. (*She bursts into tears.*)

HAZZITALL: There, there.

MARIANNE: (*Through tears.*) He's been arrested for rape.

HAZZITALL: (*Madly glad.*) Bingo!

MARIANNE: Claude was initiated into a Satanist's club. The police found the remains of the animals used in their rituals.

HAZZITALL: What'd he do to the poor critters?

MARIANNE: He's been charged with rape because he married a sixteen-year old girl from the Satanist's Club.

HAZZITALL: Isn't he married to you?

MARIANNE *breaks into tears.*

MARIANNE: No. (*She sobs.*) We never got married because he convinced me that marriage was a ploy by society. To enslave our desires. I feel like such a fool now.

MARIANNE *throws herself into* HAZZITALL'S *arms.*

HAZZITALL: Now, don't.

MARIANNE *lets out a short series of deep sobs. She cries in* HAZZITALL'S *lap.*

HAZZITALL: *(Continues.)* So many, many tears.

> HAZZITALL *tries to raise* MARIANNE'S *head from his lap, but her head is heavy and he can't pull her up from him.*

I'm sorry, Marianne, but you're getting my shirt sleeves all wet. And the salt and the water. It isn't good for my eczema.

> HAZZITALL *rolls up his shirt sleeves.* MARIANNE'S *head is in his lap, she is crying.* HAZZITALL *takes out a handkerchief and dabs the tears off his arms. He then tries to dab the tears from* MARIANNE *but she won't lift up her head. As* MARIANNE *weeps softly,* HAZZITALL *continues.*

HAZZITALL: Oh, no. You're getting my stomach wet, too.

> HAZZITALL *cannot lift her head off him. Impulsively, he tears off his own shirt. He uses his handkerchief to fan the remaining moisture on his skin as* MARIANNE'S *head slips down by his groin.*

Marianne, you've got to stop crying. It's hot and it's dangerous like that.

> MARIANNE *raises her head only for a moment to speak:*

MARIANNE: We came out here to find peace and look what happens. Claude's ruined everything.

> MARIANNE *goes back to cry in* HAZZITALL'S *lap.*

HAZZITALL: At least a human wasn't killed. Though animals aren't like blades of grass that grow back. You should try to pull yourself together.

MARIANNE: *(Muffled.)* I can't.

HAZZITALL: It's hot and wet.

> While MARIANNE *anchors her head in* HAZZITALL'S *lap and cries, she unbuttons her blouse. Then she raises her head for an instant.*

MARIANNE: Nobody loves me.

HAZZITALL: No, no. Don't think like that.

She tears off her shirt. She raises her head for another instant.

MARIANNE: You look so vulnerable. I want to show you that I am too.

HAZZITALL: I know you are. But I have a medical problem and you have a personal problem.

MARIANNE: *(Raising her head momentarily again.)* They're all the same when you look at it holistically.

HAZZITALL: I don't believe in holistics.

Pause.

MARIANNE: If you don't kiss me I don't think I'll ever stop crying.

HAZZITALL: Do I have to? It's not that I don't want to. But I'm not an animal—(MARIANNE *wails at hearing the word "animal".)* Sorry. *(Pause.)* Say, that really is an interesting necklace you're wearing.

MARIANNE: Claude gave it to me. It's a talisman. Please. *(Through a sob.)* Kiss me. Make it all go 'way.

MARIANNE purses her lips. HAZZITALL kisses her and MARIANNE's lips don't let him go for a few seconds.

HAZZITALL: *(Weakly tries to protest.)* Now, that's...

LISA enters. At first she is speechless. HAZZITALL starts to get up.

HAZZITALL: Lisa, I was only...

LISA: What—?

As HAZZITALL *rises from the chair, something from* MARIANNE'S *necklace bites into his knee.*

HAZZITALL: Ow! Ow! *(He howls from the sharp pain in his knee.)* What has stuck...? Ow! Ow! Something has poisoned me. (HAZZITALL *holds onto his knee.)*

MARIANNE: It's my talisman. The porcupine needle has come out of its pine-gum setting.

HAZZITALL: Ow! Get it out of my leg!

MARIANNE *carefully tries to extract the needle from* HAZZITALL'S *leg.*

MARIANNE: Don't push it in. It's got a barb on the end of it. Like a fishhook. The further it goes in the harder it is to get it out.

HAZZITALL: This is terribly dangerous. Don't let it near my eczema.

MARIANNE: There.

HAZZITALL *howls with pain.* MARIANNE *manages to remove the porcupine needle from* HAZZITALL'S *leg.*

Got it. It's never fallen out of its setting before.

HAZZITALL: *(Still in agony. Hyperventilating.)* Ah. Ah. Ow. Ah.

LISA: Serves you right.

HAZZITALL: *(Panting, still in pain.)* Ah... she... Ah... Claude's been arrested. He's joined the Satanist group behind your backs. Little creatures have been tortured to death. Marianne needs a lawyer.

LISA: You faithless man.

The pain subsides for HAZZITALL.

HAZZITALL: Lisa, look. My arms—I had to take off my shirt. The salt tears were all over my sores. She was distraught.

MARIANNE: I'm sorry, Lisa.

HAZZITALL: Her marriage is not a marriage. It's a holistic arrangement. She's gotten the short end of the stick.

LISA: So you're the friendly divorce lawyer. Maybe that's what we should get. A divorce. Right here in your own house!

MARIANNE: I really am sorry. Maybe it was the power of suggestion. *(To* LISA *only.)* From beforehand.

LISA: It's his fault.

> PAULINE *enters.*

PAULINE: Did you know U.F.O. sightings were at their peak forty years ago? Now human disappearances are on the rise. What's the reason people are deciding to go rather than stay?

LISA: *(To* HAZZITALL *and* MARIANNE.) You two should put your clothes on.

> LISA *leaves.* HAZZITALL *doesn't put on his shirt—it's too wet.*
> MARIANNE *puts her blouse on. Silence, then, all of sudden* PAULINE *notices.*

PAULINE: I see what's happening. *(To* MARIANNE.) You shameless hussy. You poor little mouse. *(To* HAZZITALL.) Tom, you made a vow to Lisa. To have her and hold her. (MARIANNE *sulks.* PAULINE *comforts her.)* There, there, you'll be forgiven by your husband.

> MARIANNE *wails at the word, "husband."*

HAZZITALL: Enough, Pauline. *(To* MARIANNE.) This is some kind of joke isn't it? Claude hasn't been arrested.

MARIANNE: He has. I'm sorry.

An awkward pause.

HAZZITALL: *(To* MARIANNE.*)* I'll see you out.

> HAZZITALL *and* MARIANNE *exit,* HAZZITALL *limps a little.* PAULINE *goes and gets an aerosol can of air freshener. She sprays it throughout the room.* HAZZITALL *returns, limping.*

HAZZITALL: *(Continued.)* Be careful with that stuff. You know how it gets into the cracks of my skin.

PAULINE: Well, suffer.

HAZZITALL: Why are you spraying that now? *(He means sex.)* You can't smell anything, can you?

PAULINE: I sense the unmistakable presence of mischief in this room.

HAZZITALL: Oh, really?

PAULINE: I'm disinfecting.

Lights out. End of the scene.

Entre Scene

Lights up between scenes. A chorus of some of the actors sing the song hummed earlier, "If I Was Sane It Would Drive Me Crazy".

LANCE TAIT

(Song #6: "If I Was Sane It Would Drive Me Crazy")

CHORUS (*Sings.*)
        I'm not supposed to be sore
        Or wonder what is in store.
        I pace 'cross the floor, I don't know what to do—
        If I was sane it would drive me crazy.

        How'm I supposed to be whole
        When nothing's under control?
        I tip my hand and oh, man, I'm so misunderstood—
        If I was sane it would drive me crazy.

        Can't even count you the times—
        Yeah, yeah, yeah, yeah.
        Heaven only knows the things I've seen
        And all the things I've been through, too.

        I'll write a book for the bedside
        someday if I can survive.
        A book for the fit to be tied—
        This song will be the foreword.

        I'd like things to be alright,
        I want us both to sleep tight
        But deep in the night unplanned sights
           are visited with pain—
        If I was sane it would drive me crazy.

        Can't even count you the times—
        Yeah, yeah, yeah, yeah.
        Heaven only knows the things I've seen
        And all the things I've been through, too.

        I'll write a book for the bedside
        Someday if I can survive.
        A book for the fit to be tied—
        This song will be the foreword.

CHORUS *(Continues singing.)*
> I'm not supposed to be sore
> Or wonder what is in store.
> I pace 'cross the floor, I don't know what to do—
> If I was sane it would drive me crazy.
> If I was sane it would drive me mad.
> If I was sane it would drive me crazy,
> If I was sane it would drive me mad.

(End of song. Lights fade out.)

Scene 5

In the solarium. One day soon after the last scene. Lights up. HAZZITALL *has gathered* PAULINE *and* MARIANNE *for instructions.*

HAZZITALL: It may be odd but it's all I could think of. Home justice must be found. I will teach *her* what it feels like when a spouse is wrongfully accused. Both of you, thank you for helping me. Marianne, are you all set?

MARIANNE: What if she isn't attracted to other women?

HAZZITALL: Oh, women will swerve from the path if given the chance. Most women have an innate feeling that men don't understand them. That's what attracts them to each other.

MARIANNE: *(Repulsed.)* Eew.

PAULINE: Is this a sexual fantasy of yours?

HAZZITALL: I have no one else to help me.

PAULINE: The plan is ridiculous.

HAZZITALL: *(Avoiding* PAULINE'S *look, to* MARIANNE.) Pauline, please do what you're told. You'll cite relevant scriptures from the Old Testament.

PAULINE: Is there anything about lesbians there?

HAZZITALL: Oh, just find something. It's all the same. Anything to make her feel guilty.

MARIANNE: This idea doesn't sound too original.

HAZZITALL: She's already started to remodel the basement downstairs, with the intention of living there.

PAULINE:
> I feel uneasy about this.
> Should I be part of this charade,
> To teach a man who's selfish to the point of jealousy?
> What right do I have to deceive another person?
> I know truth is what the world needs most.

HAZZITALL: So, you feel compromised. *(Pause.)* Good, here she comes. Pauline, you'd better go. Marianne, I'll stay here with you for a second. *(He notices* MARIANNE's *necklace and he cautiously backs away from it.)*

> PAULINE *exits. Pause.* LISA *enters.*

LISA: Oh, hello Marianne. How's the case going? Is Claude out yet?

MARIANNE: He's safely in a mental institution.

LISA: *(Coldly.)* Tom, I'm looking for some nails, about an inch and a half.

HAZZITALL: We were just finishing up. I'll go get them for you, sweetheart. I'll bring them downstairs for you.

HAZZITALL *exits, happy at an excuse to leave* MARIANNE *and* LISA *alone.*

MARIANNE: I just brought over the power-of-attorney papers.

LISA: Is Claude going to be all right?

MARIANNE: He's worried about the business. With you gone from the office... well, let's just say I'm thinking much more about cards that I ever thought imaginable. I like to keep things small. But when you work with cards you have to count them and sell large amounts of them.

LISA: Spending time alone working in the basement—I find myself taking a new look at my life. Maybe the past was all wrong, Marianne.

MARIANNE: I regret that.

LISA: I don't mean what happened between you and Tom.
You know, Tom and I aren't in debt. We're proud of that. But don't we owe our easy life to the people who are at the bottom rung? I see why Tom helps some of his clients for next to nothing. I understand. Other people's pain is part of the foundation of our happiness. Why is it that people turn away from truth like this?

MARIANNE: Everyone concentrates on their own problems. It's natural.

LISA: I've landed a new job.

MARIANNE: You're not coming back to the card company?

LISA: It's volunteer work. Tom found it for me without realizing it. It's a rehab center. They need an assistant manager. If there's going to be a beautiful day I'd like to say that I contributed to it. My marriage is open for analysis and so is everything else.

MARIANNE: That's like me. *(Hesitating.)* I'm still exploring. The natural. The supernatural. They're at odds with each other. It causes a healthy spark, though.

Women should be instinctual. Business is so full of... business. I'm having a hard time relaxing.

LISA: You should look over our books.

MARIANNE: I have a tense muscle right here.

> MARIANNE *is careful to keep her necklace away from* LISA. *She shows* LISA *one of her "muscles" when she bares the area near her navel.*

LISA: There aren't any muscles there.

MARIANNE: *(To herself.)* That's what Tom said too. *(To* LISA.) It's because I have a hole. Behind my ear.

LISA: You can't have.

MARIANNE: If you run your fingers through my hair you'll see it.

LISA: Claude didn't hit you with something?

MARIANNE: No. Just run your fingers through my beautiful hair. Please. You'll see.

> MARIANNE *closes her eyes. She looks like a giant wave of pleasure has overcome her.*

LISA: I don't know what you're talking about Marianne, but I'll have a look. (LISA *moves some of* MARIANNE'S *hair to one side and looks.*) I don't see anything. Except a tiny *mole.*

MARIANNE: Women don't always have to talk.

> HAZZITALL *walks in, as planned.*

HAZZITALL: There. Got you.

LISA *stops examining* MARIANNE'S *head.*

HAZZITALL: *(To* MARIANNE.) I'm shocked! *(To* LISA.) How could you two? (MARIANNE *makes sure her blouse is tucked in.* HAZZITALL, *to* LISA:) And you accused me of being unfaithful to you.

LISA: Did you get those nails?

HAZZITALL: Honey, I won't let this wreck our marriage. We'll get the best therapist.

LISA: Call one. Marianne is finally having her nervous breakdown. As for you—you're way past help.

PAULINE *enters, as planned.*

PAULINE: Don't tell me. It's all before my eyes. *(To* MARIANNE.) Iniquity, beest thou damned. *(To* LISA:)
> Dost thou know that the angels measure the
> righteous,
> That they return after each age, with their cords?

LISA: That's enough, Pauline.

PAULINE: I didn't get started on the new part.

LISA: No?

PAULINE:
> Sinner, witness the valley filled with many Babylons:
> Objects fly above, setting the landscape atilt—

LISA: Hmph.

PAULINE:
> Nowhere but near Satan's coast will you find
> So little faith and dis-sacrifices.
> Shunnest thou the path of deceit
> Shunnest thou that path O Woman.

LISA: *(To* HAZZITALL.) It's pathetic. You should take charge of *your* life.

MARIANNE: I was just leaving. It's supper time.

PAULINE: *(To* HAZZITALL.) As heaven's my witness, you've got the brain of a cactus. How she puts up with you I can't figure out.

HAZZITALL: I was only trying to bring her closer to me.

MARIANNE: I'll see you, Lisa.

> MARIANNE *exits. The phone rings.* PAULINE *answers the phone. It is another hang up call.*

LISA: I need to get out of here. *(To* PAULINE.) Are my running clothes dry?

PAULINE: Yes.

> LISA *exits.*

HAZZITALL: We did our best.

PAULINE: Sure, boss.

> *Lights out. End of the scene.*

Scene 6

*The solarium. Evening. An hour later. The sound of a distant lawnmower
or chainsaw is heard.*

Lights up. Lamps are on in the room. HAZZITALL *with* PAULINE. *Noise
from* PAULINE'S *radio is heard—this noise consists of various radio stations
mixed with radio wave-noise. The lawnmower sound fades out.*

HAZZITALL: *(Loudly.)* I was just wondering, Pauline. I haven't heard
Lisa come in. Is she back yet? It's pretty dark out there. Gloomy,
even. Pauline!

The noise from PAULINE'S *radio continues.*

Pauline, could you come out? I can't find Lisa downstairs or anywhere. She hasn't done anything rash, I hope.

*A news report, disturbed by static and radio wave interference, is heard.
The report may be read by the* LIEUTENANT *actor, in a disguised voice.*

(The Report:) "Some miles away from the town center. An act of
violence... *(The end of the sentence is rendered unintelligible by the interference.)* "It is as yet not being classified as a random act." *(Another large
radio-wave event interferes with the report.)* "The investigation continues,
the ..." *(The voice quickly fades out to unintelligibility. Other radio stations
and wave transmissions are heard.)*

HAZZITALL: We've never had problems picking up radio stations out
here. *(Shouting.)* Pauline! You don't need to play that so loud. It's
blasting through the whole house. *(The radio noise continues.)*

Life out here is supposed to be peaceful. I'm with my wife. She
makes each day lovely for me, when I think about it. Pauline! No one
is listening to me. You're drowning me out. It wasn't a good idea to
get her in a situation with Marianne. But she doesn't need to go off.
No. I'm ready to acknowledge to her that I have my shortcomings.
Pauline, turn that down!

PAULINE'S *radio switches off.*

HAZZITALL: *(Continued.)* Please come out. You know I don't like to disturb you once you're in your room.

PAULINE *enters. She is in a zombie-like state.*

Why was your radio on so loud?

PAULINE *cannot speak.*

Look, you made yourself deaf from all that noise.

PAULINE: I'm not deaf.

HAZZITALL: Have you seen Lisa?

PAULINE *gradually starts to come out of her zombie-like state.*

PAULINE: I've seen...

HAZZITALL: Lisa, where's Lisa?

PAULINE: I don't know.

HAZZITALL: Is something the matter with you?

PAULINE: I am delivered.

HAZZITALL: Look, you saw Lisa last. Where did she say she was going?

PAULINE: Gone? Oh, wow.

HAZZITALL: Where'd she go?

PAULINE: I don't know.

HAZZITALL: Is she still outside?

PAULINE: First I thought I heard a lawnmower. I have to call the newspaper. There's an ad there.

A faint muffled ruckus is heard coming from outside.

HAZZITALL: What's that, outside?

PAULINE: Outside.

HAZZITALL: Yes.

The doorbell rings.

PAULINE: I'll get it.

> PAULINE *exits to get the door. Pause.* PAULINE *comes in with the* LIEUTENANT.

This man is a police lieutenant. Excuse me. I've got to make a call.

> PAULINE *exits.*

HAZZITALL: *(Pause.)* Hello... Lieutenant?

LIEUTENANT: A crime has occurred. Not far from this house. Are you Thomas Hazzitall?

HAZZITALL: Yes?

LIEUTENANT: Maybe you'd better sit down.

Lights out. End of the scene.

Pause. The noise of radio waves fades back up. It is loud and frightening and lasts for a minute or two while the scene is being changed.

Scene 7

The pleasantly-furnished basement living space of HAZZITALL *and* LISA's *house. A staircase of several steps connects to the floor above. The ground floor (above) can only partially be seen. There are two windows placed high up on the basement walls. Before the lights come up a rain storm is heard outside.*

Lights up. HAZZITALL *very slowly limps down the stairs. His legs are terribly sore. At last,* HAZZITALL *reaches the downstairs floor. He talks to himself.*

HAZZITALL: I won't leave this room. *(Pause. Then, he says to himself what he repeatedly has told* PAULINE:*)* His lawyer will tell the court about you, Pauline. Why can't you forget about that other stuff? *(Pain shoots across his face.* HAZZITALL, *pleading, says simply to himself.)* Justice, justice for my wife.

HAZZITALL *is still. The lights fade halfway down on him. From the wings,* LISA, *a ghost, enters. She is covered in otherworldly light.* HAZZITALL *looks on, as if he is possessed by a dream.* LISA *sings. The words are to the tune of Chopin's funeral march.*

(Song #7: "Grave for the Dead")

LISA: *(Sings.)*
　　　　Grave for the dead and the dead's a grave for me.

LISA *exits. As she exits, a female sighing (recorded.) is heard. The lights on* HAZZITALL *return to normal.*

HAZZITALL: *(Horrorstruck.)* I feel like she's making fun of me.

LISA *briefly appears on stage.*

LISA: *(In earnest.)* I'm not, dear husband Tom.

LISA *exits.*

HAZZITALL: *(Closes eyes. To himself.)* So young. Taken away by a predatory felon!

PAULINE appears upstairs with feather duster in her hand. It is a problem for her that HAZZITALL is home. She shouts down the staircase.

PAULINE: Are you there?

Silence.

HAZZITALL: I have the worst nightmares. Bullets, screams, torn clothing, a gun...

PAULINE: If you are it's no good for you.

HAZZITALL: I see tens of horrors visited upon my poor wife.

PAULINE: Just because she was down there the whole last week of her life. Putting on the final touches. Never did buy that mirror she wanted.

HAZZITALL: I need to talk to you.

Pause. HAZZITALL orders her.

Down here, Pauline.

PAULINE descends the staircase.

It's called betrayal. My arms and legs don't lie, look at this—

Slowly and carefully, HAZZITALL rolls a shirt sleeve up to reveal eczema sores on his arm.

PAULINE: It *is* getting worse.

HAZZITALL: Because of you.

PAULINE: Your eczema. I'm sorry.

HAZZITALL: You know what the murderer looks like. You saw a man approach her as you went out back.

PAULINE: *(Apologetically.)* I have to tell the truth.

HAZZITALL: *(Referring to his eczema.)* It won't get better, as long as I know her killer's out there.

HAZZITALL *glares at* PAULINE.

PAULINE: I prayed for a job. There was hope. When I met Lisa and you. *(Resolutely.)* I saw what I saw.

HAZZITALL: *(With disgust.)* She was dragged into a vehicle of some kind. The breath was forced out of her.

PAULINE: It's like you have to court your wife all over again, now that she's gone.

HAZZITALL: What an odd thing to say! There's good reason you can only hire yourself out as a cleaning lady.

PAULINE: I'm much more than my job.

HAZZITALL: I can't keep employing you. You're in the way of justice. There's such a thing as the credibility of a witness. You'll destroy the case. That man should be sent to prison for the rest of his life. Don't say you left town.

PAULINE: I didn't leave town.

HAZZITALL: You saw the killer.

PAULINE: I saw a spaceship that had green wing-like thingys and purple chrome sky bumpers.

A flash of pain appears across HAZZITALL'S *face.*

HAZZITALL: You're cold. Ice. King Priam of old pleaded for his son's remains. I plead for my wife's killer to be in jail. You must testify—I mean—agree to exclude the fantastic part.

PAULINE: Is he going to show up again, I wonder.

HAZZITALL: Who?

PAULINE: Bibo, the space alien.

HAZZITALL *winces at the subject of "Bibo."*

HAZZITALL: No. (*Pause.*) The way she smoothed her hair.
    She liked to eat Fettuccini Alfredo—"heart attack on a plate"—but it doesn't do that. Okay. Vegetable soup. Green beans. Let's have some of what she liked. For lunch.

PAULINE: Good.

HAZZITALL: No. That won't cheer me up. I'll be reminded of her.

Lights down low on PAULINE *and* HAZZITALL. LISA *enters from the wings.*

(Song #8: "Mercy/Home")

LISA: (*Sings.*)
                Mercy, when you suffer,
                It's a tough one, lo—
                Mercy, when you suffer,
                It's a tough one, lo—
                My side, it's no right side
                Or a wrong side, lo—

                Home. home. home.
                Home. home. home, now home—

LISA exits. The resonance of the music accompaniment's end chord takes some time to fade. The doorbell rings, shattering that resonance. Lights up, as before, on PAULINE and HAZZITALL.

PAULINE: *(Excited.)* I'll get it.

PAULINE goes up the stairs to answer the door. The upstairs door is opened, LISA ARNY, in a wet raincoat, enters. LISA ARNY folds up her umbrella. PAULINE takes it from her and sets it down. LISA ARNY is played by the same actor that plays LISA.

LISA ARNY: Pauline. It's lovely to finally meet you. In person. This is where you work—I like to hold interviews during regular business hours. Thanks for obliging me.

PAULINE: No problem. (PAULINE *is shocked at the resemblance of* LISA ARNY *to* LISA.) Let me take your coat.

LISA ARNY: Thank you.

PAULINE is still shocked.

PAULINE: My boss is home, downstairs. *(First* PAULINE *hangs up the raincoat in a closet.)* He's home from work today. I'll introduce you.

LISA ARNY: I hope he doesn't mind.

They go downstairs. Upon seeing LISA ARNY, HAZZITALL tries to contain his shock.

HAZZITALL: Hello.

PAULINE: Tom, this is Ms. Lisa Arny. We've been talking on the phone and she wanted to come see me so I said all right.

HAZZITALL: Pleased to meet you, Ms. Arny.

HAZZITALL does a double-take on LISA ARNY.

LISA ARNY: Nice to meet you.

HAZZITALL *shakes hands with* LISA ARNY.

HAZZITALL: Excuse me, but you remind me so much of my wife

LISA ARNY: Do I?

HAZZITALL: Yes.

LISA ARNY: That's very interesting.

PAULINE: That's what she always says, Tom. "Interesting." She's a writer.

HAZZITALL: My wife has just recently passed away.

LISA ARNY: How terrible. I'm so sorry.

PAULINE: *(To* LISA ARNY.) Lisa was his wife's name.

LISA ARNY: If this is not a good time to visit I can...

HAZZITALL: No, stay.

HAZZITALL *notices* LISA ARNY's *hands.*

HAZZITALL: Such beautiful hands. *(They remind him of his wife's hands.)* At the time of her death she was wearing brightly-colored Isolda jogging gear.

PAULINE: Light blue, with stripes of pink in it.

HAZZITALL *glares at* PAULINE *with her deft description.*

HAZZITALL: She'd start for the golf course. To run along the boundary. She never got that far. Maybe 'cause someone called out to her for directions. She tried to be helpful when she could.

LISA ARNY: Violence is so... it's hard to prevent.

HAZZITALL: I'm the one who wanted to move to this town. Because it was so safe!

PAULINE: *(To* LISA ARNY.) We call this the basement suite, at least Lisa and I did. Maybe you can interview me down here while Tom attends to his things upstairs.

HAZZITALL: Interview? About Lisa's death? We haven't settled the issue between us.

LISA ARNY: I didn't know about her death.

HAZZITALL: *(Angry.)* You didn't know? It's been in all the papers.

LISA ARNY: Not mine.

HAZZITALL: It was there. You just didn't read.

PAULINE: Tom, she comes from fifteen hundred miles away. She's just got into town.

HAZZITALL: (LISA ARNY.) You're coming fifteen hundred miles to interview my cleaning lady? About what, detergent?

PAULINE: *(To herself.)* I should've postponed it.

LISA ARNY: *(To* HAZZITALL.) I'm a free-lance writer. I have a contract with Tantris Press. There are a number of people that have gotten in touch with me who are willing to relate their experiences.

HAZZITALL: Experiences of what?

LISA ARNY: Personal experiences.

LISA ARNY *refuses to divulge anymore information.*

HAZZITALL: *(To* LISA ARNY.*)* May I ask how you first contacted Pauline?

PAULINE: *I* answered a small classified ad in the National Express.

HAZZITALL: The National Express?! *(To* LISA ARNY.*)* So you work for them? Stories about celebrity swing parties and saucers in space.

LISA ARNY: I just took out an ad there.

PAULINE: Ms. Arny's come all this way to interview me. Since she's got a busy schedule it's best to start with the interview right away.

HAZZITALL: Says who? *(To* LISA ARNY.*)* She needs to dust.
   The problem is: for me and for my recently departed wife, Pauline's fantasies are a stumbling block to the successful prosecution of a man for murder.

LISA ARNY: Pauline's fantasies?

HAZZITALL: Let's call them fantasies for the moment. This is a life and death situation. *(As if to "bribe"* PAULINE *with a promotion.)* Pauline may have started out as a cleaning lady around here but she quickly evolved into an indispensable housekeeper.

PAULINE: I've been waiting for you to acknowledge that fact since my second week here.

HAZZITALL: You cannot interview her, I'm afraid, now, or ever.

LISA ARNY: I understand. Everything will be done anonymously.

HAZZITALL: Not even that.

PAULINE: But she flew fifteen hundred miles...

HAZZITALL: So do sparrows. She has other informants who have answered the ad.

LISA ARNY: *(Pause.)* Well, ah... I don't have any other informants. (HAZZITALL *looks at her, surprised.*) Everyone who answered the ad turned out to be a fake. And I have a book contract.

HAZZITALL: Tear it up.

LISA ARNY: But a contract...

HAZZITALL: Is there no dignity even in death? Contracts can be broken.

PAULINE: I'm sorry, Lisa. When you said I was to be your most important informant I didn't know I was going to be your only informant.

LISA ARNY: The book is basically your life.

HAZZITALL: Why don't you make the story up yourself?

LISA ARNY: I'm a stickler for documented facts.

HAZZITALL *lets out a sound of exasperation.*

PAULINE: I'll take you upstairs and you can interview me there.

HAZZITALL: No.

PAULINE: Then we'll go down to the Sand Pier and talk.

HAZZITALL: Neither one of you is going anywhere. To blab a story about extra-terrestrials. *(Pause.)* You're both under... house arrest.

LISA ARNY: You can't do that.

HAZZITALL: No? Just try to leave up those stairs. I'm bigger than you both. At last I see there is some evolutionary advantage to being a man.

PAULINE *and* LISA ARNY *look with pity at the distraught* HAZZITALL.

The telephone rings.

HAZZITALL: *(Continued.)* Pauline, please get the phone.

PAULINE *answers the phone.*

PAULINE: Hello. *(Pause.)* It's for you.

PAULINE *hands the phone over to* HAZZITALL.

HAZZITALL: *(Into the phone.)* Thomas Hazzitall speaking. *(Pause.)* Yes, Lieutenant. *(Pause.)* You hope the prime suspect is the right man? *(Pause.)* He is. *(Pause.)* Also, you have a report on a future kidnapping? Of a striking young woman, an independent writer from out of town? *(Pause.)* How do you... *(Pause.)* State-of-the-art police work? Then what's keeping you from tying up my, I mean, my wife's case? *(Pause.)* There is no substitute for *(He looks at* PAULINE.*)* *credible* testimony. *(Pause.)* All right. Good-bye.

HAZZITALL *puts the telephone down.*

Back to square one. Or should I say, *(He looks at* LISA ARNY.*)* square two.

LISA ARNY: I'd like a cup of coffee.

PAULINE *starts to get it.*

PAULINE: I'll get it for you.

HAZZITALL: *(To* PAULINE.*)* Don't go up there. Please get me the remaining clothesline. In the utility closet.

PAULINE: Why?

HAZZITALL: I'm going to tie you up. And keep you quiet. Sorry. This is no time for a book. But a meal—yes. Seeing you Ms. Arny makes me strangely hungry again.

PAULINE: *(To* LISA ARNY.*)* He hasn't been able to eat since what happened to his wife.

LISA ARNY: What if we don't want to be tied up?

PAULINE: *(To* LISA ARNY.*)* He's had a rough two weeks, he'll snap out of this. Let him eat.

Lights out. End of the scene.

Entre Scene

Between scenes, lights up on the actors who play MARIANNE *and* CLAUDE. *They sing, "A Ball of String." They dance/mime to the song.*

(Song #9: "A Ball of String")

MARIANNE and CLAUDE: *(Sing.)*
> A ball of string has been unwound,
> It hangs in the air,
> Hmm, connecting seed from my mind
> to the seed from your mind, hmm.
> Look there, there, there,
> It's there, right there,
> the thread, if you're gonna spin it,
> rope, if I'm gonna need it,
> Line, if you're gonna toss it over,
> it's just an inch away.
> What do I do to make you see,
> What can I say, oh—

(End of song. Lights fade out.)

Scene 8

Same as the last scene, the basement living space. Music fades in, the kind heard at a planetarium show.

Lights up. LISA ARNY *and* PAULINE *have been tied in chairs for an hour. The clothesline is tied in a comic, haphazard manner. If the women wanted to they could lift the rope and free themselves. The women are gagged. They listen carefully to make sure* HAZZITALL *is still upstairs. Then they take out their gags and talk.*

PAULINE: It wasn't as high tech as I would've expected. I mean in a spaceship not of this world. Oh. The top was vaulted. Jewels in the roof.

He laid me down on a table and examined me. He set his rod down. I looked across at the milky white walls. He waved his hand and healed this little bump I've had on my leg for four years.

LISA ARNY: Did you have to take off any clothing?

PAULINE: No, he let me keep my clothing on.

LISA ARNY: How did you know it was a he?

PAULINE: Because the way he spoke was like a man.

LISA ARNY: What did he say?

The women hear HAZZITALL *approach the top of the stairs. The planetarium music fades out.* HAZZITALL *descends the stairs. He is more limber now. The women quickly stuff the gags back in before* HAZZITALL *reaches the bottom of the stairs.)*

HAZZITALL: How are we all doing? I'm so happy. I've been able to eat, at last.

HAZZITALL *removes the gags from* PAULINE *and* LISA ARNY.

221

HAZZITALL: I'm sorry, Lisa.

LISA ARNY: I bet you would've liked to do this to your wife sometime.

HAZZITALL: *(First, embarrassed. Then:)* It's all for a very good reason.

LISA ARNY: Of course.

HAZZITALL: A "space alien" will not get in the way. *(Pause.)* If you and
I were to go out for a drink in five years, you'd admit that you did
this for the money. *(Pause.)* What have you written about before?

LISA ARNY: It's my first book contract.

HAZZITALL's *disapproving silence.*

My *only* contract.

HAZZITALL: Look, come work for me. I'll make a job for you.

LISA ARNY: I won't work in an office. I'm interested in contemporary
phenomena.

HAZZITALL: *(To himself.)* She won't go work in an office. *(Pain registers
across his face.)* You want a leave of absence.

PAULINE: *(Warning him not to think of the past.)* Don't, Tom. You just
were able to eat.

HAZZITALL *looks briefly into* LISA ARNY's *eyes. The doorbell rings.*

HAZZITALL: Excuse me.

HAZZITALL *makes his way up the stairs and answers the door. He lets the
very large* LIEUTENANT *in.*

But Lieutenant, what are you doing here?

The LIEUTENANT *stands in place but takes the liberty to glance around the room.*

LIEUTENANT: The prime suspect, as you know, was freed from jail three days ago. We warned him not to leave the area but he left.

HAZZITALL: I thought you were going to keep track of him.

LIEUTENANT: We did. And he left.

HAZZITALL: Great. Fabulous.

LIEUTENANT: I'm here to check a few facts. Let's be friends. Do you mind if I sit down?

HAZZITALL: Yes.

LIEUTENANT: I won't sit on your chair and break it.

HAZZITALL: I would prefer if you leave.

LIEUTENANT: Do you have something to hide?

HAZZITALL: I'm the innocent one.

PAULINE: *(To* LISA ARNY, *asking her to not say anything.)* Shh. He's been through so much already.

LIEUTENANT: Would you by chance... *(The* LIEUTENANT *discreetly cranes his neck around in an attempt to see downstairs.)* ...be holding two ladies against their will, down in your basement?

HAZZITALL: I think you'd better go now.

LIEUTENANT: Well, if you aren't then, you don't mind me going down into your basement suite?

HAZZITALL: It's too dirty to receive visitors.

LIEUTENANT: But isn't that why you have a cleaning lady in?

HAZZITALL: Pauline is a *housekeeper*. Lieutenant, unless you have a search warrant you're not going downstairs.

LIEUTENANT: *(Looking in the direction of downstairs, then:)* You don't see much of that Marianne woman anymore do you?

HAZZITALL: She was my wife's friend, that's all.

LIEUTENANT: You've found other avenues of physical adventure? I'm a strapping man. Get it, *(Gestures a strap or a belt.)* strap, strap?

HAZZITALL: Why have you come here?

LIEUTENANT: You want them at your mercy. *(Pause.)* We've located the prime suspect.

HAZZITALL: I thought you said you lost him.

LIEUTENANT: I said he left the area.

HAZZITALL: You'd better be hanging on to him.

LIEUTENANT: He's not going anywhere.

HAZZITALL: Good, good.

   Pause.

LIEUTENANT: He's dead.

HAZZITALL: The prime suspect? What happened?

LIEUTENANT: He drove his car into a concrete wall.

HAZZITALL: Why'd you let him do that?

LIEUTENANT: The lawless are a law unto themselves.

HAZZITALL: You let the prime suspect kill himself?

LIEUTENANT: If he was the killer, he would have been filled with pain and remorse and that would have led him to...

HAZZITALL: *(Outraged.)* Pain? Remorse? You're supposed to find murderers alive, not dead.

HAZZITALL: Get out!

LIEUTENANT: *(Jealous.)* You had a beautiful wife.

    The LIEUTENANT *exits.* HAZZITALL *slowly walks downstairs.*

PAULINE: A step towards resolution, Tom.

    HAZZITALL *reaches the basement floor.*

HAZZITALL: The prime suspect! I wanted the whole truth to be told!

PAULINE: Sometimes you have to live with pieces of the truth.

HAZZITALL: Be quiet. *(To* LISA ARNY.) And it doesn't help that you showed up here either. *(Suddenly polite.)* I'm sorry.

LISA ARNY: No, I'm sorry. Please, consider me your friend.

HAZZITALL: You don't blame me for tying you up?

LISA ARNY: It's not so bad being snug, secure.

HAZZITALL: But...

LISA ARNY: I've been tied up before.

HAZZITALL: You have?

    HAZZITALL *raises an eyebrow.*

LISA ARNY: I've been busy.

HAZZITALL: With another man?

LISA ARNY: Sometimes with more than one.

HAZZITALL: (*Crushed.*) What?

LISA ARNY: May I speak freely?

HAZZITALL: You're as free as the day you were born.

LISA ARNY: Pauline and I think you're... cute.

Pause.

HAZZITALL: (*Pleased.*) I'm... (*Appalled.*) cute? (HAZZITALL *thinks to himself. He explodes.*) I'm so unfaithful!

LISA ARNY: What?

HAZZITALL: To my Lisa. She can love nobody else, yet here I am, a few days after she's gone, beginning to... It's not right. What's come over me?

PAULINE: It's natural, in a way.

HAZZITALL: It's time to untie you both.

LISA ARNY: You don't care about my interviewing Pauline?

HAZZITALL: What's the point in stopping you now? She won't need to testify. Pauline, do you think the prime suspect really ran himself into a wall out of remorse?

PAULINE: People are more human than you think sometimes.

LISA ARNY *and* PAULINE *untie themselves.*

LISA ARNY: I'd like to ask... I ah... I've been sitting down here for quite a long time. Could you tell me where the ah...

PAULINE: The bathroom down here isn't fully redecorated. Go up and look for the first door on your right.

LISA ARNY: Thank you.

LISA ARNY *goes upstairs to exit within.*

PAULINE: She'll be in town for three days. Isn't that nice? When the rain dries up we can go show her the rocks.

HAZZITALL: Meanwhile you'll show her the rocks in your head, Pauline.

PAULINE: Bibo the space alien, was a messenger. From the Eternal. We have another sign now. She's the spitting image of your wife. God is trying to get through to you, Tom.

HAZZITALL: By killing my wife?

PAULINE: I kind of think Bibo might have dropped her down.

HAZZITALL: Dropped her down?

PAULINE: *(Thinking.)* Yeah, Bibo did it probably.

Pause.

HAZZITALL: Ms. Arny couldn't be an alien from outer space. *(Pause.)* She goes to the bathroom!

PAULINE *looks away. She thinks: "Tom, don't think you know everything."*

Lights out. End of the scene.

End of Act I

ACT II

Scene 1

The basement living space, as at the end of act 1. PAULINE *is off stage, but sings. Only a little light illuminates* LISA, CLAUDE *and* MARIANNE *as they sing:*

(Song #10: "Moan, Member, Moan")

LISA:
>   Tell-a me who that had a rod?

PAULINE, CLAUDE AND MARIANNE:
>   Moan, member, moan.

LISA:
>   It was Moses, child of God.

PAULINE, CLAUDE AND MARIANNE:
>   Moan, member, moan.

LISA:
>   Who that hit that mighty rock?

PAULINE, CLAUDE AND MARIANNE:
>   Moan, member, moan.

LISA:
>   Moses strike one, heaven clock.

PAULINE, CLAUDE AND MARIANNE:
>   Moan, member, moan.

LISA:
>   Struck it one and struck it two.

PAULINE, CLAUDE AND MARIANNE:
>
> Moan, member, moan.

LISA:

> Watch out Moses what you do.

PAULINE, CLAUDE AND MARIANNE:

> Moan, member, moan.

Lights up on the basement living space. PAULINE *enters. She picks up a feather duster and starts to dust. A massage table is now part of the furniture downstairs.*

LISA:

> Struck it three times, ring-a-ring.

PAULINE, CLAUDE and MARIANNE:

> Moan, member, moan.

LISA:

> Watch them healing waters spring.

PAULINE, CLAUDE and MARIANNE:

> Moan, member, moan.

LISA:

> Come, or are you going to stay?

PAULINE, CLAUDE and MARIANNE:

> Moan, member, moan.

LISA:

> Way behind on the blessed day.

PAULINE, CLAUDE and MARIANNE:

> Moan, member, moan.

PAULINE:

> Hypocrite, you're losing room...

Lisa, Marianne and Claude:
>Moan, member, moan.

Pauline:
>To repent this side of doom.

Lisa, Marianne and Claude:
>Moan, member, moan.

Pause. Pauline *sets down her duster.*

Pauline: *(Singing.)*
>Wasn't long before she came back

Lisa, Marianne and Claude: *(Singing.)*
>Moan, member, moan.

Pauline: *(Speaking.)* For good.

Lisa, Marianne and Claude: *(Singing.)*
>Moan, member, moan.

Pauline *folds and arranges what appears to be her own personal effects.*

Pauline: *(Speaking.)* Two years have passed.

Lisa, Marianne and Claude: *(Singing.)*
>Lisa Arny, hmm.

Lisa, Marianne *and* Claude *exit.*

Pauline: *(Speaking.)*
>Not only has her book flopped.
>Not only has she left the writing field altogether.
>And moved to this, a new place.
>Not only has she gone to school and gotten a
>>diploma in massage therapy,
>In order to have a skilled, satisfying job,
>She has husband Tom to contend with.

PAULINE *pulls out a hidden battery-powered "smokeless" ashtray and turns it on. She takes out a cigarette, lights it, takes a few puffs.*

> Tom, Tom, what can we do?
> You have wedded bliss.
> But something's wrong.
> You take to out-of-doors wandering.
> Wandering and pondering
> And neglecting your new wife.
>
> Who is this Lisa Arny, you wonder,
> Why is this Lisa, you ask,
> You distrust the situation.
> Your body of abrasions drags through the desert.
> You're out there with no tent at all.

PAULINE *glances over to the staircase and puts her cigarette out.*

God watches over you, Tom. No matter if you think so or not.

PAULINE *kneels down on one knee. She bows her head slightly.*
> I am grateful for the many gifts granted me, dear
>   Lord.
> I am thankful for the appearance of Bibo and his
>   spaceship—
> But when's he coming back?

Lights out. End of the scene.

Scene 2

The basement, soon after the last scene. Later in this scene, the rear of the house will be represented briefly. A small playing area—not the main playing area—will be used for this.

Lights up. Lisa Arny *fidgets. The* Lieutenant *looks around the room.*

Lieutenant: *(Stiffly.)* Attractive—the way you've remodeled your house down here. As a place for your business.

Lisa Arny: We didn't do much, really.

Lieutenant: I know.

Lisa Arny: You do?

Pause. The Lieutenant *goes through his pockets.*

Lieutenant: I have this. *(He holds out a coupon.)* Would now be a good time for my free introductory massage?

Lisa Arny: *(To herself, unhappy.)* You saw that advertisement? *(To the* Lieutenant.) I didn't know you were interested in getting a massage.

Lieutenant: That's why I wanted to talk to you down here.

Lisa Arny *thinks quickly.*

Lisa Arny: I don't have the time for you now.

Lieutenant: But you had the time to let me in. We can talk about the situation while I'm on the table.

Lisa Arny *pretends to look in her appointment book.*

Lisa Arny: *(Still looking in her book.)* You don't talk with the therapist while you're getting a massage. It breaks the concentration during repetitions.

LIEUTENANT: I myself have been concentrating on the repetitions taking place in this household for some time.

The LIEUTENANT *moves over to the massage table and lies on his back. He looks forlornly at* LISA ARNY.

It is after all a coupon redeemable only here.

LISA ARNY *takes the coupon from the* LIEUTENANT.

LISA ARNY: *(Innocently.)* My, you're a big man.

The LIEUTENANT *innocently smiles.*

I only have time to check your spine. *(Hoping it is so.)* If you have an ephemeral-vertebral condition then there's no point in going any further... First turn over. (LISA ARNY *helps him move over to be on his stomach. She feels his back over.)* Oh, no. Everything seems to be okay.

LIEUTENANT: Tom doesn't sleep with you anymore. He can't resolve the loss of his first wife.

LISA ARNY: Should that be a concern of yours?

LIEUTENANT: Tom, I mean the case of Tom's first wife—her death— is still open.

LISA ARNY: Open? Why?

LIEUTENANT: There was no confession in the case.

LISA ARNY: So what? You know who did it.

LIEUTENANT: Do you want me to take off my shirt *(Before* LISA ARNY *can say no, he quickly removes his shirt.)* There's an urgency.
LISA ARNY: Treatments don't always work fast, Lieutenant.

LIEUTENANT: But on a daily basis...

The LIEUTENANT *returns to lie on his stomach.* LISA ARNY *begins to massage him. He softens.*

LIEUTENANT: I need to tell you something.

LISA ARNY: *(To herself.)* Oh, God, what? *(To the* LIEUTENANT.*)* Take care, Lieutenant, to respect my job description.

LIEUTENANT: Still, you have to understand, while you have people in certain positions...

LISA ARNY: We can always move you.

LIEUTENANT: No. There are criminals all around us. Each out for himself. *(Pause. Returning to the subject, in an afraid voice.)* You promise you won't tell anyone?

LISA ARNY: Nothing that gets said within these walls goes any further.

LIEUTENANT: I thought you'd understand.

LISA ARNY: *(To herself.)* Here we go.

LIEUTENANT: You're special. Something very special. Ah... *(He hesitates, then:)* I... it's of a fearful private nature.

LISA ARNY: I'm sure it is.

LIEUTENANT: We can't proceed any further. Until I've cleared the air.

LISA ARNY: Oh?

LIEUTENANT: I've been taunted for my... well, the thing that's in question.
LISA ARNY: I'm sorry to hear that.

LIEUTENANT: Most of the taunting has come from myself, of course.

LISA ARNY: Of course.

LIEUTENANT: You see, I have a defect, it's more in the nature of a problem, I guess.

LISA ARNY: Yes, yes, yes.

LIEUTENANT: I feel so vulnerable now.

LISA ARNY: *(Reluctantly.)* Let it out.

LIEUTENANT: You won't think badly of me?

LISA ARNY: *(Reluctantly and detached.)* Do I look like that kind of person?

LIEUTENANT: No. Well. It's about my... handwriting. It's too feminine. I've tried to change it. But I can't. It's more than a failing.

LISA ARNY: It's a humiliation.

LIEUTENANT: Precisely.

LISA ARNY: Lieutenant, relax. Some day you'll come to terms with it. We all have our idiosyncrasies.

LIEUTENANT: That's not exactly the word for it.

LISA ARNY: Of course it isn't. Handwriting's a very intimate subject. Plenty of room for pain there. As a kid I hated to give away anything I wrote. Not because of what I was saying. I was proud of my penmanship, I would have *sold* my writing—to me it was as valuable as a Picasso.

LIEUTENANT: That's just the point. My writing is too beautiful.
LISA ARNY: *(With great understanding.)* That's horrible, isn't it?

LIEUTENANT: Yes. (*He clears his throat.*) Apparently Tom's ordered someone to make a statue of the first Lisa.

LISA ARNY: A statue?

LISA ARNY *stops massaging him.*

LIEUTENANT: Yes. (*Pause. Disapproving.*) He's been at the premises of an artist.

HAZZITALL *enters upstairs.*

LISA ARNY: (*Flustered.*) An artist? (*There is no way to get the* LIEUTENANT *fully clothed and standing right away. To herself:*) I thought I reminded him too much of her.

LISA ARNY *instinctively steps away from the table. Coming down the stairs,* HAZZITALL *sees the* LIEUTENANT.

HAZZITALL: (*To the* LIEUTENANT.) You? (LISA ARNY *thinks she means her. She rushes over to* HAZZITALL. *He ignores her.*) You? Have you no honor? Shame? Out of Lisa Arny's office! Bad man!

The LIEUTENANT *picks himself up off the table and puts his shirt back on.*

HAZZITALL: (*Back on the track he has been on.*) I've been thinking. All the disenfranchised people dreamed up Heaven—the idea—

The LIEUTENANT *rolls his eyes upward when he hears the word, "idea." He does not straighten up himself anymore. He nods politely to* LISA ARNY *to say good-bye. He starts up the stairs.*

... as a way to get back at those who enjoy life too much.

LISA ARNY: Do you enjoy life too much?

HAZZITALL: Don't start it with me.

"To be grateful is to recognize the Love of God
In everything He has given us—
And He has given us everything."
—This is in the literature that Pauline leaves lying around the house.
I know death is supposed to bring me closer to her God but it hasn't.

The LIEUTENANT *lingers near the front door.*

LISA ARNY: Tom, you've been outside, long—

HAZZITALL: I won't be forced to believe in something that doesn't come naturally to me. Nature, that's what she ignores. If there is a God then God is Nature. I mean, all the tiny things on stems, in seeds, or with wings. And trees, they're just a taller form of truth, if there is any truth.

LISA ARNY: I'm glad you're home.

The LIEUTENANT *exits.*

HAZZITALL: That Lieutenant. He hasn't even gotten to the reptile stage yet.

LISA ARNY: *(Nicely.)* You've had a tiring time out among the stones and rocks and sand.

HAZZITALL: He knows too much. Or thinks he does. Evil humans know too much—you know what I mean.

LISA ARNY: I'm not sure.

HAZZITALL: Lisa would.

LISA ARNY: Is that why you're having a statue made?

HAZZITALL: A statue?

LISA ARNY: The Lieutenant said you're having a statue made of her.

HAZZITALL: He's wrong. I mean, he's a little right. Look at this. *(He points to his skin sores.)* It's like lava from a hole in the ground. Eczema. Psoriasis. A pitched battle on my skin. Worsened by...

The sound of something like a chainsaw is heard. Also heard is an angelic voice repeatedly intoning a word that sounds somewhere between "grin" and "green."

What's that?

LISA ARNY: Where's Pauline?

LISA ARNY goes over to the window.

HAZZITALL: The neighborhood doesn't have any lawns. We're known as the rock garden capital of the world around here.

LISA ARNY: *(Looking out the window.)* It's hard to see anything. Pauline—where is she?

HAZZITALL: Maybe dusting. *(Motions his hand like he's got a feather duster in it.)* Dust. Dust. As she strives to cleanse her mind of sinful thoughts, while waiting for "Bibo" and his space explorers to visit the back of the house once more and give her a good goosing.

LISA ARNY: *(Yelling.)* Pauline! *(Pause.)* She's not up there. *(She runs up the stairs and looks outdoors through a window.)* I can see the street as far as a quarter of a mile.

HAZZITALL: What about a lawn mower?

LISA ARNY: Don't you remember?

HAZZITALL: What?

The angelic voice and the chainsaw sounds end abruptly.

LISA ARNY: That was the sound of *him*. Before and after his visitation to earth. Pauline heard it. I wrote about it. My book—don't you remember? *(Shouting.)* Pauline! *(Pause.)* They've taken her prisoner.

HAZZITALL: *(Sarcastically.)* She went on her own free will before. Please come down here. This is all nonsense. *(Forcing himself to apologize.)* I'm sorry. It's mythical. In the modern sense.

LISA ARNY *comes down the stairs.*

LISA ARNY: But where is Pauline?

Upon LISA ARNY's *reaching the lower floor* PAULINE *comes in upstairs and heads downstairs.*

PAULINE: Yoo-hoo—

PAULINE *shuts the door. She starts down the stairs to the basement suite.*

LISA ARNY: Pauline, we heard *the sound.*

PAULINE *does not respond. A smile is pasted on her face.*

The sound of *them.* Or *him.*

PAULINE *is still silent.*

LISA ARNY: *(Continued.)* Bibo! *(Almost pleading with* PAULINE.*)* Didn't you hear?

PAULINE: *(Smiling.)* Yes, in fact, I've got him standing right here.

Lights out on HAZZITALL *and* LISA ARNY. *They freeze. A strange light covers* PAULINE. *The unseeable Bibo is at her side. She steps away from the basement apartment and goes for a walk with Bibo.*

PAULINE: *(Continued.)* Bibo, when you come back, after your day in

China... no, I'll tell you now. There's a few things about us humans. For your research. *(Pause.)* These are the pelvic muscles. Some of the strongest muscles in the body. I use them all the time. Doing work around the house. They also can be used to put a lot of pressure on the bottom of your lungs. Underneath the lungs is where the womb is. That's where the next generation grows. In females.

(She is attempting to be scientific, not trying to betray any possible reproductive motives.) Like me. Like in Tom's wife Lisa. When the new human's big enough, the female opens her legs and breathes in to bear down on the bottom of her lungs. Then the new human comes out. If you ever hear Lisa Number Two complain, it might be because she can't get this thing started. Because of Tom. *(Pause.)* Well. I know you have to go. So. Have a safe journey. And see you soon?

> PAULINE *winds up at the back of the house. Lights up on a rock, one foot tall, and on an elbow-shaped gas main or water main pipe coming out of the ground. Darkness covers* HAZZITALL *and* LISA ARNY *and the basement living space.* PAULINE *looks skyward. She dances and sings:*

(Song #11: "Bibo Song")

PAULINE: *(Sings.)*
> Things we read in the paper,
> Noise heard in town,
> Jams up our living radios.
> How sad it is that one begets the other.
> It all piles up to an inner tower of woe.
>
> Bibo, you are the rise,
> The rising of the special
> Balm for all eyes.
>
> The day has come:
> Humans will be free
> As long as they respect each kind,
> And eachkindly alien category.

Though PAULINE *is finished singing, the music continues for a while, then fades out.*

Lights fade to black. End of the scene.

Scene 3

Back inside the basement. The next day. Lights up. PAULINE *is dusting.* HAZZITALL *is trying to talk some sense into her.*

HAZZITALL: Pauline, he didn't come before. And he's not coming again. Do you understand?

PAULINE *sets down her feather duster.*

PAULINE: Maybe I should take a another shower...

HAZZITALL: I'll never forget. This is the same sort of thing that stood in the way of speedy justice for her killer. I hate to rehash old times.

PAULINE: *(Not hearing.)...* not for vanity's sake. I've got to be cleansed. If I could, I'd get as pure as... Sometimes I pray that I could get changed into fire.

HAZZITALL: You don't have to go that far. Think of me.

PAULINE *takes out a pack of cigarettes.*

It's hard to find an honest housekeeper.

PAULINE *removes a cigarette. She sets the pack down on the nearby massage table. Overly excited, she lights her cigarette with her shaking hands.*

HAZZITALL: What, you're smoking? I never knew you smoked.

PAULINE: You think you know everything about me.

HAZZITALL: Doesn't this fly in the face of your desire to be purified?

PAULINE: I'm nervous.

> PAULINE *gets a small suitcase she has stored under the massage table. She opens it up, checks the contents inside, and closes it.*

HAZZITALL: You shouldn't be nervous. If I feel rotten it's because of something beyond my control. Even a doctor's control.

> PAULINE *smokes her cigarette to relax. Something seems to take hold of her.*

It's hereditary, isn't it? Isn't almost everything these days?

PAULINE: Can you feel anything in your legs?

HAZZITALL: Nothing outside the normal lacerations.

PAULINE: I can't in mine. Am I levitating?

HAZZITALL: *(Exasperated.)* Unbelievable.

> *There is a strange sound of high rumbles.* PAULINE *still smokes, but sometimes places one hand to her forehead as she concentrates on what is supposedly being said to her. Sometimes she affects a different tone when relaying some of Bibo's words.*
>
> *Pause.*

PAULINE *(Jolted.)* He's talking to me.

HAZZITALL: He?

PAULINE: My preceptor, Bibo, the space alien.

> *Pause.*

HAZZITALL: I hear nothing.

PAULINE: Turn the radio on high volume and play with the dial. You might trap some of what he's saying.

HAZZITALL: *(Sarcastically.)* What would he be saying now, Pauline?

Pause.

PAULINE: Greetings from the place called Zuala Ret.

PAULINE *again puts her hand to her head.* LISA ARNY *enters the house and comes downstairs.*

LISA ARNY: I had to go out and buy a tape recorder.

HAZZITALL: *(To* LISA ARNY.) To replace the one you gave away? You quit writing.

LISA ARNY: With this happening, I need to be ready to dictate.

HAZZITALL: *(To* LISA ARNY.) She's not receiving telepathic signals.

LISA ARNY: Fantastic!

PAULINE: What do you want to ask him?

LISA ARNY: Wonderful! (LISA ARNY *switches on her tape recorder.)* Ask him if we can see his space ship.

HAZZITALL: *(Sarcastically.)* Ask him if he knows anything about a lawn mower or a chain saw in the area. Ha!

PAULINE: One question at a time. *(She receives the reply. To* LISA ARNY.) Someday you'll see his spacecraft. (PAULINE *receives another reply. To* HAZZITALL.) The power mower sound is the sound of their clock chiming. He's sorry it's so loud.

LISA ARNY: Ask him—what's the greatest truth he's learned about us?

Pause.

PAULINE: Only one thing can be perfectly attained on the earth: Death.

HAZZITALL: *(Not impressed.)* What else is on his mind?

Pause. PAULINE *is perplexed.*

PAULINE: Hmm. *(She gets it.)* There. Resistance throughout the lung is caused by increased convection.

LISA ARNY: *(To* PAULINE.*)* Sounds like he's examining you from afar.

HAZZITALL: He wants to gauge your ability to breathe heavily. He's going to jump your bones...

LISA ARNY: Oh, Tom!

HAZZITALL: ...but the smoke's getting in the way of his going through with it. Pauline, I'm allergic to your cigarette. Take it outside.

Silence from PAULINE.

LISA ARNY: She can't.

HAZZITALL: Why not?

PAULINE: I'll go out and sit by the one flower and talk to him.

LISA ARNY: No. I don't want you to go out there alone.

There is a tapping sound on the basement window.

I guess he's coming in for you.

PAULINE: I'll meet him outside.

LISA ARNY *approaches the basement window.* HAZZITALL *would never admit he is nervous about what is going on. There are two more taps at it. There is another tap and* HAZZITALL's *skin on his forearm reacts painfully to it.*

HAZZITALL: Ow! *(He coughs from the cigarette and sends* PAULINE *out.)* The sooner the better!

PAULINE *casually takes the suitcase in her hand and creeps up the staircase.* LISA ARNY *looks around the basement window casing to figure out just what is making the sound.* PAULINE *exits upstairs within to get to the backyard.*

HAZZITALL: *(Groping for logic.)* A breeze must be blowing something against the window.

HAZZITALL *rests against the massage table. He tries not to let on that the tapping sound unnerves him. He is occupied with his own thoughts. Startled,* LISA ARNY *switches off her tape recorder.* HAZZITALL *pays no attention to what* LISA ARNY *is doing or saying.*

LISA ARNY: *(To the other side of the window.)* You want to tell me something? In person? *(With the intonation of "you can't".)* We're expecting visitors. *(Pause.)* From where? *(Pause.)* Out of town. *(Pause.)* You don't want your men to see you in the front of our house? *(Pause.)* Then leave, Lieutenant! *(Pause.)* What is it you must tell me? *(Pause.)* A surprise?

LISA ARNY *leaves the window. She goes over to* HAZZITALL.

Forget about the tapping. Where did Pauline go?

HAZZITALL: *(Caught up in his own thoughts.)* She's outside smoking.

LISA ARNY: I told her she was not to.

We hear a great explosion out in back of the house. HAZZITALL *and* LISA ARNY *freeze. Lights out. Music. Lights fade up on* PAULINE *who enters barefoot, near a rock in the backyard area of the house. Two pipes are seen through light smoke. One is a large elbow-shaped main pipe and another follows closely next to it. The large pipe is split open and water is trickling out of the smaller pipe.*

PAULINE *faces the audience as she talks to the unseeable Bibo. The* HELIUM CHORUS *(consisting of the actors who play* CLAUDE *and* MARIANNE.*) is just offstage. The CHORUS's "im-man-ee's" are intoned on various high pitches.*

PAULINE: It's so warm. But the flower's not burned up. Bibo, are you behind that flower?

HELIUM CHORUS: Im-man-ee, im-man-ee, im-man-ee.

PAULINE: Yes, there you are.

HELIUM CHORUS: Im-man-ee, im-man-ee.

PAULINE: I'm glad to get my shoes off. The road's been rocky and rough at times. (PAULINE *studies Bibo.*) I'm ready for the final journey.

HELIUM CHORUS: Im-man-ee, im-man-ee, im-man-ee, im-man-ee, im-man-ee.

PAULINE: Why do you call me precious?

HELIUM CHORUS: Im-man-ee, im-man-ee, im-man-ee, im-man-ee. Im-man-ee, im-man-ee, im-man-ee, im-man-ee, im-man-ee.

PAULINE: Because "Faith gives meaning to suffering, faith redeems death, and I have faith?" That's so sweet.

PAULINE *looks over to the elbow-shaped water main pipe.*

PAULINE: *(Continued.)* Oh, look—there's some water sprouting out. It must be the water main's sprung a leak. First the fire cleans me. Now some water. All this in one day.

HELIUM CHORUS: Im-man-ee, im-man-ee.

PAULINE: Yes, you can kiss me, if only it's on the hand. *(She holds out her hand. Pause. There is no kiss.* PAULINE *is flustered.)* Bibo, where'd you go? Have you forsaken me? No. I've come this far—*you've* come this far—Sure, I could always atone more, but... I am what I am. *(The unseeable Bibo kisses her with force on the cheek.)* Wow, that was some kiss. I guess my hand was not...

HELIUM CHORUS: Im-man-ee, im-man-ee, im-man-ee, im-man-ee, im-man-ee.

PAULINE: "There are many more muscles and nerves in the face." Yes, you're right. But God clothed me, and clothed I stay. *(Coquettishly.)* So, mind your manners.

A beautiful phrase of harp music is heard.

Ah, these harps are nice sounding. Look how the sea of glass swells. When will the foundations and the walls and the gates come up?

The music continues.

I have to pray. Do what you will with me, O Lord!

Lights out on PAULINE, *music stops.* PAULINE *exits. Lights up on* HAZZITALL *and* LISA ARNY, *who unfreeze.*

HAZZITALL: What was that?

LISA ARNY: A big whooshing sound.

HAZZITALL: Stay right here.

LISA ARNY goes to the window.

LISA ARNY: It wasn't out this side.

LISA ARNY cranes her neck around to get a view.

HAZZITALL: Be careful.

LISA ARNY: It's, it's... *(She switches her hand-held tape recorder back on. She speaks into it.)* Something's happened out in back.

HAZZITALL: Yes?

LISA ARNY: *(Always speaking into the tape recorder.)* A glowing mass of thin wadding.

HAZZITALL: Let me see.

HAZZITALL goes over to the window. He cranes his neck around to get a view.

LISA ARNY: I hesitate to use the words "fireless smoke".

HAZZITALL: A billow. Of misty flame.

LISA ARNY: Don't you see, it's *color* that looks like its burning, but it's really...

HAZZITALL: It *is* burning, and floating, and disappearing up.

LISA ARNY: Atomizing blue. Effervescing yellow. A cloud cremation of purple.

HAZZITALL: It started by the gas main.

LISA ARNY: *(Looking.)* Withdrawing. From the backyard. So quickly. The atmosphere. It's tinged *(Searching for the right word.)* ...amber!

LISA ARNY: *(Turns to HAZZITALL.)* Tom!

HAZZITALL: *(Horrified.)* Oh, no.

LISA ARNY: It's vanishing into the heavens.

HAZZITALL: I know what's happened out there.

LISA ARNY: He's taken off, launched by an explosion.

HAZZITALL goes away from the window. There is a sound of leaking water.

HAZZITALL: The water pipe's been split open. The water runs next to the gas main. Now I know why they built it that way. It's a cheap, automatic sprinkler system. There must have been a tiny bit of... Gas! Pauline's cigarette! (HAZZITALL *puts his hands in his face.*) Oh!

Lights out. End of the scene.

Scene 4

Minutes later in the basement. Lights up. HAZZITALL, *in short sleeves, wears rubber gloves to safeguard his skin. He is mopping up.* LISA ARNY *is wiping off the downstairs walls and furniture. Wet rags and a mop pail are in view. The whole room is wet.* PAULINE'S *pack of cigarettes is on the massage table where she left them.* HAZZITALL *and* LISA ARNY *take a break from mopping up.* HAZZITALL *takes off his rubber gloves.*

HAZZITALL: I didn't smell any gas escaping out back. Must have been some sort of freak leak.

LISA ARNY: *(Grieving.)* PAULINE. She's a scoop of wet ashes out by the gas main.

HAZZITALL: You called the Lieutenant, right?

LISA ARNY: He was already not far from the area.

HAZZITALL: Then what's keeping him?

LISA ARNY: *(After a brief glance over to the basement window.)* He muttered something about a whole new way of looking at life.

LISA ARNY tries to tidy up by the massage table.

HAZZITALL: Oh, I told the artist to destroy the statue of Lisa.

LISA ARNY: *(Pleased.)* Thank you, Tom.

The doorbell rings.

It's the Lieutenant—at last.

LISA ARNY picks up the pack of cigarettes PAULINE left behind. She suppresses a sad feeling. She puts the cigarettes away. She goes upstairs and opens the door. The LIEUTENANT enters.

LIEUTENANT: Hello, Lisa. Sorry I'm late. Curious reports. UFO's. Time-wasters.

LISA ARNY: Come downstairs. My husband can't make the trip up right now. His legs.

LIEUTENANT: *(To LISA ARNY.)* I do have something to say to only you, but...

They walk down the stairs.

HAZZITALL: Mind the water, Lieutenant. The explosion put a crack in the water pipe.

LIEUTENANT: *(Seeing HAZZITALL.)* I offer my condolences.

The LIEUTENANT swiftly goes to HAZZITALL.

LIEUTENANT: *(Continued.)* Let me embrace you, you poor man.

The LIEUTENANT *bearhugs* HAZZITALL *supposedly to offer his condolences.* HAZZITALL *writhes in pain—the* LIEUTENANT *also squashes his foot.*

HAZZITALL: Ow, Lieutenant, thank you, but...

The LIEUTENANT *releases him but continues to stand on* HAZZITALL'S *foot.* HAZZITALL *recoils.*

You're still on my foot!

LIEUTENANT: *(Falsely apologetic.)* You're not feeling well.

The LIEUTENANT *gets off* HAZZITALL'S *foot.*

HAZZITALL: Ouch. You oaf.

LIEUTENANT: I understand. *(He won't elaborate.)* I'm a little nervous.

HAZZITALL: You, *nervous?* *(Pause.)* Maybe now we can get down to taking care of what's left of Pauline.

LIEUTENANT: I have some papers here. Statements to be signed. Here, take my fancy ink pen.

The LIEUTENANT *takes out his fancy fountain pen. Accidentally, ink squirts out of it and lands on one of* HAZZITALL'S *arms.* HAZZITALL *shrieks in pain.*

HAZZITALL: What have you done? Ow, ow—it's squirted all over my...

The LIEUTENANT *lets the papers drop to the floor.*

LIEUTENANT: Please let me help you.

The LIEUTENANT *bends down with a handkerchief to the wet floor. He quickly moistens the handkerchief. He rises and begins to dab at the ink on* HAZZITALL's *arm.*

LISA ARNY: Oh, don't use water on his arms, Lieutenant. It causes him pain.

HAZZITALL: *(Crying out in great alarm.)* Agony! Agony!

LIEUTENANT: You'd better come over here.

The LIEUTENANT *grabs* HAZZITALL's *wrist to guide him over to the massage table.*

HAZZITALL: Don't you understand? *(Howling.)* Hands off!

LISA ARNY: Lieutenant, he's very sensitive.

LIEUTENANT: I know. I'm very sensitive as well.

The LIEUTENANT *steps on a mop that has been resting against the massage table. The mop handle hits* HAZZITALL *in the head. It trails down across* HAZZITALL's *arm as it falls to the floor.*

Let me get that—

The LIEUTENANT *bends to pick up the fallen mop. As he picks it up, it swings around and knocks* HAZZITALL *to the wet floor.*

HAZZITALL: No. Ow. (HAZZITALL *starts hyperventilating.*) The pain. It's... it's...

LIEUTENANT: I must help you up on the table.

HAZZITALL *is in so much pain that he doesn't feel what is being done to him. The* LIEUTENANT *helps him up to the massage table.* HAZZITALL *lies on the table in shock.*

LISA ARNY: What should I do, Tom?

"Delirium" music begins.

HAZZITALL: Get a dry towel and wipe me off.

LISA ARNY: They might all be used up.

LISA ARNY goes into the corners of the room in search of a towel or dry cloth.

HAZZITALL: Oh, God, the pain. God, God, God.

As HAZZITALL says "God" repeatedly, Lights pointedly grow dimmer. "Delirium" music continues. HAZZITALL sinks into an altered state.

God, God, God, God. *(etc.)*

A light continues to shine on HAZZITALL. The LIEUTENANT is visible in the dim light. He snoops around the room. LISA ARNY approaches HAZZITALL with a dry towel in her hand. She dabs at the water that is on him. The ghost of PAULINE, barefoot, enters. She approaches HAZZITALL and appears to only him.

PAULINE: Many things die, but life is eternal.

HAZZITALL: Ow, ow, ow.

PAULINE: Wash your feet with water as you wait for the Lord.

HAZZITALL: *(Writhing.)* Are you crazy? I've already got too much water on my skin.

PAULINE: What you're experiencing is transitory.

HAZZITALL: I hope to Christ it is.

HAZZITALL continues in excruciating pain.

PAULINE: To Christ? You're not a believer.

HAZZITALL: At this point I believe in anything.

PAULINE: You really have to believe it. Or it doesn't count.

HAZZITALL: You're kicking me when I'm down, Pauline.

LISA ARNY: Tom, you're delirious.

PAULINE: With God as my witness, I reach out to you.

PAULINE *starts to reach out.*

HAZZITALL: Keep hands to yourself.

LISA ARNY: I'm only trying to help.

PAULINE: Don't fear death.

HAZZITALL: I don't fear death. I'm in agony.

PAULINE: You've had a thing about death.

HAZZITALL: About *Lisa's* death, yes. It has been a little rough. I was her husband.

LISA ARNY: You still are my husband.

PAULINE: But life is for the living. Court in session. All rise.

HAZZITALL: What?

PAULINE: You're going to be judged. The Final Judgment.

HAZZITALL: I'm not dead. I'm alive. I know because I'm still in horrible pain!

LISA ARNY: Settle down, Tom.

PAULINE: That's how you define life?

HAZZITALL: In my more uncomfortable moments.

PAULINE: Why do you say God only in anger or in pain? What do you believe?

HAZZITALL: I see the spirit in all things, not to mention the colors, especially green.

PAULINE: You'll have to do better than that.

HAZZITALL: The beauty and organization of the world is obviously beyond any rational understanding. You see, I'm not completely a doubting Thomas.

PAULINE: You're pathetic. Tom, come out of the eternal cold.

HAZZITALL: It's a burning sensation, Pauline. Sort of like your Hell.

PAULINE: How would you know since you're a... Pantheist, it seems? *(Pause.)* This isn't the Final Judgment. Look, admit that you've done wrong.

HAZZITALL: Ow. Yes, of course I've done wrong. Hasn't everybody? While we're at it, admit that as a citizen of this land I'm free to have my own beliefs.

PAULINE: It's sad, very sad. Lisa Number One didn't need to go jogging that evening. But you upset her so.

HAZZITALL: Don't you think I've thought of that?

PAULINE: You can cause a lot of pain, you know.

HAZZITALL: *(Rare admission.)* I do know.

PAULINE: What are you going to do? With your life, I mean—you got a second chance—Lisa, all over again. You're blowing it. *(Frustrated, concerned.)* I don't know why you got a second chance. God has a lottery or something. And you won.

Pauline *slowly exits to the wings.*

Hazzitall: *(Exasperated.)* Where are you going? God!

Lisa Arny: Tom, I'm right here.

Hazzitall: *(In pain.)* God. God. Oh. God. God. *(On the final "God's" he breathes a sigh, a release from the pain.)*

> *Lights progressively come back up on stage, to* Hazzitall's *"Gods". The "Delirium" music fades out.* Hazzitall *comes out of his altered state. He stops writhing on the massage table.*

Let me stand on my own two feet.

> *The* Lieutenant *approaches* Hazzitall.

Lisa Arny: Not yet. I'm not finished.

Hazzitall: Ow.

Lisa Arny: There, you can get up now if you want to.

Lieutenant: I'll help.

Hazzitall: Not on your life.

> *Relieved, yet exhausted,* Hazzitall *slowly gets off the table and onto his feet.*

Lisa Arny: I'll go upstairs and get your tincture of cortico-alcestis.

Hazzitall: And leave me down here with him? No. I'll get it myself. And don't either of you even think of helping me up those stairs.

> Hazzitall *ascends the staircase faster than one would normally expect. Once he has exited the* Lieutenant *speaks.*

LIEUTENANT: *(First clearing his throat.)* There is something that I have to tell you. You only.

LISA ARNY: What *is* it?

LIEUTENANT: It's a... ah... well... hard to...

LISA ARNY: Is it what you said was a surprise?

LIEUTENANT *is silent.*

LISA ARNY: Something about seeing the world differently now?

LIEUTENANT: Yes. I might as well spit it out. *(Blurts out:)* I've tried everything, to get you out of my mind. But it's no use, no use at all.

LISA ARNY: What?

The LIEUTENANT *gets down on one knee.*

LIEUTENANT: O Helen, Helen of Troy—the face that launched a thousand ships.

LISA ARNY: My name isn't Helen.

LIEUTENANT: I'm saying I love you.

LISA ARNY: But you don't even know me!

LIEUTENANT: *(Trying to prove her wrong.)* We have records on you going back only two years. *(He's discovered her identity.)* But I think I know who you are.

LISA ARNY: You do? You're in love with a vision.

LIEUTENANT: Aren't we all?

LISA ARNY: It's wiser to love a person. Ask my husband. As you may not have noticed, he's been struggling through that concept, Lieutenant.

LIEUTENANT: Call me Tiny-kins.

> HAZZITALL *appears at the top of the stairs. Behind him stands the ghost of* PAULINE, *dressed from head to toe in the vestments of the Intergalactic Pope. This ghost of* PAULINE *is not seen by any of the characters.* HAZZITALL *proceeds nobly down the stairs.* PAULINE *is solemn and follows at a careful close distance, as if ready to offer advice or service to him if he needs either. Upon stepping down from the bottom stair* HAZZITALL *speaks in a stately manner.*

HAZZITALL: Something's different about my medicine today. Has anyone tampered with my tincture?

LISA ARNY: Not that I know of.

HAZZITALL: So strange. Wonderful. I am resolved. Resolved, in earnest. I'm a changed man. I'm certain, fully certain, that life won't be lived in shambles. Pauline may be gone. Darkness *(He looks briefly at the* LIEUTENANT.) may lurk in the background, but...

LISA ARNY: You and I are going to take it easy for a few days.

HAZZITALL: Yes.

LISA ARNY: Lieutenant, would you pick up your papers and leave us?

LIEUTENANT: Pauline's remains need to be summarized.

LISA ARNY: *(Practically shooing him out.)* Do have a look on your way out. We'll sign the papers later at the station.

HAZZITALL: Yes, Lieutenant. Go to your job. Go do what you do best. There's no reason to be embarrassed for what's happened. *(In a normal, unstately manner, to* LISA ARNY.) What's happened?

LISA ARNY: *(To* HAZZITALL.*)* You've mentioned change. *(To the* LIEUTENANT.*)* Good-bye Lieutenant. Now be obedient.

LIEUTENANT: *(Crestfallen.)* Good-bye.

> *The* LIEUTENANT *walks up the stairs. He mumbles and throws a nasty look at* HAZZITALL *and says to him:*

Faker.

> *The* LIEUTENANT *sternly looks down towards the basement apartment. He then exits the house.* HAZZITALL *shudders. Though the solemn ghost of* PAULINE *is close by,* HAZZITALL *loosens up and begins to sound like his old self.*

HAZZITALL: Hmm. Pauline. It's going to be quiet not having her around. And potentially filthy. I pray that everything is well with her.

LISA ARNY: Pray?

HAZZITALL: In a manner of speaking. If there's a journey for her, I hope it's a happy one.

LISA ARNY: What kind of journey?

> HAZZITALL *does not elaborate. The sound of rain is heard.*

Oh, listen to that.

HAZZITALL: In our little desert. Let it rain! We can splash through it. *(Pause, to listen.)* Feeding the earth. Those little drops. Rivulets. Growing in our path. See them pushing through the gravel, leaving their fleeting signatures in the sand. Great water. A flood though, we don't want a flood, Noah's flood, on the rocks, flood—roof, door, carpet, flood.

LISA ARNY: Are you all right?

HAZZITALL: *(Expansively.)* Lisa, the world is wide. Too wide to know all. Somehow the shoulders of my hunchbacked mind have been straightened.

LISA ARNY: You're not all right.

HAZZITALL: I stand bolt upright. Nothing to gain but eternal salvation from my conversion.

LISA ARNY: Conversion? I'd better run and check your medicine.

HAZZITALL: It still gets me, though. Before you, came... came a lovely woman very much like you.

LISA ARNY: Yes, that's true.

HAZZITALL: Oh, no. The medicine's wearing off some. I'm wondering again.

LISA ARNY: Tom, don't feel bad about asking questions. I want you be just who you are. Everybody does.

HAZZITALL: Everybody? Who's everybody?

LISA ARNY: All of us.

HAZZITALL: Us? Now, who would "us" be? *(Pause.)* You're with *them*, aren't you?

LISA ARNY: Make sense, Tom. Make sense.

Pause.

HAZZITALL: You're not a space alien, are you?

More silence from LISA ARNY. *The doorbell rings.*

LISA ARNY: *(Flabbergasted.)* The Lieutenant, again!? Just because the rest of the world bows down to him, it doesn't mean we're going to.

HAZZITALL: We'll pretend we're not home.

LISA ARNY: He knows we're here.

HAZZITALL: He's got some excuse. They always do. An umbrella—he wants to borrow one. Well, he can't.

LISA ARNY: If Pauline were here—oh, Pauline! If she were here I'd have her answer the door. She'd find some way to deal with him.

The ghost of PAULINE *obligingly goes to the door and opens it.* CLAUDE, *a little wet, appears, carrying a parade-size American flag on a pole. It is mounted in a flag harness, with the holder down by his crotch.* MARIANNE, *also a little wet, wears a colorful blouse and coat made from pieces of another American flag.*

CLAUDE: It's some wind we're having, Marianne. Blew the door right open.

PAULINE steps aside as CLAUDE *comes rushing in with the flag.* MARIANNE *trails quickly behind him.*

Hello! Hello! Quite a storm out there.

HAZZITALL: *(To* LISA ARNY.*)* Claude? *(To* CLAUDE *upstairs.)* All your legal fees are paid. We're square. Marianne's been mailing them in. What's the problem?

CLAUDE: Oh, you're down there. Let me unholster my flag.

CLAUDE tries to take his flag out of his harness but it is stuck.

It's stuck. For a second. I'll get it. Since I'm out...

MARIANNE: He's on a furlough.

CLAUDE: ...I've come to pay my respects to your new wife. I know she isn't new to you anymore. It's been two years, my fellow American.

HAZZITALL: American?

> CLAUDE's *entire attention is on his crotch area where he is trying to disengage himself from the flagpole.*

MARIANNE: Claude hasn't given up his spiritual side. He and the director of the mental hospital, they're both on a patriotic kick. They think the U.S. gets a bum rap in the world. *(Pause.)* If he can't get the flag off, why don't you come up stairs? We'll have some coffee.

> HAZZITALL *and* LISA ARNY *go to the base of the stairs and look up to see* CLAUDE *and* MARIANNE.

HAZZITALL: We can't. I was just asking my wife a question. And the gas isn't hooked up.

> CLAUDE's *attentions are still at his crotch area. He yells without looking down the stairs.*

CLAUDE: I've heard she looks a lot like Lisa.

LISA ARNY: *(Still downstairs.)* Not only that, my name is Lisa.

HAZZITALL: Yes, Lisa.

LISA ARNY: *(To* HAZZITALL.*)* You didn't call me Lisa Arny—

HAZZITALL: I didn't, did I?

> CLAUDE *raises his head from the harness and flagpole and glimpses* LISA ARNY *downstairs.* CLAUDE *is shocked at the resemblance of* LISA ARNY *to* LISA.

CLAUDE: Oh, my God! This is unbelievable.

> CLAUDE, *amazed at the appearance of* LISA ARNY, *loses control of himself. His legs wobble and the flagpole almost hits* PAULINE. *The flagpole scraps against the door or the floor;* CLAUDE *loses his balance and he*

tumbles down the stairs into the basement apartment. MARIANNE *runs down the stairs to help him up.*

HAZZITALL: I beg your pardon, but what brings you here?

CLAUDE: I told you. She was my most prized employee.

HAZZITALL: Who?

CLAUDE: Your wife. As any good red-blooded American business-man I want to demonstrate that I value my employee's hard work. Even if she is no longer with us. Therefore, I've come to honor her.

HAZZITALL: But she quit your company before she died.

CLAUDE: She took a leave of absence.

HAZZITALL: She wasn't working... at your *card* company.

CLAUDE: All right, that does it. We'll step outside.

HAZZITALL: I'm not going anywhere.

CLAUDE: Then we'll fight right here.

HAZZITALL: Now, now, getting in trouble the minute you're released only gives strength to the argument that we're soft on our criminals.

CLAUDE: That really does it.

HAZZITALL: Shouldn't peace be the goal of all *Americans?*

MARIANNE: Tom, I think we got him into the wrong place. He was actually more together before he went into the hospital.

CLAUDE *is up on his feet now, totally in control of his flag. He deftly rolls the flag around the pole. He starts tapping* HAZZITALL *with the pole, then he takes a few light jabs at him.* HAZZITALL *picks up the mop to defend himself.*

HAZZITALL: Now, stop that.

CLAUDE continues to talk as he "fences" with HAZZITALL.

CLAUDE: It shouldn't matter what anybody does for a business just as it shouldn't matter if a Lisa is a Lisa or a Lisa. The important thing is to love this country like a newly arrived alien. And never let your bloodline's pride decay.

MARIANNE: Claude, you're going to hurt yourself and somebody else, too.

CLAUDE: I've made mistakes. But this glorious land is a land where you get even a third or fourth chance in life. Some people use up their mistakes. It never occurs to them that they have fabulous opportunities here for failure over and over again. *(To HAZZITALL.)* You spit on our nation's Pursuit of Happiness.

HAZZITALL: How?

CLAUDE: You have a lack of appreciation. That's your one big mistake.

HAZZITALL: Really?

CLAUDE: You godless, countryless, good-for-nothing!

HAZZITALL: I was good enough to get you transferred into a mental hospital.

LISA ARNY: Claude, you're talking about my husband.

CLAUDE: *(To LISA ARNY.)* I'm sorry, but you're not the woman you once were. *(Changes his mind.)* I didn't mean that. *(To HAZZITALL.)* I never liked you either. Imagine how humiliating it was for me to have to ask you to become my savior.

CLAUDE continues to "fence" with HAZZITALL.

LISA ARNY: Now, boys. *(To* CLAUDE.*)* If you won't listen to me, for Lisa's sake, please stop this.

CLAUDE: No, sorry. There's no other way I can win you, Lisa.

He starts to sob, he stops "fencing" with HAZZITALL, *his flag unravels. Once the flag unravels,* CLAUDE *wraps himself up in it, he falls to the floor in great emotional distress.*

(He voices the word with anguish.) Lisa. He was right, Marianne. Partly right. I did want an affair with Lisa, but Lisa wouldn't have me. *(Sobbing.)* What am I going to do? I'm such a mess.

MARIANNE: *(Calming him down.)* I think it was a little too early to release you, Claude.

CLAUDE: I know.

MARIANNE: The intentions were good. We'll have you back there in no time.

CLAUDE *weeps. Then he looks at* LISA ARNY.

CLAUDE: *(To* LISA ARNY.*)* Why him?

LISA ARNY: Marianne, you help Claude up the stairs.

MARIANNE: *(To* CLAUDE.*)* You can settle into your soft cotton straightjacket, Claude.

MARIANNE *bundles* CLAUDE *up the stairs. They exit past the front door.*

HAZZITALL: God knows why I ever kept him as a client. I suppose I did it for Lisa. But now, I've got you. You're not going anywhere. No one's going to bust in upstairs, a least for a minute. Humor me, okay? Before we were interrupted, I asked you... if you were a space alien.

LISA ARNY: It's absurd, isn't it?

HAZZITALL: Unreasonable, yes.

LISA ARNY: Still you want to know, though? Why bring more stress into your life? And your medicine, it's had unusual side effects lately.

HAZZITALL: Just for sport, tell me. Let's not blame the medicine.

LISA ARNY: When you first met me you said you wanted mystery in the woman that you would love.

HAZZITALL: I never said that to you. I said that to my first Lisa.

LISA ARNY: Those were very romantic times.

HAZZITALL: And how would you know?

LISA ARNY: Tom, you got what you wanted. But where was your follow through? You let what you wanted die. Then, the long nightmare over it all. Well, it had to be that way. For you to learn.
   It wouldn't be smart for me to answer your question about me. Do you really want to risk so much between us?
   (*Pause.*) You drove your wife crazy by not paying attention to her. Couldn't you see she was only naturally reaching out, in a barren desert, to the people nearest, for friends and company? You made fun of her interest in the paranormal. To her a séance was a pastime, barely believable, but you made her feel like an ass. She was beautiful. You didn't do anything about it except be jealous.
   You had it all: beauty, mystery. You frittered it away. It's not a wife's duty to sit around and radiate charm. You have to put something into a relationship for it to flower throughout the seasons. Oh, but you found it easier to indulge in work. And we think Claude has problems, you're not immune. Oh, and you blamed your illness for anything you did wrong.

HAZZITALL: I'm sorry. I won't do that again. And I won't question you anymore about whether or not you're a you-know-what.

LISA ARNY: *(To the audience.)* Look, I'm not advocating that relationships get organized along the lines of one person, usually female, having all the beauty and mystery. And the other person earning most of the money. Everything should be done on a case-by-case basis. As there is enshrined in our Constitution tolerance for different religious beliefs, there should be tolerance for different types of relationships between lovers.

Frankly, I think the kind of marriage that Tom's been involved in is old-hat. Maybe it was the Conservative era that encouraged him. They had a *maid?* They didn't even have kids yet! But obviously the whole set-up here smacks of some elaborate joke created to show that Tom was neglecting not just his wife, but also the spiritual, irrational side of his *life*. So you see, dear Tom is not undeserving of all the trouble he got. I'm sorry to see that characters had to be killed to prove a point. At least no real blood was spilled.

Ah, how men are slow to change. Sometimes we can feel sorry for them. *(To* HAZZITALL.*)* So what are we going to do?

HAZZITALL: For starters I would like a light, festive atmosphere. If it's not too much to ask. It's been way too heavy around here.

LISA ARNY: Agreed.

HAZZITALL: But still, we do have a slight mess on our hands.

Music starts.

(Song #12: "Fire and Water")

LISA ARNY: *(Sings.)*
> Fire, there's so much water in sight,
> Fire and water.

(Spoken.) Tom, this place is such a fright.

(Sings.)
> Shouldn't try to do ev'rything alone
> When you can get someone to help you.

LISA ARNY: *(Continues singing.)*
>Why would you ever want to do it alone
>When someone's out there looking for a home,
>When someone's out there looking for a home.
>
>Think, we could leave this room for someone else.

MARIANNE, CLAUDE, *and the* LIEUTENANT *enter and come down the stairs. They hold sponge mops upside down, against their shoulders.* CLAUDE's *mop has a little American flag dangling from it. These three are led by* PAULINE.

>Shouldn't try to do ev'rything at once—
>Brother that puts you in one big bind.
>Shouldn't try to do the impossible
>When there's so much that's possible.

The CHORUS *consists of the characters* MARIANNE, CLAUDE *and the* LIEUTENANT.

CHORUS: *(Sings.)*
>We will sing to cheer the weary trav'ler,
>The weary trav'ler upon this globe.
>And if the trav'ler doesn't want to hear us
>We will sing, sing, sing anyway.

HAZZITALL: *(Exasperated, speaks:)* Mop now, sing more later.

Instead of speaking in tongues, the CHORUS *apparently sings in tongues:.*

CHORUS: *(Sings.)*
>You-ee-lye, he lye, heel lye.
>Heel lye, he rye he rye.
>
>Choose the in, the out you will not find.
>You should get someone to help you.
>Surrender to the roller coaster ride,
>Ride, we say, ride, we say, ride, we say ride.

HAZZITALL *joins in, singing for the first time.*

CHORUS, LISA ARNY and HAZZITALL: *(Sing.)*
   Moan, member, moan.
   Moan, member, moan, member
   Moan, member, home.

The song ends but music continues.

HAZZITALL: *(To the others, spoken.)* All right, friends.

HAZZITALL *manages a smile to the others.*

Lights out. End of the scene.

End of Act II

End of the Play.

READ TO ME

a one-act play

Remembering O. Henry
(William Sidney Porter, 1867-1910)

Characters

JOHN   Male. 30s-40s.

BARBARA   Female, 20s.

Place: In a city.
Time: Present.

Notes

The minimal and non-naturalistic set of the play help with the simple storytelling aspects of *Read to Me*. With little effort John turns from talking with the audience to being in the scene with Barbara. Barbara at first appears to be a character type more than a character—even though she pointedly does not speak in slang. She is after all a worker, on the job, wanting to satisfy her customer. However the orphic power of music slams her and she cannot help but be herself. Partly I see John as the traveler/wanderer figure we see in noh plays who discovers a situation that both provokes contemplation and radiates beauty. What better way to hope for beauty than to borrow an excerpt of beautiful writing from François René de Chateaubriand—from his *René?* I use a translation of Chateaubriand, but it still works well. Thanks for permission to quote goes to the University of California Press. They publish F.R. Chateaubriand, *Atala and René*, edited/translated by Irving Putter, copyright 1952, The Regents of the University of California.

Read to Me was first presented in a reading by Matt Pepper and Kristin Geber at the Rocky Mountain Book Fair, Denver, Colorado, on March 4, 2001.

Read to Me

Street noise. Sounds of cars and a few peoples' voices. The scene is an imaginary street: no stage representation of a street is necessary. We also see a coat rack on stage.

Lights up. JOHN *walks along the street. He wears an overcoat. He carries a book. The street noise fades out.* JOHN *stops and turns to the audience.*

JOHN: I'd asked a few people to read to me. But they had no time. Certainly I could read to myself, and I do, often.

In my opinion, the skill of reading is often wasted. But don't get me wrong. I didn't want those people I knew to read to me in order to prove how wonderful reading is to them and the world. I'm more selfish than that. I have my own pleasure in mind.

I wasn't looking for someone to read to me on a regular basis. Though I admit I was thinking of tape-recording somebody reading to me so that in the future I might be able to relive the experience, if I ever really could relive the experience.

Obviously it wasn't because of a lack of education that my people could not read to me. They simply wouldn't. I wondered if any of these people had missed being psychologically imprinted, as a child, with the pleasurable sensations produced by being read to. Did they never revel in having a story or poem read to them? Have too many things intruded into their lives to cause them to forget this delight? Does becoming an adult mean that such a thrill must never be sought again? I suppose because one learns to read as a child that many people take it to mean that they no longer have to be read to. Is this part of what it means in our society to became an individual: we now can read for ourselves, and nobody has to read to us anymore?

Pause.

JOHN: (*Continued.*) Does school really want to prepare us only to read stuff that'll get us a job, and help us hang onto that job? The literature we're destined for is material on business, money and machines. And office procedures. This is not reading. I don't know what it is except it's something geared for the robot in you.

JOHN *goes over to the coat rack. He takes off his coat while still holding on to the book he has in his hand.*

Well, I became desperate to hear somebody else read. I needed a person reading to me.

Street sounds fade up. The volume of these sounds is softer than before.

Barbara, as she called herself, was a prostitute who was standing on the corner of X Street and Y Street. Forgive me for not mentioning the real name of these streets, but the real names aren't important. I will tell you however that I was staying nearby in a hotel called "The Visitors'". I can also tell you I was actually born in the city where The Visitors is located. As is often the case nowadays, I was born in this city but grew up entirely somewhere else. For the record, I have no relatives or friends in this city. As far as I am concerned, this town could be any town, anywhere.

Now "The Visitors'" hotel was fairly cheap. This was important. I was just starting to travel a lot and was on a limited budget. A number of the rooms in the hotel were dirty. In fact, I saw three before I settled on one I thought was okay. No telephone was in the room. This would influence how I'd find the prostitute. I was in fact forced to the

streets to get my girl. I actually preferred this method as opposed to the blind-date set-up that would be the case in an arrangement made by telephone.

Being that "The Visitors" was shabby, and in the central part of the city, it comes as no surprise that two blocks away, prostitutes could be found. Certainly the more expensive prostitutes didn't work on the street. I'd have to be fairly lucky if I was going to get what I wanted where I was looking. The prostitutes' exaggerated way of dressing up wasn't particularly sexy but it did serve to identify them in their trade. Barbara looked a little classier than the rest. I wondered why she was making herself available this way, instead of by phone. I never found out.

I guess I was lucky: here she was. Here for the clients, those faceless motorists in from the traffic. Here for those who'd take her for their satisfaction. This purportedly took place about seven blocks away in an empty parking lot.

The street sounds fade out. Upbeat music fades in as JOHN *continues.*

Barbara: almost knee-high white boots, a red mini-skirt, a tight black sweater, and actually, a young and tender-looking face. I was pretty sure as soon as the hotel clerk set eyes on her he'd tell her to leave. Though the hotel had notions regarding noise limits, dust, smells and bed-quality that were not obvious to me, most certainly they'd have a policy towards prostitutes. This'd be rooted in the hotel wanting to have as few headaches with the public—and police —as possible.

I approached Barbara. It was no surprise to find out that she could read, but still I was relieved. I haggled with her over her price. Afterward, I realized that she'd only led me to believe I'd been haggling. Barbara had her set prices based on time and exactly what she did. She thought I was some kind of freak. But I wasn't too dangerous or she wouldn't have taken my money. By a stroke of great fortune when we got the hotel lobby the clerk was busy in an adjoining room. Though he heard a bell jingle when we entered the old heavy door, he didn't come out right away. I quickly got Barbara out of the lobby and up the stairs. As we moved down the hall, the thought occurred to me that she'd been in The Visitors' before. Well, I didn't ask her, that's for sure. Getting her through the door seemed to me to be my greatest accomplishment of the past month. *(Pause.)*

The upbeat music ends. BARBARA *enters and stands comfortably, at ease. A purse is on her shoulder.*

JOHN: (*Continued.*) Now, what would I have her read to me? I men-tally rubbed my hands together in anticipation. Certain pieces of lit-erature flashed across my mind. Would she be interested in any of them? Probably not. Would she feel any connection to them? I doubt it. But they were favorites of mine. I would enjoy listening to them. Could I really find pleasure in the various English pieces I was think-ing of—in the setting of this drab hotel? Well, I tried hard not to get ahead of myself. I knew the pieces I had in mind had music to them. I assured myself that this music in the literature would blast thor-ough any disagreeable setting.

Lights come up on a portion of the stage previously not lit up. The scene is a room. There is a bed, a chair, a suitcase, a dresser or table with a radio/CD player on it. Alternatively, a curtain can open to reveal this room.

I looked at Barbara's face as she glanced over the room. I didn't want whatever she read to me to somehow be a negative comment on our situation. I didn't want her reading something that'd cause her to make any deep associations between it and her own life—of which I knew nothing. I didn't want to surprise her with intimacy— because, after all prostitutes have feelings, and it seems to me there's an unwritten code between prostitute and john. One should steer clear of arousing at least the feelings of the prostitute. Having said that though, I didn't want Barbara to read something to me that was so fabulously detached from emotional life that it would have all the sensuality of a VCR owner's manual. I also had another problem: I couldn't choose something that'd make my hotel room sound like a classroom. I can hear what she'd say now.

BARBARA: I hated school.

JOHN: This'd mean I would not have her read to me Andrew Marvell's poem, "To His Coy Mistress" with its marvelous "But at my back I always hear/ Time's wingèd chariot hurrying near". Nor would I be able to have her read me the divine "John Barleycorn Must Die" by Robert Burns. She might not get the point of it, and for sure, she'd stumble over the Scottish bits. Certainly it would mean that sections from the "Second Shepherd's Play" were completely out of the question: Ah, she'd never know the delight of hearing that

JOHN: *(Continued.)* three medieval English shepherds could time-travel to Roman-era Bethlehem in order to pay their respects to the baby Jesus.

Thinking in more modern realistic terms, it did cross my mind that perhaps I should have her read to me O. Henry's "The Furnished Room," Mostly because it is a fist of a story, clutching a great passion, and boy do I love to hear this sort of tale. I've always believed the great passion of this story is not necessarily the young man's passion for one Eloise Vashner, as the author himself would have us believe. Instead I think the great passion is the O. Henry's passion for art. Those descriptions of the hallway of the rooming house—those are not descriptions invented by some skilled commercial writer. They are depressing particulars lived daily by the highly sensitive O. Henry himself, in pursuit of his art. And the theme of the lovers' separate suicides...it all makes me think of Vincent Van Gogh, and that painting of his, of his bedroom at Arles.

No, it wasn't a good idea to read that story. Not here.

Well, I decided on something from not even the English or American world, but from the French. Wouldn't it be wonderful to hear some of Chateaubriand's "René", I thought. The story'd take us to several outdoor locales in the 18th century, including along the banks of the Mississippi, and on the Atlantic seacoast of France, where Amelia's convent was located.

I'd only had the chance to read the story once before and was impressed.

(To BARBARA:*)* Here's the money. *(He gives her the sum of money they apparently agreed on. She puts it in her purse.)* Please, sit down.

BARBARA: Okay. *(She sits down in the chair.)*

JOHN: I've got a book here. I've made up my mind what we're going to do.

BARBARA: Whatever you want, lover.

JOHN: Oh, is that what you call people like me?

BARBARA: It's what you call a boyfriend, isn't it?

JOHN: I'd like us to take our time.

BARBARA: You got the money, I've got the time.

JOHN: All right.

BARBARA: That means when you take more time, it costs more money.

JOHN: I'm on your ...wavelength.

She stands up.

BARBARA: What do you want me to take off first?

She places her hand on her breast and moves her hand around in a circular motion.

JOHN: Nothing.

She looks over and sees his radio/CD player.

BARBARA: So you're a slow one. You want me to strip to music?

JOHN: I did tell you that you were only going to have to read to me.

BARBARA: Yeah, what's it going to be, lover? *(She runs her tongue over her lip.)*

JOHN: None of that.

BARBARA: Whatever you say.

JOHN: Well, here it is.

He gets the book out of his suitcase and gives it to her.

BARBARA: Thanks, lover.

JOHN: You don't have to call me that.

She has the book in her hand. With her thumb, she flicks through all of the pages in about three seconds.

JOHN: Excuse me, I'm going to lie down on the bed.

BARBARA: You want me to lay down with you?

JOHN: No, I want you to sit right in that chair. I don't think your standing up and reading will be the best. What I want you to read is the part that's called "René." Can you find it?

BARBARA: Well, we'll just see. *(She looks in the table of contents and finds where "René" is.)* Got it.

JOHN: Good.

From her shoulder she takes off her purse and puts it on the dresser or table.

BARBARA: *(After a pause.)* Okay. You're kidding me. You're trying to have a laugh at a working girl.

JOHN: I suppose you do get abused from time to time.

BARBARA: Hey, that's out of line, okay?

JOHN: You're right. Sorry. You have your rules. Makes sense.

Pause.

BARBARA: Do you want me to get down on my knees? And come over to you?

JOHN: Actually, no.

Pause. She thinks.

BARBARA: You are kidding me, aren't you?

JOHN: What makes you think I'm joking?

BARBARA: Okay, let's get going. I'm ready for almost anything.

JOHN: *(Sarcastically.)* Well, you don't have to sound so excited about this.

BARBARA: You're the boss.

JOHN: Just relax, okay? I really just want you to read the story to me. And you don't have to play my mother, or my sister, or a babysitter—you know what I mean.

BARBARA: Okay.

JOHN: Just start reading "René" from the top.

BARBARA: Gotcha.

> *She begins to read. She is not bad or hopeless, just not very good at the task. Sometimes she runs through sentences and over periods in the text. More than once she protects herself from making mistakes by an almost staccato reading; or she attacks a section with a rhythm or mood that is inappropriate for that section. Of course there are pauses for mistakes and corrections, some of which are suggested in the text below. Once in a while she gets through a sequence of sentences all right and is almost pleased with herself.*

BARBARA: *(Reads.)* "On arriving among the Natchez René was obliged to take a wife in order to confirm (BARBARA's *mistake.*)... to conform to the Indian customs; but he did not live with her. His melancholy nature drew him constantly away into the depths of the woods. There he would spend entire days in solitude, a savage among the savages. Aside from...Chactas, his foster sa *(Another mistake.)*... father, and Father Souël, a missionary at Fort Rosalie, he had given up all fellowship with men. These two elders had acquired a powerful influence upon his heart, Chactas, through his kindly indulgence, and Father Souël, on the contrary, through his extreme severity. Since the beaver hunt, when the blind sachem... Sachem?"

JOHN *nods "yes".*

JOHN: It means Indian chief.

BARBARA: "...sachem had told his adventures to René, the young man had constantly *(A mistake.)*... consistently refused to talk about his own. And yet both Chactas and the missionary keenly desired to know what sorrow had driven this well-born European to the strange decision of retiring into the wildernesses of Louisiana. René had always claimed that he would not tell his story because it was too insignificant, limited as it was to his thoughts and feelings. "As for the circumstance... circumstances... *(She reads again, she was right the first time.)* circumstance which induced me to leave for America," he added, "that must forever be buried in oblivion."

Thus several years went by, and the two elders were unable to draw his secret from him. One day, however... *(She loses her place and starts further down in the text.)* ...on the twenty-first day of the month the Indians call the "moon of flowers," René went to the cabin of Chactas. Giving his arm to the sachem, he led him to a spot under a sassafras tree on the bank of the... Meschacebe?"

JOHN: It's another Indian word for the Mississippi. Can you give me the book, please? I'll read some. *(She gives him the book.)* A really good part comes after that. It's when he starts to open his heart to them.

(Reads eloquently.) "Sometimes we strolled in silence hearkening to the muffled rumbling of the autumn or the crackling of the dry leaves trailing sadly under our feet. In our innocent games we ran after the swallow in the meadows or the rainbow on the storm-swept hills. At other times we would whisper poetry inspired in us by the spectacle of nature. In my youth I courted the Muses. Nothing is more poetic than a heart of sixteen in all the pristine freshness of its passions. The morning of life is like the morning of the day, pure, picturesque, and harmonious."

Pause.

Here, maybe you can try again. Start where I left off.

He gives her back the book and points to where he left off. She finds her place and begins to read:

BARBARA: "On Sundays and holidays I often stood in the deep woods as the sound of the distant bell drifted through the trees, calling from the temple... of the man... *(A mistake.)*... to the man... of the fields. Leaning against the trunk of an elm, I would listen in rapt silence to the devout tolling. Each tremor of the resounding bronze would waft... *(This has been pronounced as "whaaft". Then she pronounces the word as wäft—"a" as in the word "after".)* waft... *(She then quickly goes back to pronounces it as she did originally.)* ...waft... into my guileless soul the innocence of country ways, the calm of solitude, the beauty of religion, and the cherished melancholy of memories out of my early childhood..."

JOHN: Okay, that's enough. I'm sorry. It's not working. *(Pause.)* Let me think. Stay there. *(He reaches over and turns on some music on his CD player. Though repetitive, the music is soft and cuts right to our hearts. He then says to himself:)* What do I do now? *(Looking up to the ceiling.)* It's not working!

BARBARA's *cool exterior is melted by the soft pleasant music. All of a sudden, she starts to tear up.*

JOHN: I'm sorry.

BARBARA: For what?

JOHN: For being so harsh about how you were reading.

BARBARA: You were right about it.

JOHN: I could've been a little more... diplomatic.

She cries softly.

You don't have to cry.

BARBARA: I'm not crying about you criticizing me.

JOHN: Oh.

BARBARA *sits down and continues to weep.*

I guess you should just let it flow. I mean, sometimes that's what we need, a good cry.

BARBARA: *(Pause.)* Yeah, like you know. My make-up's running.

She gets her compact out of her purse and looks at herself and tries to erase some of the damage.

JOHN: I don't cry much myself. Not in that way. In my own way, though.

BARBARA: Like there's other way?

JOHN: Oh, I mean something like "crying inside."

BARBARA: Men are like that. Look I won't charge you for the time now. I don't know what's happening to me.

JOHN: It was a beautiful story, wasn't it?

BARBARA: It was all right.

JOHN: What we heard of it anyway.

She cries.

I'm sorry I said that.

Pause.

I like the music.

BARBARA: I want you to turn it off. But then I don't.

JOHN: It's calming. But also it sometimes makes me a little depressed. I wonder why that is? (*Pause.*) I shouldn't have said that either. (*Pause.*) Look we'll just wait here a few minutes. Let the music play. I thought this would turn out... differently. I didn't realize that I might be so particular about how it was read.

BARBARA *gets up, walks away from* JOHN *and the scene. She addresses the audience:*

BARBARA: I need a rest. I'm supposed to be free.

Before, when I worked in those offices—I wasn't working as a whore, but I was still a whore. Every job I had before this was more degrading than what I go through now. They took my time, my soul. The stupid things they made me do! God, I was just dirt to them!

The bosses, they made a hundred times more than me. Finally in the last job, they didn't want to give me a forty-cent raise. So I quit. I couldn't live on what they paid anyway. In this city, forget it. And with a three-year old kid, double forget it.

Pause.

Well, you're not going to get from me some speech in dialect like: (*She speaks in some kind of dialect.*) "last night, in some alley, Maury and Nicolette came by with some crack cocaine and some brandy in a bottle with a brown paper bag wrapped around it..." That's not me. How could I hang on to my daughter if I was like that?

Pause.

I guess I was crying because I'm tired and the story made things a little out of control—and the music, yeah it was the music. Now I'm all together in a strange way. Miles away. Away from being hassled by the pimps. Pimps. You name the business, they're in it.

She now goes back to being in the scene with JOHN. *She is not crying, but she is still upset.*

JOHN: I should turn this off. It'll make you more like the Vikings.

He turns off the music.

BARBARA: What?

JOHN: Vikings. The Viking raiders. From Norway. They were strong.

BARBARA: What the hell are you talking about?

JOHN: They were strong because they didn't have the kind of music I have. *(Pause.)* I guess they weren't always *that* strong. They couldn't have been every time. Picture how it must have been for them. For some of them, sometimes: They're big galoots, these Vikings... They're sacking some town. It's 1000 A.D. They have to approach the town carefully in the moonlight. But they're bumping into trees on the way into the village. You know why they're bumping into trees? And even bumping into each other? It's not a full moon, but it's a pretty decent moon for marauding. You've got Vafthrudnor knocking into Thorolf. Styrbjorn the Grey bouncing off Halfdan the Black. Ulfhedin Ketilsson's just about ready to punch Grim Geitskor right in the nose, because he stepped on his foot which is very sensitive from the last campaign. Why is this happening? Why can't they stay in some kind of formation on their way into the attack zone?

BARBARA: I don't know.

JOHN: It's because they need eyeglasses. It's 1000 A.D. and eyeglasses have not been invented yet.

BARBARA: Are you trying to make me laugh?

JOHN: It's just a story. The Vikings had eye problems too.

BARBARA: There's nothing wrong with my eyes.

JOHN: Whatever you say.

BARBARA: I was crying. I've stopped now.

JOHN: At least we didn't get to the incest theme of the story. I mean, with the René, not the Vikings. (BARBARA *just looks at him, not sure what he's trying to say.*) Actually I don't know what I'm taking about. I shouldn't be trying to be wry about incest. I know in your business...

BARBARA: ..."the hookers have been victims of incest."

JOHN: That's not what I mean to say.

BARBARA: Then what did you mean?

JOHN: Look, I wasn't thinking.

BARBARA: Yeah, and you said you wanted to think.

JOHN: You could read again. I could coach you. Maybe you'd get the hang of it.

BARBARA: *(The cool exterior starts to form again.)* Whatever the customer wants.

JOHN: I'm sure it's not *whatever* the customer wants.

BARBARA: *Almost* whatever he wants, lover.

JOHN: Let's just sit here for a minute, okay? It's nice to have you around, Barbara—it doesn't matter if that's really your name. You know, I don't have much money. But it doesn't matter. I've got my books. They're the crown jewels to me. The story we were reading—well... it's pretty amazing to be able to go the banks of the Mississippi and sit there with an old Indian chief, even if I don't like the gruff Catholic priest with him. 'Cause there's other things there—like the poetry. And there's this, well it's an interesting tactic—you see, René at first doesn't want to confess what went on. He stalls by describing the trees, the bushes, his childhood—anything he can describe—in order not to get to the part that you and me never got to... which is actually not the best part because it seems so contrived. Because it's all about his sister longing for him. Incest was a fashionable theme in those days.

JOHN: *(Continued.)* You must think I'm silly telling you I've got the crown jewels. I'm sure you've had rich men that love to brag about how rich they are. I'm not bragging. The price I pay for reading is well beyond the price you see on the back of a book.

Long pause.

BARBARA: I'll be going?

Pause.

JOHN: Yeah.

She takes up her compact again and looks at herself in its mirror. She repairs some of the damage to her make-up. After this she says:

BARBARA: Well, take it easy.

JOHN: You too. (BARBARA *gathers up her purse and leaves.* JOHN *is alone.*) Now, where were we?

He picks up the book and begins to read:

"...and the cherished melancholy of memories out of my early childhood! Oh! What churlish heart has never started at the sound of the bells in his birthplace, those bells which trembled with joy over his cradle, which rang out the dawn of his life, which signaled his first heartbeat, announcing to all surrounding places the reverent gladness of his father, the ineffable anguish and supreme joy of his mother! All is embraced in that magical reverie which engulfs us at the sound of our native bell—faith, family, homeland, the cradle and the grave, the past and the future."

He sets the book down and walks off stage. We hear a church bell sound perhaps six or seven times. There is silence. The lights fade to black. The upbeat music fades up for the curtain call.

End of Play.

BETSY PHILADELPHIA

a one-act play

Characters

LASKO   *Female or Male. 30s to 50s.*

EDDIE   *Male, 20s or 30s.*

DENISE/BETSY *Female. 20s-30s.*

Scenes: (Philadelphia) donut shop, a police station; neutral stage.
Time: November-December 2000.

Notes

   One purpose of *Betsy Philadelphia* is to document, for the future, some of the feelings people had during the recent presidential election. Obviously this is a partisan play. No attempt has been made to give equal time or be "fair" to the George W. Bush camp. Such fairness would destroy what I'm trying to do. Did Bernard Shaw try to be fair to those whom he thought were a danger to the world?

   The play's first two scenes are fairly realistic, and full of talk of politics. As the play progresses, it goes more into Genet- and Aristophanes-like territory. For the Hand, I am indebted to a nineteenth century French puppet play. *Betsy Philadelphia* was first presented in a Moving Parts reading on March 25, 2001 in Paris by Bill Dunn, Mike Morris and Lori Lamb. The play is dedicated to Yvonne Shafer.

Betsy Philadelphia

Scene 1

A counter in a donut shop. Three members of the Philadelphia Police, in uniform. Lights up. LASKO *stands separate from the scene.* EDDIE *and* DENISE *are seated, coffee and donuts are on the counter in front of them.* DENISE *has a southern accent, not thick.*

LASKO: There's a slogan that the managers of Philadelphia have come up with, to promote our fine city to tourists and residents alike. The slogan is: "Philadelphia—the place that loves you back." More about that later. There could be another slogan for the city, something like, "Philadelphia—the place where politics have never been a small matter." That's not so catchy-sounding, I admit.

So here we are in Philadelphia. At a time when American democracy is hard at work. Two members of the Philadelphia police department patrol are on a break now. We're not surprised to find them in a donut shop. I give you Eddie, and Denise.

LASKO *exits.*

EDDIE: *(To* DENISE.) There's plenty of reason to be upset. If Bush wins then he gets to appoint three Supreme Court justices. You, as a woman, should be concerned about that, because if Bush gets in, abortion may be illegal again.

DENISE: I'm not sure abortion should be legal.

EDDIE: How can a Republican government logically outlaw abortion? Bush's party is for the government staying out of citizens' lives. Isn't the abortion situation sheer hypocrisy?

DENISE: No, it's different.

EDDIE: Oh, it's different. Bush doesn't follow through with the logical conclusions of his arguments. Because they run counter to his emotions.

DENISE: It's important to have a heart, Eddie. That's why Bush is talking about compassionate conservatism.

EDDIE: He wasn't so compassionate *before* he was in public life. Remember what "Talk" magazine says. Bush cheated that rancher in Texas to get that land for his baseball stadium's parking lot. And the rancher finally beat Bush in court and got an award of three and a half million dollars.

DENISE: That magazine's run by liberals.

EDDIE: Yeah, sure. They all are. The compassionate stuff is plain garbage. The first thing he wants to do when he gets in office is give a tax cut to the rich. That's what we need, a larger gap between the rich and the poor in this country.

DENISE: The tax cut's for everybody.

EDDIE: The only people it makes any real difference to is the rich. Meanwhile a program like Headstart for children can't find funding. It makes me sick.

DENISE: Don't get upset.

EDDIE: No? Bush moves to the center and takes over Gore's policies. He says anything to get elected. I wish people would listen to where he was last month, and the month before, when he said he's born-again, that he no longer drinks and that all his past wrongs are somehow erased from the record on account of his relationship with God.

DENISE: That's what God does.

EDDIE: And when he said, "I'm running for President because I want to help usher in the responsibility era, where people understand they are responsible for the choices they make and are held accountable for their actions." What a snowjob. He's great at not being held accountable himself. How he stopped people from thinking about his earlier use of cocaine seems to be the greatest political achievement of his life.

DENISE: Everybody makes mistakes, Eddie.

EDDIE: Some get caught and some don't. Think about the four million people in this country who've been caught with drugs and now they can't vote because they've been convicted of a felony. If Bush had been caught he wouldn't be allowed to vote, let alone run for president.

DENISE: None of his drug use has been proven.

EDDIE: Exactly. *(He drinks from his coffee.)* I like when he says he'll bring all opposing sides together, to make one effective government. He says he's good at that. But how's he going to do that? The real George W. Bush takes extreme positions on the issues.

DENISE: Well, he's not so extreme. If he is...

EDDIE: So you admit it. Listen, Denise. He's arrogant. He knows what's best for us. He's part of the group that always knows what's best for us. But what happens to be good for us also happens to be best for his rich cronies. That's why he wants to reward them immediately with a tax cut. You know what Gore's first act as president will be? To enact campaign finance reform. So the rich can't play such a big part in choosing the president.

DENISE: Not all rich people are voting for Bush.

EDDIE: Thank God.

DENISE: People, not dollars, elect the president.

EDDIE: You are sadly mistaken.

DENISE: We don't need our government funding our elections for us. If we're for a candidate, we should be able to donate our money to them. Campaign finance reform, it's another excuse for big government. There's no reason why the government should be expanded, like Gore wants it to be.

EDDIE: Gore doesn't want to expand the government!

DENISE: New programs, that's what he says. He and Clinton very carefully try and hide that kind of thing.

EDDIE: Our government now is the smallest government in 30 years. The Democrats are only trying to make sure the Republicans don't do things like siphon money away from the public school system. Did you go to public school?

DENISE: Of course.

EDDIE: Don't look for your old school to be alive if Bush gets in.

DENISE: You're exaggerating.

EDDIE: We have a big country. We can't have a tiny government. And the *government* pays people like you and me to do a service to the community.

DENISE: They don't pay enough.

EDDIE: That's one thing we can agree on. You almost need to get a second job in our "profession." *(Pause.)* Do you think you'll ever moonlight?

DENISE: I have enough to do.

EDDIE: I might have to take something sooner or later.

No, I can't believe anything the Republicans say. They complain about government waste and they waste forty million dollars on trying to bring down Clinton because they don't like him. The Democrats have kept things rolling along better than Bush's father did.

DENISE: I know you don't like Bush.

EDDIE: It's peoples' *fears* that he keys into.

DENISE: I know you don't like him, but he's not what you think he is.

EDDIE: He's some kind of holy-rolling confidence game. Another great accomplishment of his: he's no longer a mean drunk! Hey, what does he know about foreign policy?

DENISE: He'll look out for our national interests. There are terrorists out there who'd sooner kill us than look at us.

EDDIE: I bet you think we're the number one country in the world.

DENISE: Why do you say that?

EDDIE: Well, I bet you do.

DENISE: Yes, I do.

EDDIE: You see, that's the problem. Everybody thinks their country is number one. Actually, according to the United Nations, Canada is the number one country in the world.

DENISE: Then why doesn't the U.N. move their offices to Canada?

EDDIE: Have you ever been abroad?

DENISE: What's that got to do with anything?

EDDIE: Then how do you know we're number one?

DENISE: I know.

EDDIE: George W. Bush has never been abroad that I've heard of. So you may have more things in common with him than you think.

DENISE: He's been abroad. Enough to know that there are other countries that hate us because we're number one.

EDDIE: I can't believe you're saying that.

DENISE: Let's change the subject. I'll be glad when this election is over.

EDDIE: Nobody challenges Bush on his m.o. You know it's just not right if someone has to have two different personalities to make his way through the world.

DENISE: All politicians are two-faced.

EDDIE: Not to the extent of Bush. The networks should get into this. But they're afraid of him.

DENISE: What is there to be afraid of?

EDDIE: If you have to ask, then you'll never know.

DENISE: All right, that's enough. It's time to change the subject. *(Pause.)* How's your dad doing?

EDDIE: The doctor's letting him out of the hospital *just so he can vote!*

DENISE: Good.

EDDIE: You bet it's good.

DENISE: Is he okay then?

EDDIE: Tests. There was something in the last CAT scan. He's going back in, *right after he votes.*

DENISE: I really hope he'll be okay, Eddie.

EDDIE: Thank you.
I couldn't become a Republican! It's the dark side of human nature. That's what the Republicans are part of. Greed, selfishness, fear, ignorance.
What bothers me is there are those Reaganomic types, too young to remember the inflation and unemployment, the crime, the tent cities, the national debt of the Reagan years.

DENISE: Like you remember?

EDDIE: Yeah, I remember. You're just trying to flatter me.

DENISE: I'm not.

EDDIE: See, you weren't old enough to witness the suffering of those times.

DENISE: Where I lived everything was fine.

EDDIE: The suburbs?

DENISE: Well, sort of.

EDDIE: Were there other kids around?

DENISE: Yeah, plenty.

EDDIE: That's good.
But what do kids know? They're vessels. They're tanks for the filling. Especially consumer products. If Pepsi gets you as a seven year old, it's got you forever, and Coca-cola's out of luck.

DENISE: Watch out, Eddie, you're becoming an old fuddy-duddy before your time.

EDDIE: No, I just realize that the hand of corporate America is at my throat.

DENISE: Maybe you should vote for Ralph Nader.

EDDIE: No third party candidates for me. It's not rational. You're only throwing your support behind the guy you don't want.

Pause.

DENISE and EDDIE: Okay, where to now?.

They laugh at the oddness of them both saying the same thing at the same time.

DENISE: We should head over to Girard Avenue.

EDDIE: You want to drive?

DENISE: Sure, I'll drive.

EDDIE: You know, there are a lot of vulnerable people in this country. A lot of people are in debt over their heads. Even the Democrats haven't been able to change this. We only barely have affordable housing in Philadelphia. It's far worse in a lot of other cities. People forget how much can really go wrong.

DENISE: Come on, Eddie.

They get up and leave.

Lights out. End of the scene.

Scene 2

At the counter in the donut shop. Coffee and donuts. Lights up. EDDIE *is talking on a cell phone.* DENISE *sits next to him. He ends the phone call. There is a piece of campaign literature in front of him which he will read from a little later on in the scene.*

DENISE: How's he doing?

EDDIE: Dad's excited. Gore won the election but Bush is stealing it, he says. I think they should count all the Florida votes over by hand. It's the only way we'll ever know. Bush doesn't want that though. In the recounts that *have* started, Gore's picking up votes. Meanwhile, the Russian Government has offered its assistance in helping to oversee the recounts.

DENISE: I never heard that!

EDDIE: Most of the media aren't reporting it. It's too embarrassing.
 Do you think that Bush might be humbled by the fact he lost the popular vote by a half a million people? That he might just keep quiet for a while? No, he declares himself the winner. He was such a loser six days ago when it came out that he had a drunk driving conviction. And Cheney, too—what an even bigger loser: arrested *twice* for drunk driving. You know, I've never been arrested in my life. Plenty of people I know have never been arrested. Don't get me wrong. It's not the worst thing in the world to be arrested... but these guys are holding themselves up as being virtuous men!
 Listen to this, *(He reads.)* "The governor believes very strongly and very sincerely that America's leadership and its moral values and its economic values are also a central part of American foreign policy." Who is this guy? This has all the depth you get out of a fortune cookie. It's scandalous how far he's gone in life. But again, his name is Bush, and he's tight with the millionaires.

DENISE: About half of the country voted for him and most of those people are not millionaires.

EDDIE: Hasn't Bush been saying all along that we should trust the people? But now, when more counting will show the people might be against him, he doesn't want to trust the people.

Keep the people stupid. Republicans don't want to invest in education. It's easier to control stupid people. To scare them, rile them up. Respond purely on emotional grounds to the masquerader George Bush because they're not educated enough to analyze anything.

DENISE: So now it's the uneducated who voted for him.

EDDIE: I don't know who it is! Who in their right mind would vote for George W. Bush?!

DENISE: Me.

EDDIE: I don't understand you. But I do know you were impossible to understand even before the Republicans held their convention here thinking they might get a few more people from Pennsylvania to vote for them.

DENISE: I'm glad we can still be friends even though we don't agree on politics.

EDDIE: Yeah right.

DENISE: Now, don't be sore.

EDDIE: People are too stupid to realize that they're being bought by the millionaires.

DENISE: Oh, come on.

EDDIE: Advertising works. Otherwise there'd be no such thing as advertising agencies.

DENISE: Gore advertised.

Pause.

EDDIE: I want a smart person with broad interests to be president. Somebody who I think's a lot more intelligent than I am. Somebody who doesn't change personalities with the weather. Somebody not in a state of arrested development. George W. Bush still listens to the same music he listened to when he was in college.

DENISE: I still listen to the same music that I did when I was in high school.

EDDIE: You're not running for president. *(Pause.)* Man, I have two years of college. I guess it's time to go back. Change my career maybe, yeah— I'll have to save up some money, if that's possible in this world.

DENISE: You might need it if you're going to get married some day.

EDDIE: Married? What makes you say that?

DENISE: Well, you might find the right girl.

EDDIE: Okay, this is not a favorite subject of mine. I'm currently on another problem—a problem which I do not wish to have, if I ever get married. That is: I hope not to settle for less, as we might do if George W. Bush gets in as president.

DENISE: Don't worry. You'll see. Bush'll be fine.

EDDIE: He'll never be fine. He's a predator. His people are predators. The purpose of government is to serve the people so that the people can be safe from oppression. The only thing the Republicans make the world safe for is big business. And this winds up hurting the people, always.

DENISE: Like the democrats are much better?

EDDIE: Let me tell you about the Democrats. They're always there, ready with an innovative plan after the Republicans have had their hands on the economy and screwed it up. This scenario repeats over and over again in our country's history. And I appreciate the Democrats for more than just their ability to get this country on its feet whenever it's been in the dumps. They're the only ones who've proved they have a little bit of *heart*.

Once, when Carter was President, man, he was a good man and I can't stand it when people criticize him... when Carter was President, my dad took me and my mother to New York City. We saw a musical called Nine. Something you couldn't see in Philadelphia. We wanted to see another show, but things were expensive. Dad found a show. It was an opera. In English. A comedy. By Mozart. It was cheap. It was happening because at that time the economy in New York was not good and Carter implemented a program called CETA. There was this CETA orchestra for unemployed musicians. They were the ones that gave the concert version of the opera. It was fantastic. We enjoyed it as much, maybe more, than the Broadway show.

Oh, and before you criticize it as some kind of pork barrel thing, let me tell you that the musicians were being paid minimum wage, less than a lot of janitors. It was no gravy train. The musicians needed to be kept in New York because New York is New York and certain democrats knew this and consequently had a *vision*, and I don't mean some bullshit vision about tax cuts, but a vision that had to do with jobs and with service to the community that already works their butts off.

Yeah, I like the Democrats. They're more likely to widen your horizons. What do Republicans do for you? They want you to be able to have the latest model of a new cell phone.

DENISE: So that's what you think, Eddie.

EDDIE: Yeah, it's what I think. I want to keep on thinking. I don't want to shut off thinking, like the Republicans always want to do. They say the vote counting should not go on for long— that we have to pick a winner for the purposes of finality. If it's only finality they want, then why not choose Gore? He won the national popular vote.

Lights out. End of the scene.

Scene 3

Neutral stage. Lights up. LASKO *is wearing a black gown printed with crescent moons, planets and stars. S/He wears a cone-shaped hat. S/He is supposed to look like a magician/astronomer.*

LASKO:

> It's a little breezy.
> Despite the city lights, constellations can be seen in the sky.
> Perseus, Pegasus. Cassiopeia.
> Tonight they're not blotted out by the moon.
>
> What a great distance it is
> That separates us from those stars.
> The distance creates a space for us to think very freely...
> That is, if someone else is not always trying to tell us how to think.

Pause.

> Philadelphia.
> Here we are in the cradle of democracy.
> How good is our democracy?
> Is it working well?
> We know we're supposed to have rights.
> The Conservatives'll tell us there should be more talk about responsibility than rights.
> Yeah, sure—
> Those control-freaks.
> Their point sounds very interesting at first,
> Until we realize such a statement might mean giving up the little power we supposedly have...

Pause.

LASKO: (*Continued.*)
>
> Politics can be a pain in the ass.
> But we have to be politically minded
> Or a tyrant will seize power.
> It's as simple as that.

Pause.

> Let's look up again at the stars.
> (*Looking upward.*) There. I can see Camelopardalis,
>   Auriga, Taurus.
> Orion is on the rise.
> Oh, how I love to engage with the stars.
> But you have to be careful and not to overdo it.
>
> Oh, I want to dream. I will dream.
> Man is a dreaming animal who wants the Good Life.
> One can die trying to get it,
> Is it really possible we can get it?
> Are we dreaming too much to want it?
> Is it a weird dream,
> Like falling into the Delaware River
> And being rescued by a New Jersey submarine?

Pause.

> Tonight, after being asleep for a couple of hours,
> Eddie's dreaming is not smooth...
> I can tell you that all the chamomile tea dreamed of
>   on South Street
> Couldn't buy him a sound sleep this night.
>
> Eddie dreams of Philadelphia,
> The streets and the homes,
> The good parts and the bad,
> The flowers in the park and the weeds in the empty
>   lots.
> But he doesn't dream of small boats on the
>   Schuykill

LASKO: *(Continued.)*

Like he did when he was a youth.
No, now he dreams of the police station.

In his dreams comes talk of Denise—
Talk from the cops at the station.
Some say Denise is a mother hen.
Whenever a guy comes into contact with her he feels
    like he's supposed to fall into her brood or what-
    ever you call the groups of chicks that a hen has.
There's other talk.
The other theory has it that Denise is available for a
    good time—
Just not with people from work.
Now, Denise has a defender—sort of—
One cop says Denise is okay
And to just stop talking about her.

Then Eddie walks in.
The men look at him.
They ask him about her.
He says I'm her partner,
I'm not saying anything.

But Eddie does know one thing.
He knows that Denise has eyes for him and he's not
    interested.
Then the scene changes in the dream:

Denise is sitting next to him in the patrol car.
They're moving very slowly.
Like the final moments of a rolling bowling ball on
    grass.
Their car windows are down.
Their heavy car proceeds syrup-thickly through an
    intersection
In a less-than-safe section of town.

LASKO: (*Continued.*)

> They hear a disembodied call from the side of the street.
> It's supposed to be the voice of somebody who knows Denise.
> They call for her to come out of the car and say hello.
> Denise thinks she recognizes the voice.
> She gets out of the car.

DENISE, *in uniform, enters, finds a spot on the stage and stands.*

> Eddie waits.
> He sees her go to the side of a building with them.
> Then she's out of sight.
> He can only hear her.
> And what he hears is this:

DENISE: Hey, how'ya doin'?

EDDIE, *in uniform, enters, finds a spot on the stage and stands.*

LASKO:

> Normally, you never let your partner out of your sight.
> Eddie's mind goes off in another direction.
> He thinks of his dad.
> His father says he feels better and wants to buy a new sport coat.

Pause.

DENISE: Let me go.

LASKO:

> —Denise cries out.
> If your partner goes out of sight, you get out of the car and go to them.

DENISE: Eddie. Eddie!

LASKO:
>Eddie hears his name.
>He's still thinking of his father.

DENISE: Help me, Eddie.

LASKO: Eddie remains in the patrol car.

DENISE: Help. Please. Now.

LASKO: Eddie hears her. Unlike George W. Bush who moves in on the presidency as quickly as he can, Eddie is going nowhere.

DENISE: Eddie, where are you?

LASKO: Yes, Eddie, where are you? Can't you help your partner? Can't you help someone in need? This is supposed to be the City of Brotherly Love.

DENISE: Eddie!

LASKO: Go to her.

EDDIE: I can't.

DENISE: Eddie!

LASKO: Go.

EDDIE: My body won't move.

LASKO: Move, dammit!

EDDIE: My legs won't move.

DENISE: He's got a knife, Eddie.

LASKO: Why, Eddie, why?

EDDIE: We can't be friends. She voted for Bush. Bush is evil. Terrible things are going to happen in the world now. And I don't just mean that more land in Alaska is going to be opened up for drilling oil.

DENISE: They're laughing at me. They say they're going to cut off my trigger finger.

EDDIE: Let 'em cut off your fingers. You deserve it.

LASKO: What!?

EDDIE: You heard what I said. (Pause.) I could care less what happens to her. As far as I'm concerned, she's garbage. She's contributing to the destruction of the world.

LASKO: (Facetiously.) How do you *really* feel about her, Eddie?

EDDIE: Oh, no. No!

LASKO: Eddie starts to talk while not yet finished dreaming.

EDDIE: It's hell, man, it's hell! Florida! Florida! Things would be different if the Governor of Florida wasn't a Republican, and also didn't happen to be George Bush's brother. And guess whose voting machines malfunctioned in Florida? Not the rich people's voting machines. They worked fine. It was the machines that the poorer people had to use. Districts that vote Democrat. That's where the uncounted votes are. Bush knows he'll lose. That's why he's messing up the process. Now he's only ahead by three hundred votes. We've got to count all the votes. Look, everybody on the inside, both Republican and Democrat, knows that Gore won.

LASKO: Oh, boy. Philadelphia is a place where politics are taken seriously. And that's good.

EDDIE: Politics are not taken seriously just in Philadelphia, Lasko. Not just in Philly!

Lights out. End of the scene.

Scene 4

At the police station. In Sergeant LASKO'*s office. Lights up.* EDDIE *sits down with* LASKO *at her/his desk.* LASKO *is now in uniform.*

LASKO: Why don't you want to be on patrol with her?

EDDIE: I just don't think it's right.

LASKO: What do you mean, right? What's gone on between you two?

EDDIE: Nothing.

LASKO: Then why are you requesting another partner?

EDDIE: I don't think she's the best partner for me.

LASKO: Something's happened between you.

EDDIE: Not really.

LASKO: I don't buy it. Tell me what happened. *(Pause.)* You must have a reason.

EDDIE: I do.

LASKO: Then what is it?

EDDIE: It's stressful to be around her.

LASKO: So?

EDDIE: Maybe it's because she's from the South.

LASKO: That's no reason at all, man. You don't have anything against Southerners that I know of, do you?

EDDIE: No. Probably not. I voted for a Southerner.

LASKO: That's all there was to vote for. So are you gonna sit here and waste more of my time? Or are you gonna tell me what's up?

EDDIE: It's just not working out between her and me.

LASKO: Like for example...?

EDDIE: Well, I got an indication...

LASKO: What did she indicate to you?

EDDIE: Nothing.

LASKO: You told me you got an indication.

EDDIE: Not from her.

LASKO: From one of the other guys?

EDDIE: No.

LASKO: From a little bird, then, huh? Eddie, come on, I don't have all day.

EDDIE: The indication's about the firmest indication you could ever have that things won't work out. But the indication itself, is, I admit, a little out-of-the-ordinary.

LASKO: This is some kind of sex thing, isn't it? We thought she was interested in you. Did she make a pass? Did you make a pass?

EDDIE: No, nothing like that.

LASKO: Then what is it?

EDDIE: Can't you just do me a favor, Lasko, and split us up?

LASKO: It's not an easy thing to do! Where's the problem here? What's the reason? Tell me. Straight up.

EDDIE: The thing is, I can't be *there* for her. That's why I can't be on patrol with her.

LASKO: You have to be there for her. She's your partner. It's your job.

EDDIE: I know, but I can't be.

LASKO: Look, I need to know why. And these things have to be written down.

EDDIE: You can't write it in a report.

LASKO: Try me.

Pause.

EDDIE: I had a dream. I didn't help her. I couldn't get out of the car when she was being attacked. I've got this thing against her. And I know it's not going to go away.

LASKO: What have you got against her?

EDDIE: It's gonna sound stupid.

LASKO: Yeah?

EDDIE: It's her politics. She voted for Bush.

LASKO: Oh, boy. *(Pause.)* Well, I have to think about this, Eddie. Having a dream isn't going to be much for the captain. If there was something else...

EDDIE: Not really.
    (Pause.) Hey, did you hear the news? Dick Cheney should never even have been running for Vice President because for the last eight years he's been a resident of Texas. And federal law bars a President and Vice President being from the same state. A law of common sense: you don't want some kind of pre-formed gang coming to the White House.

LASKO: The news never stops.

EDDIE: Cheney changed his address five months ago when he found out about the law. But I'm afraid they're going to get away with this. They're old hands at abusing the law. *(Pause.)* Well, thanks, I'll shove off now.

> EDDIE *is just about to leave when* DENISE *passes by on her way out of the precinct station. She is in civilian clothes.*

DENISE: Hey, Eddie, how's it going?

EDDIE: It's going fine, Denise. How ya doin'?

DENISE: Great.

LASKO: Speaking of great, you look great.

DENISE: Well, somebody noticed. *(To* EDDIE.*)* Hope you have a good night. *(To Both.)* Bye.

> DENISE *leaves.*

EDDIE: Why'd you have to say that?

LASKO: Because she looks great.

EDDIE: Yeah? Whatever.
   There's something even besides her politics that rubs me the wrong way. I don't know. I feel she's kind of phony. Maybe that's not the word. We sit around. I feel like I'm only talking to half a person. Where's the other half of her? Am I looking for a more interesting half, a more humane half? I can't say exactly what I mean. She's strange. I don't want to get to know her any better. I'm afraid of what I'd get to know.

LASKO: Okay, okay. I don't want to hear anymore about her now. *(Pause.)* Hey, what's up with your father?

EDDIE: Well, I'm having dinner with him. He's going to show me some more clippings. *(He laughs.)* That's where I get a lot of my information from, from him. He collects everything you'd ever want to know about George W. Bush.

LASKO: I know enough about him and what I know I don't like.

EDDIE: Dad says the worst is yet to come. See you later.

LASKO: Bye.

Lights out. End of the scene.

Scene 5

News report: "Bush declared victor after Gore concedes, etc."
Neutral stage. Lights up. EDDIE *and* LASKO *in plainclothes. They talk to themselves but at times also talk to the audience.*

EDDIE: Who were we kidding? There's no way Sergeant Lasko was going to be able to get me teamed up with someone else—because of a dream I had! He *(Or "She" depending on the sex of the actor.)* told me finally that as the country was going to have to put up with Bush as President, I would have to put up with Denise. And that if Denise was ever in trouble I'd have to be there for her or there'd be grave consequences. As a result I've thought maybe I should find a new job.

LASKO: Now that's very extreme.

EDDIE: Things are extreme these days.

LASKO: You're not quitting your job, Eddie, forget about that. Even though things are extreme. They're not *extreme* extreme.

EDDIE: Hmm.

LASKO: I know you're wound up. All of us are. You'll be all right. And our country will survive the bastard Bush.

EDDIE: But I'm worried what we're going to do to other countries.

LASKO: It won't be easy to keep track of the underhandedness that Bush'll use abroad. It's hard enough to do it right here.

EDDIE: All the talk in the past about our Right Wing subverting elections abroad. Now we get to see how its done right here at home. "A machine count is the only reliable measure. A hand count is open to too much subjectivity." What garbage. Somehow it worked for them, though. I thought the highlight was when those Republicans stormed into the county building and shut down the count in Miami. Of course that was until the U.S. Supreme Court got into the picture. My father was right. The worse *was* yet to come. And it did come. Lasko, you and I deal with the courts in Philadelphia on almost a daily basis. And we've seen judges throw their weight around. We've seen them be rude. And it is *not* cool.

LASKO: No.

EDDIE: But until I heard the Supreme Court this past Monday, I thought they'd be different from what I sometimes encounter. When Judge Anthony Scalia of the U.S. Supreme Court told Gore's attorney that he was not being "rational", he sounded like a judge in the old Soviet Union. Where they used to dehumanize and silence their adversaries by labeling them insane and sending them off to be insane.
  You know, the decision that Scalia and his pals made, if followed logically, renders null and void every election that has ever taken place in the U.S. to date?
  Scalia and his cronies. Conservatives. This proves that conservatism's as bad for American democracy as communism would be. Conservatism is a way of thinking that's too easily hijacked by an exclusive group. The Republicans have made a big mistake by embracing it. If we had fewer credit cards reality could wake us up

EDDIE: *(Continued.)* and make our stomachs sore from hunger. Then we'd rebel against the idiocy of conservative theories.

LASKO: Well, my friend, the election fell off the back of a truck. Bush picked it up and ran with it. It's a sham he wouldn't let its rightful owner be determined. The Supreme Court helped him beat the clock during his run with it.

EDDIE: George Bush wants people to trust him. After cheating his way to the top? He delivers his first address to the country as President elect and has the gall to say that he believes "there is a reason" for him being elected. Yeah, God wants him in the White House, he announces. Sure. This is a little too close to what royalty used to say in Europe when they claimed they had the divine right to rule.

LASKO: Eddie, here in this city where American democracy was born we won't take this lying down. If Bush isn't careful, there'll be trouble here. We might be looking at a lot of overtime. Riot duty. I hope not.

Pause.

But enough of this for the moment. Let me emphasize that we'd like you to visit Philadelphia. We've got the restaurants, and you name the country—we've got the cuisine. We're not anywhere as expensive as New York or Washington. Speaking of Washington, have you ever tried to stay there? The hotel prices are outrageous. So much for the common citizens of this country being able to see the federal government up close! Hey, I recently heard some Republicans complain that they can't afford to work in Washington for Bush. After they were the ones that created a culture of high real estate prices there!

Well, Philly's where our federal government began. "Of the people, by the people, for the people." Now we've wandered considerably from this concept. But if it's up to people like some of us, we'll steer our way back. Come to us here. Postpone your trip if we're going to have a protest, but do come—come see us right after that. Talk to us, walk among our past and present—which is your past and present—and get inspired.

Raucous music. Suddenly, DENISE *comes "floating" out. Actually she is standing on a low, small (2 feet by 2 feet.) platform with wheels underneath it. This is moved by stage hands. She is dressed as a dominatrix, and also wears black leather gloves. She carries a whip and an unlit cigarette.*

BETSY: How the mice will play while the cat's away! What's this crap about coming to Philadelphia and getting inspired?

I just like the way you've changed gears from being police officers for the city of Philadelphia to being defenders of American democracy. And you have guns and badges that seem to make you real important. Down on your knees!

EDDIE: I'm not entirely surprised you've shown up looking like you do.

BETSY: Down, I said.

EDDIE *humors her.* LASKO *follows and does the same— they both go to their knees after a moment.*

EDDIE: Okay.

BETSY: *(Facetiously.)* Oh, you have so much power. You can scare all those people on the streets. Lock 'em up when they do wrong. But you know what? You're mistaken. The big guys use you. *They* have the power. *(To the audience.)* I guess you're wondering what this is all about. It's the American way: to have a second job. *(To* EDDIE *and* LASKO: Now, lick my boots.

EDDIE: What?!

BETSY: You've been bad, speaking your mind, Eddie. "Make Philadelphia your Philadelphia", that's what you tell them! I'll tell you who your Philadelphia is. It's me, Betsy Philadelphia. And you're going to do what I tell you to do, here in my dungeon. You want politics? I'll give you politics. Vote for my cigarette. Go on, light it!

She gives LASKO *a match or lighter to light her cigarette and s/he does as commanded.*

BETSY: *(Continued.)* All right. *(She smokes the cigarette and appears to relax for a moment.)* All this talk about the election. The United States. Democracy. Stay down on the ground, Eddie. And say that word for me, will you, Eddie?

EDDIE: Which one?

BETSY: The d-word.

EDDIE: Democracy.

BETSY: A useful word to confuse and fool the people. *(Smokes.)* You're all fools. *(Pause.)* Eddie, get it now. *Fetch* it. Go get the *hand*.

EDDIE: What's that?

BETSY: You heard me. The hand.

EDDIE: I don't know what you mean.

BETSY: You know. You're a policeman.

EDDIE: I don't know.

> BETSY *threatens him with her whip.*

BETSY: You lie, you piece of dirt! Get it. Get the hand. Betsy Philadelphia says get the hand now or I'll put this cigarette out on your face!

> EDDIE *does not comply, though he stays down on the ground.*

LASKO: Look, I'll get the hand.

> LASKO *leaves momentarily and finds the hand. S/he comes back with a giant picture of a hand, an image of a hand in salute.* LASKO *stands holding the picture of the hand.* BETSY *sticks her face in* EDDIE's *and blows cigarette smoke at him.*

BETSY: Virginia, North Carolina, Tennessee. Greetings from the tobacco states. They know the hand well. *(To* LASKO.*)* Find a stand. A hand-stand for it.

> LASKO *leaves momentarily with the picture of the hand.* BETSY *waits impatiently.* LASKO *comes back with the picture of the hand and a painter's easel. S/he sets up the easel and puts the picture of the hand on it.*

Now, a firm hand is required to guide the human race. We all know that. Let's not forget it. You've heard of a helping hand? That goes to the children. Well, we're all God's children, aren't we? Hah, hah, hah. *(To* LASKO:*)* Sniff my glove. *(He sniffs her glove.)* Nostalgic, isn't it? How you love the smell of power. Mama's power, which is greater than the hydrogen bomb.

(Pause.) Eddie. It's obvious that you don't fit in. I know you want to fit in. Gaze at the hand, necessary to man. Gaze at the hand while I whip your behind. Yes, the pain is necessary too. Maybe Mama ought to make you suck the handle of her whip first though. *(She grabs hold of* EDDIE'*s head.)* Turn your head. Look to the hand for guidance. Now, stand up, Eddie. I want you to stand in agony, to stand there and strain like an animal who was only meant to crawl.

> *She lets go of him.* EDDIE *gets up off the ground, almost casually, certainly without her help.* BETSY *paces a little while she speaks:.*

> > Let us worship the hand.
> > O Hand, more powerful than God.
> > The hand that settles elections in one fell swoop
> > The hand that brings a Yugoslavian peace to families.

(To EDDIE.*)* You're standing up but you're not in pain.

EDDIE: No, I'm not.

BETSY: You must worship the hand.

EDDIE: No.

BETSY: That's the law in my dungeon. You disobey, you're punished. I am the truth and the law here.

EDDIE: Well, you've revealed yourself as Betsy Philadelphia. Now it's time for me to take off my mask as it were, and reveal just who I am. I'm not just Eddie, Philadelphia policeman.

BETSY: I know you have grander aspirations.

EDDIE: I guess you could say I have a second job, too. It's not really a second job. It's more like the inner core of me, the highly concentrated me, that comes out in difficult situations like this. I like to think that the inner core of me has something to do with the Good in humanity.

BETSY: I'll give you a core. And you'll need cuffs, too. Your grand aspirations are all to be found, guided by the hand.

EDDIE: No, they're not. My aspirations are grand, I admit. Though I must say, *I'm* not grand, I am myself of the Little People.

BETSY: Ha! That's right, you're a scrawny little flea.

EDDIE: No, I am of the Little People who are on guard against false gods.

He runs up to the poster of the hand, picks it up, and throws it to the ground and stamps on it.

EDDIE: There's the hand for you. You are fear upon the land. You are ignorance. You are boring. And you are smaller, much smaller than even the Little People.

BETSY: You're totally without discipline. Get down on the ground again.

EDDIE: No way. *(Pause.)* Lasko, you've been silent. What's going on?

LASKO: A man must work. But he also must wonder. I haven't been saying anything because a person cannot think and talk at the same time.

BETSY: With the hand to guide you there's never that problem.

LASKO: I've decided I don't like the hand.

BETSY: The hand feeds us.

LASKO: No, we feed the hand. *(Pause.)* And we damage ourselves with it.

BETSY: There's no damage done by the hand that's not rewarded by some sort of money.

LASKO: That's the problem, isn't it? *(Pause.)* Well, Betsy, you and this hand, I have to thank you, really. The way you've both set me to thinking in very earthly terms. Wow. I feel I'm practically being sent back to some kind of infant stage. To re-think me and my surroundings. I feel like saying, first, I am Lasko. It's a pretty good name to greet the world with. It's easily remembered—not that I have some big desire to be remembered, but I'd like to be recognized by a person who might see me again sometime.

BETSY: This is outrageous! The hand! The hand! If anyone ever needed it, you need it, now!

LASKO: My name is Lasko. Your name is Betsy Philadelphia. I respect that you have this name. So we are... Lasko... and Betsy.

BETSY: You're absolutely... melting down. The hand! The hand! Where is it? And by the way, it's *Betsy* and Lasko!

LASKO: But what about Eddie?

BETSY: He's a little guy. He doesn't count.

LASKO: So we have here Betsy, Lasko and Eddie. Eddie's not saying anything at the moment. I bet he's thinking. It was like when I was quiet. I wasn't saying anything because I needed to think.

BETSY: I'm telling you, the hand allows you to talk and think at the same time!

LASKO: How could that be?

BETSY: It's because the hand is really doing the thinking for you.

LASKO: *(A revelation.)* Of course!

BETSY: It's fabulous, isn't it?

LASKO: No. *(Pause.)* Betsy, it occurred to me while I was thinking that you want us to worship the hand, but you don't want people to count election votes by hand. Funny isn't it?

EDDIE: The hand does not acknowledge paradoxes, *(To* BETSY.*)* does it?

LASKO: If the hand's doing the thinking for us we're not really thinking. It's ghastly, isn't it? The hand lives on and on in its horror.

EDDIE: Betsy, you went to a lot of trouble, I'm sure, of getting dressed up to play this part of yours, but there's no role for you here. We reject you. We reject what you stand for. We reject the more mundane form of you: the police woman Denise who demonstrates obscene obedience to whatever the Republican party says. And we reject the manifestation of arrogance and power that is forced upon us in the person of one Mr. George W. Bush.

There are many things left for us to do. We will work against Bush junta doing its damage to the planet and the peoples of the world. Our land will not give into the hand. We will guard against mental depression the days to come. We will not forsake honesty. Nor will we stand by idly while people such as ourselves are be ridiculed for being sensitive or complex. We will not live at ease with the vampires around us who ship their blood off to the hand. We will

EDDIE: *(Continued.)* survive the deadly influences of conservatism and greed. We shall pursue joy in our lives in various life-affirming ways.

Betsy, or Denise, or whoever you are, you are ejected from this artistic work. Get out before we throw you out.

BETSY: *(With dignity.)* Remember. Remember. The hand. It disciplines and guarantees life, health and wealth.

LASKO: Sure, right. Tell that to the folks who know it well in South America.

EDDIE: That's enough. Leave!

BETSY *leaves in a huff.*

Lights out. End of the scene.

End of Play.

Acknowledgments

I have been very fortunate to have so many talented people help in the creation of these plays and this book. Thanks to Walter Teres, Lise Geurkink and Bill Dunn for their editorial assistance, as well as their fabulous work on other facets of this project. I thank Michelle Powell, Martin Lockley and those already mentioned in the previous pages for such wonderful work, including Jo Oskoui at www.2celldesign.com for web design, and Mayam Oskoui. I would also like to thank Bruce Boswell, Bill Troop, the Taits, Kevin Hankel and John Murphy; Yves and Sophie Gaudin; Linda Jones at Enfield Publishing; Frank and Jean Hoff, Joseph Meeker, Darko Suvin, Domenico Pietropaolo, Derek Walcott and Boston University; Michael Moss, Jim Cooke and other Boston Equity actors now forgotten by me; Joan and Walter Luikart, Stephen Fitzstephens, Gordon Rogoff; American Repertory Theatre's Robert Orchard, Arthur Holmberg, Megan Uebelacker, actors Jeremy Geidt, Karen MacDonald, Justin Campbell, Gin Hammond, Rachael Warren and Ben Evett; Paul Scallan, Bruce McIntosh, Joe Marinelli, John Robert Hood, Natalia Golimbievskaya, Gretchen Minnie, Rick Barbour, Chris Citron and Mary at the Colorado Center for the Book; Isla Eckinger, Don and Gail Elwell, Wanda Ivey, Linda Tyrol; Lucy and Julian Cook, Jim Shutt, John and Chris Thomas; Patrick Barrows, the Segarnicks, the Motsingers, Chris and Laurie Brown; Jean-Pierre Martin, Gwylene Gallimard and Jean-Marie Mauclet, Sally and Dave McFall, Patrice and Maria Villaume, Bille, Johannes Kühl and the Goetheanum; Christian Meyer, Arthur Pritchard and Bretton Hall College; Odile Trufanow and Hazel Lee.

Hazel Lee

LANCE TAIT is a graduate of Bard College. As a singer/songwriter, he has performed solo in London, England, New York and Los Angeles. His plays have been performed or have received public readings in Boston, Los Angeles, Denver, Toronto, Paris, the United Kingdom and at the American Repertory Theatre and Harvard University. He has an M.A. from Boston University where he studied with Nobel laureate Derek Walcott. His other books, published by Enfield, are *Miss Julie, David Mamet Fan Club, and Other Plays* and *Edwin Booth: A Play in Two Acts.* He has been a visiting lecturer in theatre at Bretton Hall College, Leeds University, in England. His website address is www.lancetait.com.